瑷珲海关
历史档案辑要

海务港务（下）
（第六卷）

黑龙江省档案馆　编译

社会科学文献出版社
SOCIAL SCIENCES ACADEMIC PRESS (CHINA)

目录

专题三

港口事务

1. 为戊通公司码头修建事

Taheiho Harbour. + Wut'ung Co's Jetties. Aigun Office to con-
mendation to remove, + posting
appointment of an expert to decide in the
matter, suggesting

2309.

I. G.   H A R B I N   29th January, 1921.

Sir,

I have the honour to forward, appended

hereto, copies of Aigun Despatches Nos. 299

and 301 to this Office,

reporting that the Wutung Steamship
Co. during the winter of 1919 - 1920
had built a jetty of some 275' in
length at Taheiho for the protection
of their steamers wintering there and
that the question of extension of the
jetty this winter had been made the
subject of considerable informal discussion between the Wutung Co. and
the Aigun Assistant in Charge; that
experience during the last summer had
shown that the current, which sets
to the Taheiho side of the river
strikes this jetty, is causing silting
of the Harbour; and recommending the
immediate removal of this jetty;
suggesting dredging operations by the
Customs or the Wutung Co. or still
better the making of a winter harbour
below Taheiho as shown on sketch

and

The Inspector General of Customs,

        P E K I N G.

and recommended by Mr. Wallhgren, the Senior Officer; reporting that two former Russian officials of the Amur River Conservancy Bureau who were asked to give an opinion and point out a suitable location for a winter harbour, pronounced that the present jetty was detrimental to the Harbour, that the bunding of the foreshore at Taheiho should not be delayed too long, that it would be advisable to dredge a channel across the spit, where it joins the island, that there is a suitable place below Taheiho between the island and the mainland for making a winter harbour and that the water front of the island opposite Blagovestchensk could be utilized for wharves; reporting that the main points are being referred to the Taoyin and that the question of bunding will be taken up with the Taheiho merchants and that the Wutung Co. has been informed of the opinion expressed by the two Russian experts.

As these matters are not of my competence and should be treated by an expert I beg to inquire whether the Inspectorate is still thinking of appointing a successor to the late Mr. Garden, River Inspector, who was detached

for

for duty at Taheiho and had received instructions
to make a survey of the Taheiho Harbour and
attend to Harbour questions generally.

At the beginning of the autumn I sent
Mr. Grundt, Assistant Boat Officer, for duty at
Taheiho to attend to these matters but I doubt
Mr. Grundt is qualified for such responsible
and expert work. It must also be taken into
consideration that the question of Aids to
Navigation on the Amur River and other boundary
Rivers may again be taken up by the Chinese
Government and that without the presence of an
expert on such matters nothing can be done.

In this connection I beg to point out
that an excellent opportunity now offers for
the Chinese Government to secure the services
of two Russian experts on Amur River Conservancy,
Messrs Krynin and Ignateff who have been
engaged on such work as Director and Inspector
respectively for the last 15 years and who
have applied for appointment in the Chinese

                                    Government

Government Service.

A Copy of this Despatch is being forwarded

to the Coast Inspector.

I have the honour to be,

Sir,

Your obedient Servant,

(Signed)   R. C. L. d'ANJOU,

Commissioner.

A P P E N D I X N O. 1.

THE SENIOR ASSISTANT, AIGUN, to HARBIN COMMISSIONER.

No. 299.

Harbin.

Aigun / Taheiho, 11th December,1920.

Sir,

1.   The question of extension of a jetty or breakwater this winter has been the subject of considerable informal discussion between the Wutung Co. and myself and the Company having decided to refer the matter to Harbin for discussion with you I have the honour to put before you the viewpoint of this office of the situation.

2.   Last winter, without asking the permission of the Customs, the Wutung Co. built into the River a jetty of some 275' in length to protect their steamers wintering here and which would be endangered when the breakup of the ice came in the Spring. A sketch map is enclosed, drawn up by Mr. Wahlgren, Senior Officer, showing the position of the jetty and its relation to the rest of the harbour. By referring to this sketch it will be seen that a point is gradually shoaling up the harbour and is a very serious menace. Experience this past Summer has shown that the current, which sets to the Taheiho side of the River, strikes this jetty, swirls, has its speed retarded and deposits silt on this point.

3.   Copy of a report drawn up by Mr. Wahlgren

is

is also enclosed.   The "River experts" he refers to
are the officials who were formerly at the head of
navigation affairs on the other side of the River.
However, a layman can easily see the detrimental
effect of the jetty.   It would seem that rather
than extend the jetty the present one should be
removed immediately.

4.   However the question is complicated by the
lack of winter harbour facilities and some steamers
should winter here.   If either the Customs or
Wutung Co. could maintain a dredge here or even
rent one occasionally from Blagovestchensk, the
shoaling could be kept under control and the jetty
could remain.   But with the passing of time no
doubt other Steamship companies would want to build
similar jetties and silting would then go on at
too rapid a rate.

5.   The alternative is to build a winter harbour
below Taheiho (there is no place above) and the
possible location for such a harbour is indicated
on the sketch.   The Wutung Co., however, say this
place is impractical but I do not know how sincere
they are in their assertions.   It would seem as
if when the Railway from Harbin eventually comes in
that all yards, docks, etc., will have to be below
Taheiho and that the present location of Wutung Co.
will be found to be impossible.

6.   Now that the river is frozen and it is not
possible to take soundings nor go into the
proposition of a winter harbour this winter, it
would seem as if the question would have to lie

over

over until Mr. Boat Officer Grundt can go into it next Spring (in conjunction with Wutung Co.).

7.   Formerly the Ferry followed the line now marked "Winter Road" on the sketch but its course has had to be shifted to the line indicated. It would be a great benefit to the harbour if a channel could be dredged through this shoal and a great convenience to the Customs if the Ferry landing could be restored to its old position (next to the Custom House). Perhaps the Blagovestchensk Government would let us use a dredge without charge for a short time, the expense of working it to be advanced from Suspense A/c and eventually recovered when a system of dues to improve the harbour is installed.

8.   With your permission I could make some preliminary enquiries on this point, have the Taoyin take it up officially if it seemed practical and eventually lay before you an estimate of what needed to be done and what it would cost.

                    I have, etc.,

            (Signed)   R. M. TALBOT,

                          2nd Assistant, A.

THE SENIOR OFFICER, AIGUN, to AIGUN ASSISTANT.

MEMORANDUM.

                    Taheiho, 6th November, 1920.

    The Wutung Steam Ship Company are contemplating during

during this winter to lengthen their breakwater,
now protruding in Amur River above their wharf in
Upper Harbour Reach, by another 35 feet. As it
is considered by river experts that their present
mole (a timber caisson 275 feet long by 30 feet
wide, filled with stones, of which at average
normal water mark 265 feet comes out in the river)
is harmful to the Harbour and if lengthened would
be still more so, on account of the loose matter
carried by the water in the River on striking
this obstruction begins to whirl and then settle
lower down, specially on the bank which is located
in lower part of Harbour, very near in line with
the utmost point of the breakwater, thereby causing
the best part of the Harbour to be gradually
silted up while the mole only is useful as
protection in spring time for Wutung vessels against
drift ice, it would be of great advantage to
future shipping if this mole could be removed
altogether instead of being lengthened.

Attached please find a rough sketch map of the
Harbour on which are indicated Wutung breakwater,
sand bank in lower part of Harbour and site where
a suitable winter dock could be built at very low
cost by ship owners who wish to lay up their
vessels for the winter at Taheiho.

(Signed)   O. W. WAHLGREN,

Chief Examiner, B.

APPENDIX.

A P P E N D I X NO. 2.

THE SENIOR ASSISTANT, AIGUN, to HARBIN COMMISSIONER.

No. 301.

Harbin.

AIGUN / TAHEIHO, 12th January, 1921.

SIR,

With reference to Aigun Despatch No. 299 to Harbin of 11. December, 1920:

> Harbour: Wutung Co. jetty: scheme of extension of criticised. Dredging of, permission to make certain inquiries as to cost of, requesting:

I have the honour to address you supplementing the above despatch.

On the 31. December, 1920, two former Russian officials of the Amur River Conservancy Bureau, Mr. P. P. Krynin, the Director, and Mr. P. T. Ignateff, the Chief River Inspector, both engaged in the problems of conservancy and lighting of the Amur River and its affluents for the last 15 years, escaped from Russia and came to Taheiho enroute to Harbin. Knowing their qualifications and intimate knowledge of the Amur at this point I asked their opinion on several questions affecting the Harbour and their idea of a suitable location for a winter harbour. Mr. Ignateff spent half a day visiting and inspecting the proposed site for the latter. The following is a resumé of their report.

> (a) The present Wutung Jetty is not good for the Harbour. Just below the jetty there was formerly 15' of water but now there is only 2' at the same level.

level. The jetty is, however, not so dangerous for the lower part of the Harbour unless it was extended when it would cause the lower part of the Harbour to silt up also.

(b)   The main force of the current on the Amur is bearing against the Taheiho side.   During the last ten years a deep inroad has been made into the river bank and in another ten years the bund will disappear and the foundations along it will be undermined. To remedy this the whole water front should be bunded at once.   The Wutung Co. have this year bunded part of their foreshore and the bunding they have done would be cheap and effective for the balance of the foreshore.

(c)   It would be advisable to dredge a channel across the spit, where it joins the island, in front of the Custom House.   Such a channel would greatly improve the Harbour as the Ferry and steamers could then berth in the lower part of the Harbour near the Custom House.

(d)   There is an ample and very suitable place below Taheiho between the island and the mainland for making a winter harbour for vessels (vide sketch plan enclosed in Aigun Despatch No.299

quoted

quoted above) wintering in Taheiho.
Some heavy expenses would, however, have
to be incurred to make this a first
class anchorage.

(e)   The water front of the island
opposite Blagovestchensk could be utilised
for wharves its nearness greatly
facilitating transhipping.

The above five paragraphs need very little
enlarging.   It can be seen that, as I stated in my
previous despatch on the subject, the Wutung jetty is
damaging the Harbour and its extension would be out
of the question, the question of bunding should be
taken up at once, that a channel dredged across the
spit would advantageously serve the lower part of
the Harbour, that a winter harbour could be
constructed behind the island below the town, and the
future place for the expansion of shipping facilities
is the island.

At present the island is only cut off from the
mainland by a channel when there is high water.   If
a channel is cut across the base of the spit, the
dredgings from it as well as from the proposed
winter harbour could be used in making the island
part of the mainland and when the proposed Harbin -
Taheiho Railway is built tracks could be run out to
the docks it would be possible to build opposite
Blagovestchensk's shipping center.

With reference to my request in the previous
despatch on this subject that the question of the

use

use of the dredge be taken up with the
Blagovestchensk Government. I am assured by the two
men mentioned above that the Far Eastern Republic
is most anxious to enter into an agreement with
China as to the Amur. Whether it is best to await
for a formal agreement or to approach them informally
for the use of a dredge is a question. I presume
you will advise a waiting policy.

I am referring to the Taoyin the main points
of the despatch and those of my previous one and
expect that he will take up at once with the
merchants the question of bunding, the material for
which will have to be bought this coming summer.
On receipt from him the measures the merchants are
willing to adopt, I will submit them to you. I
am also acquainting the Wutung Co, informally, of
the opinions of Messrs. Krynin and Ignateff as to
their jetty and they will no doubt forward the
information to their Head Office at Harbin.

In conclusion I should say that it is the
opinion of the two experts mentioned above, who are
very familiar with the problems we have to face,
that constant dredging and heavy expense will be
required to keep the present Harbour in navigable
shape but I gathered that if the island was used
as the shipping center these problems would largely
disappear.

I have, etc.,

(Signed)   R. M. TALBOT.

2nd Assistant, A.

True copies:

2nd Clerk, C.

No. 2477   Commr.

Harbin   No. 82,629

                    Inspectorate of Customs,

                          Peking, 17th February, 1921.

Sir,

I am directed by the Inspector General to acknowledge receipt of your Despatch No. 2309: forwarding with your comments, copies of Aigun despatches Nos. 299 and 301 criticising the proposed extention of the Wutung Steamship Company's jetty built in the winter 1919-1920, recommending its removal, suggesting dredging operations by the Customs or the Wutung Company, bunding of the foreshore and the making of a winter harbour below Taheiho, etc., and pointing out, in connection with the appointment of a successor to the late Mr.. Garden, River Inspector, the opportunity that offers for the Chinese Government to secure the services of two Russian experts on Amur conservancy, Messrs. Krynin and Ignateff:

                                  and

The Commissioner of Customs,
    H A R B IN.

and, in reply, to say that the Assistant-in-charge at Aigun was right to draw attention to these matters, all of which are important; but the Customs cannot undertake bunding, dredging or construction of a winter harbour for the very *good* reason that there are no funds, It seems necessary to define responsibility as soon as possible. The Customs will attend to harbour control and the provision of the neccessary harbour aids to navigation, but there our functions cease, and the responsibility for the rest lies with the territorial authority, presumably the Taoyin.

You are to veto at once any further extension of the Wutung jetty and place on record this veto, at the same time pointing out that the existing jetty is a menace to navigation and public rights, and ought to be removed. You are further authorised to take up the question of the appointment of Mr. Ignateff as River Inspector submitting your proposals officially, and stating if there would be any objection to his holding concurrently the position of Harbour Master at Aigun.

A

A copy of this despatch is being sent to the Coast Inspector.

I am,

Sir,

Your obedient Servant,

(Signed) C. A. V. Bowra,

Chief Secretary.

True copy:

Unclassed Assistant.

HARBOUR TAHEIHO: RIVER INSPECTOR AND HARBOUR
MASTER: appointment of non-Russian, with Mr.Ignateff
as Assistant, recommending and veto of the extension
of Wutung Co's jetty, reporting..

2333.

I. G.   Harbin, 3rd March, 1921.

Sir,

         I have the honour to acknowledge receipt

of I. G. Despatch No. 2477/82,629 (in reply

to Harbin Despatch No. 2309),

                   pointing out with regard to Conservancy
                   and Harbour matters at Taheiho that
                   the Customs cannot undertake bunding,
                   dredging or construction of a winter
                   Harbour for lack of funds; defining
                   responsibility e.g. Customs will attend
                   to Harbour Control and Harbour Aids
                   to Navigation and the rest lies with
                   the territorial authorities; instructing
                   me to veto at once in writing the
                   further extension of the Wutung Co's
                   jetty and ask them to remove the
                   present jetty; and authorising me
                   to take up the question of the
                   appointment of Mr. Ignateff as River
                   Inspector and perhaps also as Harbour
                   Master at Taheiho.

         In reply I beg to place on record that I

                                                   have

The Inspector General of Customs,

               P E K I N G.

have communicated with the Wutung Steamship Co. vetoing any further extension of their jetty at Taheiho on the ground that the existing jetty is detrimental to the Harbour and have asked them to remove the present jetty without delay.

With regard to the question of appointment of Mr. Ignateff as River Inspector I am of one mind with the Coast Inspector (and with the Tidesurveyor whom I have consulted) that it would be inexpedient to appoint a Russian to fill the post for which the late Mr. Garden was nominated. A Russian River Inspector no matter what his qualifications may be would be at a great disadvantage when coming into contact with his national Authorities, especially under the present Bolshevik regime at Blagovestchensk. Mr. Ignateff is more or less a run-away from the Bolshevik regime; his presence at Taheiho in such a high official

capacity

capacity as River Inspector in the Chinese
Government Service might cause us embarasment
and perhaps difficulties. My idea from the
start was that a non-Russian River Inspector
be nominated in replacement of the late Mr.
Garden and that Mr. Ignateff be placed under
him where he would render invaluable services
owing to his intimate knowledge of the Rivers
forming the boundaries between China and Russia,
owing also to the former's non-acquaintance
with the Russian language.

With regard to the suggestion put forward
to appoint Mr. Ignateff as Harbour Master the
argument put forward in what precedes applies
still more strongly. A Russian Harbour Master
would find his authority constantly challenged
by his nationals in charge of vessels. In
short my recommendations are as follows; the
immediate appointment in replacement of the
late Mr. Garden of a non-Russian River
Inspector who would also be Harbour Master

at

at Taheiho and the appointment on terms
to be settled of Mr. Ignateff as Assistant
River Inspector. The appointment of the former
should be made without loss of time as
Harbour Regulations for the Port of Taheiho
will be enforced if approved by you at the
beginning of this season (in April) and as
many matters regarding conservancy and Harbour
improvements are coming for discussion and
execution this season for which we will
need technical knowledge.

A Copy of this Despatch is being
sent to the Coast Inspector.

I have the honour to be,

Sir,

Your obedient Servant,

(Signed) R. C. L. d'Anjou,

Commissioner.

呈海关总税务司署 2309 号文　　　　　　　　哈尔滨关 1921 年 1 月 29 日

尊敬的海关总税务司（北京）：

　　兹附上瑷珲分关致哈尔滨关第 299 号及 301 号呈抄件：

　　　　"戊通航运公司于 1919—1920 年冬季在大黑河修建一处长约 275 英尺的码头，用于冬季存放该公司轮船。戊通公司提出于今年冬季扩建该码头，因此瑷珲分关帮办与之进行多次私下协商。依据去年夏天之经历，江水在流动过程中会不断冲刷该码头，导致淤泥堆积于大黑河港口。本署兹建议立即拆除戊通公司所建码头；由海关或戊通公司出资疏浚河道；或者根据超等关员华格伦（Wahlgren）先生之提议在大黑河下游另选一处冬季港口（参阅简图）。兹汇报，瑷珲分关曾就修建冬季港口一事请教两名前俄阿穆尔水道局（Amur River Conservancy Bureau）官员，他们认为大黑河下游有一处位于小岛和大陆之间的土地适宜修建冬季港口，戊通公司码头阻挡了该港口发展。这两名俄籍专家给出如下建议：立即在大黑河口岸修建前滩；疏浚与小岛连接的航道；可在布拉戈维申斯克（Blagovestchensk）对面之水域修建码头。现已将两名俄籍专家之建议告知道尹和戊通公司；修建前滩码头之事已由大黑河商人着手筹备。"

　　本署并非航务专业人士，因此需听从航务专家建议。请问贵署是否仍在考虑派遣巡江工司至大黑河口岸任职，以此填补已故贾登（Garden）先生的空缺，调查大黑河港口实际情况并参与研究港口问题等。

　　今年秋季初，本署派遣四等总巡谷兰体（Grundt）先生前往大黑河口岸任职，并参与上述港口调研等工作。但本署仍一直担心其无法胜任如此需要专业技能的工作。兹认为中国政府必然考虑黑龙江及其他边界河道上的航务工作，但是若无航务专家的帮助，则难以开展航务工作。

　　有鉴于此，兹建议海关可将两名俄阿穆尔河水道局（Amur River Conservancy Bureau）的俄籍专家推荐给中国政府，负责黑龙江上航务工作。过去 15 年来，柯宁（Krynin）先生和易保罗（Ignatieff）先生一直担任俄阿穆尔水道局（Amur River Conservancy Bureau）督办和巡江工司，负责俄国航务工作的同时亦为中国政府工作。

　　此呈抄件已发送至巡工司。

您忠诚的仆人

（签字）覃书（R. C. L. d' Anjou）

哈尔滨关税务司

附录 1

瑷珲分关超等帮办致哈尔滨关税务司

呈哈尔滨关 299 号文   瑷珲分关／大黑河 1920 年 12 月 11 日

尊敬的哈尔滨关税务司：

1. 入冬以来，本署一直就扩建码头或防波堤一事与戊通公司进行私下协商。现戊通公司已提出将该问题送至哈尔滨关与贵署商议。现汇报瑷珲分关对此事之意见。

2. 去年冬季，戊通公司未经瑷珲分关准许便于黑龙江上修建一处长约 275 英尺的码头，用于冬季存放该公司轮船，但春季到来黑龙江开江后该码头会对航运造成威胁。兹附上超等关员华格伦（Wahlgren）先生绘制的简图随呈附上，从图中可知该码头位置以及其与大黑河港口之关系。因在此修建码头，导致大黑河港口逐渐显露浅滩沙洲，对航行和货船靠岸造成极大威胁。今年夏天之经历表明戊通公司码头阻碍了大黑河一侧的江水流动，造成旋涡的速度减慢，因此在港口处沉积了大量淤泥。

3. 华格伦（Wahlgren）先生撰写之报告抄件也随呈附上。报告中提及"河道专家"指的是曾在俄国管理航务工作的两名俄籍官员。然而即使是对航务工作一无所知之人亦可看出戊通公司码头对航运产生的恶劣影响。兹认为应立即拆除戊通公司修建的码头。

4. 但是由于大黑河地区并无冬季港口供船只停靠，因此拆除戊通公司码头一事较为复杂。若海关或戊通公司可在大黑河或者是布拉戈维申斯克租赁一艘清淤船定期疏浚河道，则可消除大黑河港口的浅滩沙洲，亦可保留戊通公司码头。但长此以往其他航运公司必然也会计划在港口附近修建类似码头，导致淤泥迅速在港口堆积。

5. 另一解决方案便是在大黑河下游修建一处冬季港口（大黑河上游并无可用之地），可修建冬季港口之地已在简图中标出。戊通公司认为海关选择之地并不妥当，但本署怀疑其动机。若哈尔滨与大黑河铁路通车，则所有仓库和码头等都将修建于大黑河下游，现有戊通公司之码头将被弃用。

6. 由于现今黑龙江冰封，因此无法进行探测，也无法在今年冬季研究修建冬季港口之事。因此相关事宜只能待明年春季命三等总巡谷兰体（Grundt）先生与戊通公司职员一道前往大黑河下游考察后再做决定。

7. 此前的轮渡航线现在简图中标记为"冬季道路"。若海关可在浅滩沙洲中清除出一条航道,则对港口大有裨益；若轮渡靠岸地点可回到原有位置（即海关办公楼旁）,则为海关工作提供极大的方便。也许布拉戈维申斯克政府可准许瑷珲分关短期免费使用清淤船,长期使用清淤船之费用可从暂付账款中支出,并在港口修建完毕后用江捐税收填补暂付账款。

8. 待贵署批准修建冬季港口建议后,本署将就此事做初步考察。若考察结果适宜修建冬季港口,则本署将与道尹进行正式沟通并汇报修建所需准备工作及预算。

您忠诚的仆人

（签字）铎博赛（R. M. Talbot）

二等帮办前班

瑷珲分关超等关员致瑷珲分关帮办

大黑河 1920 年 11 月 6 日

戊通航运公司计划于今年冬季扩建防波堤,同时扩建其在黑龙江上大黑河港口上游的码头 35 英尺。河道专家认为,现在戊通公司码头已对港口产生不利影响（码头为一个长 275 英尺、宽 30 英尺的木制沉箱,箱内填充有石子,露出水面的部分长 265 英尺）,扩建后更不利于港口之发展。因为码头（即沉箱）中松动的石子等建材随江水冲刷移动,逐渐成为江中的阻碍物,最终随着旋涡流入下游并不断累积在港口下游江岸上,与防波堤距离极近。戊通公司码头仅为保护该公司船只可在开江之际免遭江面浮冰碰撞,但却因此造成了大黑河港口逐渐被淤泥堵塞。因此,为提升大黑河港口货运,戊通公司码头非但不应扩建,反而应予以拆除。

兹附一张大黑河港口简图,其中标明了由戊通公司修筑的防波堤,下游港口沙滩以及适宜修建冬季码头（轮船船主希望冬季可将轮船停靠于大黑河,故而所需花费均由轮船船主出资,且费用极低）的位置。

（签字）华格伦（O. W. Wahlgren）

头等验货后班

附录 2

瑷珲分关超等帮办致哈尔滨关税务司

呈哈尔滨关 <u>301</u> 号文　　　　　　　　　瑷珲分关 / 大黑河 1921 年 1 月 12 日

尊敬的哈尔滨关税务司：

参阅 1920 年 12 月 11 日瑷珲分关致哈尔滨关第 299 号呈：

"戊通公司计划扩建码头；大黑河港口现被淤泥阻塞，请求批准清淤费用。"

特做如下补充汇报。

1920 年 12 月 31 日，两名前俄阿穆尔河水道局（Amur River Conservancy Bureau）官员，督办柯宁（P.P.Krynin）先生和总巡江工司（Chief River Inspector）易保罗（P.T.Ignatieff）先生逃离俄国，准备经大黑河前往哈尔滨。此二人已在俄阿穆尔河水道局（Amur River Conservancy Bureau）工作 15 年之久，对黑龙江的航务管理和照明问题深有研究，因此本署就大黑河港口之事向此二人询问意见，同时询问修建冬季港口的适宜之处。易保罗（Ignatieff）先生用半天时间考察了拟修建冬季港口之处，两位先生为大黑河港口发展提出如下建议：

（1）如今戊通公司码头不利于港口发展。该码头下游水域深度原为 15 英寸，而如今同一水域深度只剩 2 英尺。若扩建该码头，则会导致港口下游部分淤泥堵塞，更不利于港口发展。

（2）黑龙江江水主要冲击大黑河一侧。近 10 年来，江水对大黑河沿岸的侵蚀严重；若不及时补救，未来 10 年大黑河所有堤岸将完全消失，地基也将遭到破坏。为作补救，沿岸堤坝需立即加固。今年戊通公司为其前滩修建堤岸，工程花费较少且效果极佳。

（3）兹建议在淤泥中清除出一条航道，连接海关办公楼前的小岛。此航道将极大改善港口工作，使得轮渡和轮船均可停靠于海关办公楼附近港口。

（4）大黑河下游小岛与大陆中间的水域面积广阔，足够停泊多艘船只（具体位置参阅瑷珲分关致哈尔滨关税务司第 299 号呈所附简图），为修建冬季港口的适宜地点。虽修建成本较高，但是冬季此处将成为黑龙江上最佳停泊点。

（5）有一小岛正对布拉戈维申斯克，便于运输，可在此处修建码头。

上述五段两名俄籍专家之观点可做如下提炼：两名俄籍专家与本署此前的意见一

致，即戊通公司码头对大黑河港口害处极大，不可任其扩建；应立即开展加固堤坝工程；需在淤泥中疏浚一条航道连接港口下游部分；可于大黑河下游小岛后身修建冬季港口；未来可在布拉戈维申斯克对面小岛修建码头。

现今，待黑龙江水势上涨之时，小岛与大陆之间将产生一条航道。若有一条航道可穿过淤泥，则从该航道挖出的淤泥及从拟修建冬季港口之处挖出的淤泥可用于堆积小岛。待哈尔滨至大黑河铁路修建完成，铁轨可直接铺设至正对布拉戈维申斯克的货运中心。

参阅本署此前就清淤一事所做汇报，清淤船之使用权一直由布拉戈维申斯克政府把持。据柯宁（Krynin）先生和易保罗（Ignatieff）先生称，远东共和国现急于与中国政府就黑龙江问题签署协定，因此目前难以判断海关是待正式签署协定后租借清淤船还是先私下接触布拉戈维申斯克政府租借清淤船。但本署建议贵署可先耐心等待。

本署将把本呈文要点以及此前呈文告知道尹，并希冀道尹立即联系当地商人筹集修建堤坝经费，于今年夏季购置相关建材。道尹回函称商人愿意接受海关提议，兹将道尹回函一并呈交。本署亦与戊通公司私下协商，并将柯宁先生和易保罗先生对码头一事之建议告知对方，对方已将海关意见呈送至哈尔滨总公司。

海关所面临的问题为淤泥不断在港口堆积，海关需大量钱款维持港口航运。柯宁先生和易保罗先生为河道航运专家，可帮助海关解决此问题。本署认为若将布拉戈维申斯克对面之小岛改建为运输中心，则上述问题便可迎刃而解。

您忠诚的仆人

铎博赉（R. M. Talbot）

二等帮办前班

该抄件内容真实有效，特此证明：
录事：方骏良二等同文供事正后班

致哈尔滨关第 <u>2477/82629</u> 号令　　海关总税务司署（北京）1921 年 2 月 17 日

尊敬的哈尔滨关税务司：

哈尔滨关第 2309 号呈收悉：

"兹附瑷珲分关致哈尔滨关第 299 号及 301 号呈抄件，呈中反对在 1919 年至 1920 年冬天拟建戊通航业公司码头，提议拆除该码头，由海关或戊通航业公司负责疏浚河道、修筑前滩堤岸及在大黑河下游修建冬季停泊处等工作；任命继任者接替前巡江工司贾登（H.G.Garden）先生之职位一事有利于中国政府确保两名俄国专家（柯林（Krynin）先生及易保罗（P. I. Ignatieff）先生）在黑龙江的疏浚工作。"

奉总税务司命令，现批复如下：上述事宜非常重要，瑷珲分关代理税务司予以关注之举十分正确；然因海关资金紧缺，无力承担修筑前滩堤岸、疏浚河道或修建冬季停泊处之工作，遂有必要尽快明确海关职权，海关将仅有管理港口及提供必要的港口航路标志之职责，其余职责交由当地政府（可能为道尹）。

若戊通航业公司有扩建戊通码头之意，请立即予以否决，并将该否决记录备案，对方告知现存码头危及航运及公众权利，应予以拆除一事。关于解决易保罗先生任巡江工司一事，请呈交书面意见，并汇报是否有人对易保罗先生兼任瑷珲分关理船厅一职有异议。

此抄件发送至巡工司。

您忠诚的仆人

（签字）包罗（C. A. V. Bowra）

总务科税务司

该抄件内容真实有效，特此证明：

录事：吉补思（C. S. Gibbes）未列等帮办

呈海关总税务司署 <u>2333</u> 号文　　　　　　　哈尔滨关 1921 年 3 月 3 日

尊敬的海关总税务司（北京）：

海关总税务司署第 2477/82629 号令（为回复哈尔滨关第 2309 号呈）收悉：

　　"就大黑河港口管理问题一事，本署认为，因缺少经费，故而海关无法在冬季为此港口修建堤岸或疏浚河道；但海关有义务参与港口管控、航路标志建设及其他宣誓领土主权之事；请贵署立即以向戊通公司发去信函，告知其不得继续扩建该公司位于大黑河的码头；任命易保罗（Ignatieff）先生担任巡江工司并兼任大黑河口岸理船厅。"

兹回复，本署已联系戊通航运公司，告知该公司位于大黑河的现有码头不利于港口发展，因此海关禁止其扩建，并命令戊通航运公司立即将该码头拆除，不得有误。

至于任命易保罗先生为巡江工司一事，本署与巡工司意见一致（本署也曾询问过头等总巡，其意见与本署二人一致），即任命一名俄国人填补已故贾登（Garden）先生的职位并不妥当。无论一名俄籍巡江工司有多么适任，在处理与俄国有关的工作时都很难保证客观公正。尤其是如今布拉戈维申斯克由布尔什维克党掌控，而易保罗先生可谓是布尔什维克党之叛徒，若其以巡江工司这一中国海关高级关员之身份出现在大黑河，则可能会令海关尴尬并为海关带来工作困难。本署自始至终认为应由一名非俄籍关员担任巡江工司，以此填补已故贾登先生之空缺；鉴于此前贾登先生因不熟识俄文而造成的不便，因此可令易保罗先生担任新巡江工司之属下，凭借其对中俄河界和俄文的了解为海关提供不可多得的服务。

至于任命易保罗先生为理船厅一事，本署反对的理由与上一段一致，即一名俄籍理船厅在处理俄国船只问题时难以保持客观公正。简言之，本署建议如下：立即任命一名非俄籍巡江工司（也可兼任理船厅）前往大黑河填补已故贾登先生之空缺，并任命易保罗先生为副巡江工司。若贵署批准《大黑河口岸理船章程》，则可于今年航运季开始之时（即 4 月）实施，届时急需讨论有关港口管理和改善之问题，海关也需巡江工司提供专业知识，因此对非俄籍巡江工司之任命较为急迫。

此呈抄件已发送至巡工司。

您忠诚的仆人

（签字）覃书（R. C. L. d' Anjou）

哈尔滨关税务司

2. 为完成港口测量工作及于大黑河建立水位标尺事

99.

I. G.   Aigun/Taheiho 27th February, 3.

Sir,

1.   I have the honour to report that, taking
advantage of the 1928 Agreement on Aids to Navigation
with the Russian Amur Navigation Office, I have
obtained in December last, from that Office, the
services of an Assistant Surveyor and Draughtsman
who, under the direction of Mr. Ignatieff, Technical
Adviser on Aids to Navigation, has conducted a
thorough survey of the Taheiho Harbour. The work
was started on the 19th December, and lasted until
the 30th, the Harbour being surveyed on a length of
1,300 sajen (9,100 feet) ; the basis taken for mea-
surements is the lowest level of the Amur on 16th
July, 1913 (sajen 57,562 = ft. 402.934 above the level
of the Pacific Ocean - at a point slightly above the
Custom House). - A Map, n a scale of 1 : 5000, has
                                                    been

The Inspector General of Customs,
          P E K I N G.

been compiled, and a copy of it is enclosed: I hope it will prove useful, especially when the future of the Taheiho Harbour is to be discussed.

I have issued the Russian Surveyor a daily allowance of $ 2.00, for the time he has been permanently stationed in Taheiho; the boatmen have been made use of for the work of breaking the ice, and for taking certain measurements ; but I had also to engage other and more competent workmen, for a total of $ 6.60. The total expense amounts therefore to $ 30.60.

2.   I have also to report that the arrangements formerly made for measuring the level of the Amur at Taheiho were inadequate and gave inaccurate results; and that I availed myself of the presence of the Russian Surveyor for the construction of a proper and satisfactory River-Gauge. This was completed on the 9th February, and a profile of it is enclosed. - The Surveyor worked at it for 13 days, and I issued him the same allowance as above, i.e. a total of $ 26; the expenses, including materials, amount to $ 44.78.

I have the honour to solicit your sanction
to

to the expenses incurred in the survey of the Harbour, and in erecting the River-Gauge, and to apply for instructions as to their accounts treatment.

Copy of this despatch is being forwarded to the Coast Inspector.

I have the honour to be,

Sir,

Your obedient Servant,

Acting Commissioner.

[A.—270]

No. 110 . Commrs .

Aigun No. 93,527 .

Inspectorate General of Customs,

PEKING, 15th March, 1923 .

SIR,

  I am directed by the Inspector General to acknowledge receipt of your Despatch No. 99 :

reporting that, taking advantage of the 1922 Agreement on Aids to Navigation with the Russian Amur Navigation Office, you obtained from that Office the services of an Assistant Surveyor who, under the direction of Mr. Ignatieff, Technical Adviser on Aids to Navigation, has conducted a thorough survey of the Taheiho Harbour, and soliciting authority for your expenditure in this connection amounting to $30.60; and also stating that you availed yourself of the presence of the Russian Surveyor to have a proper and satisfactory river-guage made at a cost of $44.78, for which expenditure you also request sanction;

and, in reply, to say that your idea of seizing the opportunity to have the harbour surveyed and a proper river-guage constructed was an excellent

one.

The Commissioner of Customs,

  A I G U N.

one. The Chart which has been prepared should prove very useful in the future, if the present soundings may be considered as permanent. The expenditure incurred, _viz._ $30.60 and $44.78 should be charged to your Amur River Dues Account in your Account D: Local Moneys Account.

I am,

Sir,

Your obedient Servant,

Chief Secretary.

呈海关总税务司署 <u>99</u> 号文　　　　　瑷珲关 / 大黑河 1923 年 2 月 27 日

尊敬的海关总税务司（北京）：

　　1. 兹汇报，俄阿穆尔水道局根据 1922 年航路标志协议，于去年 12 月派遣一名副测量师兼制图员至瑷珲关，在航务专门顾问易保罗（Ignatieff）先生的指导下，对大黑河港口进行了全面测量。测量工作于 12 月 19 日开始，至 12 月 30 日结束，港口测量长度共计 1300 俄丈（9100 英尺），以 1913 年 7 月 16 日黑龙江最低水位（太平洋海平面以上 57562 俄丈 =402934 英尺——略高于海关办公楼）为测量基准。大黑河港口地图已按 1/5000 之比例绘制而成，兹附地图抄件（附件 1，存档于航务专门顾问办事处），希望对大黑河将来之发展能有所助益。

　　费用方面，该俄国测量师留于大黑河期间，每日发放 2 银圆津贴；关于港口破冰及部分测量工作，虽主要由水手负责，但亦需雇用其他更有能力之工人，费用共计 6.50 银圆。因此该项工作支出总计 30.60 银圆。

　　2. 由于此前对于测量大黑河口岸黑龙江水位之工作准备不充分，以致测量结果不甚精确，故本署借此机会，请俄国测量师制作切实符合要求之水位标尺。该项工作于 2 月 9 日完工，兹附相关文件（附件 2，存档于航务专门顾问办事处）。该俄国测量师此项工作时长共计 13 天，每日发放 2 银圆津贴，共计 26 银圆；该项工作支出（包括物料费用）总计 44.78 银圆。

　　兹请示批准大黑河港口测量及建立水位标尺两项工作之支出，同时请对该两项支出之入账办法予以指示。

　　此抄件发送至巡工司。

您忠诚的仆人

包安济（G. Boezi）

瑷珲关署理税务司

致瑷珲关第 <u>110/93527</u> 号令　　　海关总税务司署（北京）1923 年 3 月 15 日

尊敬的瑷珲关税务司：

第 99 号呈收悉。

　　"汇报如下情况：根据与俄罗斯阿穆尔河航政部订立的 1922 年《航路标志协定》，奉航务专门顾问易保罗（Ignatieff）先生的命令，一名航政部副测量师对大黑河港口进行了全面测量，请示支付调查费用共计 30.60 银圆；另外，贵署趁此机会让俄罗斯测量师帮助建立适当的水位标尺，费用共计 44.78 银圆，请示批准此开支。"

　　奉总税务司命令，现批复如下：兹告知，抓住此机会调查港口并建立适当的水位标尺，您的这个主意非常棒。如果当前测探水深保持永久不变，则此图将来必定非常有用。所需费用（即 30.60 银圆和 44.78 银圆）应由贵署 D 账户暂记账中的阿穆尔河江捐账项划转。

您忠诚的仆人

包罗（C. A. V. Bowra）

总务科税务司

3. 为拆除戊通航业公司建于大黑河港口的码头所采取的措施事

Replied to in No. 129

118

. C.

Aigun/Taheiho   12th May, 1923.

Sir,

The Harbin Commissioner, in his despatch No. 2309 reported that a Jetty built by the Wut'ung S. S. Company in Taheiho was, according to experts, detrimental to the Harbour, and the cause of the silting of steamers anchorage along a considerable stretch of the foreshore. You directed in your Despatch No. 2477 / 82,629 to Harbin that any further extention of the Jetty was to be vetoed at once. This was done (Harbin Despatch No. 2333), and I have the honour to report that the Company, acting under instructions from the Customs, opened in the spring of 1921 two large passages in the Jetty, as a provisional improvement.

After my arrival, I took the question up, but was asked by the Wut'ung Co. to wait until the appointment of a Harbour Master or River

Inspector,

Inspector General of Customs,

P E K I N G.

Inspector, (which appointments were then contemplated) before deciding on the removal of the Jetty:
anyhow, no work could be done in the summer.

Later, in the winter, 1921 - 1922, I discussed this question with the newly appointed
Superintendent; but, while the point was still
at issue, the appointment of a River Inspector
was once more proposed (Aigun despatch No. 44 and
I. G. Despatch No. 58 / 90,054) and the Superintendent asked me to wait until the appointment be
made.

When Mr. Ignatieff arrived, in October,
1922, I asked for his advice, and late in
November, on the Superintendent's return from a
two months' voyage to Mukden and Tsitsihar, I
reported him the expert opinion of Mr. Ignatieff,
which was unfavourable to maintaining the Jetty.
The matter dragged along till February, when I
wrote to the Superintendent, giving Mr. Ignatieff's
opinion, and saying that the removal of the Jetty
would be less difficult this year, the Company
having no steamers wintering in Taheiho. The
Superintendent transmitted my despatch to the
Company,

Company, which stated in reply that they had
consulted competents (?) when building the Jetty,
and were told it would do no harm to the Harbour;
that the Jetty was used for sheltering Steamers
from the ice at the closing and opening of the
River, and that one dredge, the property of the
Heilungchiang Government entrusted to the Kuang Hsin
Kung Ssŭ, was moored below the Jetty. In view of
these arguments, the Superintendent again queried
whether the Jetty should actually be removed. - In
the meantime the survey of the Harbour was completed,
and the resuting map showed most clearly the damage
done by the Jetty to the anchorage just in front
of the Wut'ung Co. and the Ferry Pontoon. This
plan I submitted to the Superintendent, telling him
at the same time that, since he was still in
doubt, I would submit the question to the Coast
Inspector. - But the plan apparently had a decisive
impression on the Superintendent, who asked for a
copy for transmission to the Company. - This I
forwarded, and then the Superintendent ordered the
removal of the Jetty, and informed the Customs
accordingly. His despatch however was sent and

received

received on 18th April.

But on 17th the Wut'ung Co. was already advertising on theatre handbills and offering merchants, free of charge, the stones of which the Jetty is made, provided they would cart them away at their own expenses.

The Agent of the Wut'ung Co. was sent for at once, and it appeared that, without a word to the Customs, without any idea as to how the work should be carried on, the work had been started. The Jetty consists of a structure, divided into three parts, held together by a frame of stout wooden poles, filled in with large stones. The wooden frame of half the section more advanced into the River had been hastily removed by a dozen or so workers, and the stones had simply been scattered on the ice. The Technical Adviser, sent to investigate on the damage done and on the possible remedies, reported the fact as a catastrophe. He and the Senior Out-Door Officer estimated at 75 cubic sajens (25,725 cubic feet) the amount of stones so scattered on the ice,

ready

ready to fill the Harbour as soon as the ice
should break. - It was too late, with the scanty
means at the disposal of the Co., to remove the
whole Jetty before the opening of the River . I
therefore ordered the Company to stop demolition at
once, and to have the stones removed; but it was
clear that the Company had no funds whatever for
doing the work, and that merchants could not find
carts to transport the stones offered them free
of charge, because the soldiers of a Company about
to leave for Tsitsihar were requisitioning any carts
that appeared in the street. After a hasty understanding with the Chamber of Commerce, the Taoyin-
Superintendent promised he would support the Customs
in their protest, should any of the carts used for
the transport of stones and provided with a Customs
Flag be requisitioned. Two amongst the most powerful
merchants thus started work at once; in one instance
a few carts were stopped by the Military, but a
protest of the Chamber of Commerce to the Military
Authorities (without interference from the Customs)
obtained their release. The soldiers did not leave
after all, and the eating of stones went on at a
                                                quick

quick pace. By the end of April, before the ice
broke, all the stones had been taken away: half
the furthest section of the Jetty had been entirely
removed, the other half had been properly reinforced,
so that all danger of the Harbour being encumbered
with stones had disappeared. - I have written a
despatch to the Superintendent, explaining matters,
and asking that the remainder of the Jetty be
removed in the autumn, soon after the closing of
the River.

It is unfortunate that the Jetty could not
be completely wiped out before opening of the Navigation. However, thus reduced, it will do only
little harm, and what is left should now, without
further questions, be removed in the autumn.

Copy of correspondence on the subject with
the Superintendent is appended (Append No 1).A rough
sketch shows the Jetty as it was originally, how
it was modified in 1921, and how it is at present
(Append No. 2)..

Copy of this despatch is being sent to the
Coast

Coast Inspector.

I have the honour to be,

Sir,

Your obedient Servant,

Acting Commissioner.

呈海关总税务司署 <u>118</u> 号文　　　　　　　　　瑷珲关／大黑河 1923 年 5 月 12 日

尊敬的海关总税务司（北京）：

　　哈尔滨关致海关总税务司署第 2309 号呈中曾汇报，经专家鉴定，戊通航业公司在大黑河所建码头对港口不利，将导致前滩的轮船停泊地点被淤泥充塞。海关总税务司署致哈尔滨关第 2477/82629 号令指示，凡涉及码头扩建之事，均应立即否决。哈尔滨关致海关总税务司署第 2333 号呈回复已照办。兹汇报，戊通航业公司已照海关指示，于 1921 年春在该码头处挖掘两条宽阔水道，以作临时改善办法。

　　本署抵达大黑河后，立即着手处理该码头之问题，但戊通航业公司提出，希望待瑷珲关任命理船厅或巡江工司后，再决定拆除码头之事（因此当时方有任命理船厅或巡江工司之提议）；且因当时正值夏季，无论如何皆无法开展拆除工事，故暂行搁置。

　　至 1921—1922 年冬季，本署方与新任海关监督再次商议此事，但仍未做出最终决定，海关监督希望待巡江工司到任后，再行处理，本署无奈再次申请任命（参阅瑷珲关致海关总税务司署第 44 号呈及海关总税务司署致瑷珲关第 58/90054 号令）。

　　易保罗（P. I. Ignatieff）先生于 1922 年 10 月到达大黑河后，本署便就此事向其请教，其认为不应继续保留该码头。因此，待海关监督于 11 月末从奉天及齐齐哈尔公干两月返回后，本署便向其说明易保罗先生之意见，然此事再次被搁置。至 1923 年 2 月，本署再次向海关监督致函说明，鉴于戊通航业公司今年并无轮船在大黑河过冬，易保罗先生认为，今年更易于进行码头拆除工事。海关监督遂将本署信函转发至戊通航业公司，但该公司却称在修建该码头之前，已向有关部门进行过咨询，且有关部门认为该码头的建造非但对港口无害，而且还可以在封江至开江期间为轮船提供庇荫，使之免受风雪的侵袭，目前正有一艘由黑龙江政府委托给广信公司的疏浚船停靠于该码头。鉴于戊通航业公司的上述申辩，海关监督再次向本署确认是否应拆除该码头。与此同时，大黑河港口的测量工作业已完成，测量图纸明确显示，该码头已对戊通航业公司与渡船码头前方的停泊地点造成损害。本署遂将测量图纸发送至海关监督，并表示若其对此依旧存疑，本署可将此事呈予巡工司定夺。海关监督查看图纸后便不再犹疑，要求本署提供一份图纸抄件，以发送给戊通航业公司；本署已照办。随后海关监督便下令拆除码头，并告知海关据此行事；但该指令的公文至 4 月 18 日方发送至本署。

　　而戊通航业公司已于 4 月 17 日派发传单，告知商人可免费将码头石料运走，唯须自理运输费用。

本署知晓后，立即召见了戊通航业公司代理，结果发现，该公司在未知会海关、未做好拆除计划的前提下，已开始码头拆除工作。码头整体由硬木架支撑，内中分为三个部分，各以大块石料填充。一半的木质框架延伸至江中，现已被十余名工人拆除，废弃的石料竟随意散落在冰面上。本署遂着航务专门顾问前去调查目前已造成的损害程度，以确定是否还有何补救措施，航务专门顾问调查后称此乃灾难一场。根据航务专门顾问与超等外班关员的估计，目前大约有 75 立方俄丈（25725 立方英尺）的废弃石料散落在冰面上，一旦江面融化，这些石料必将填满港口。而戊通航业公司已然无法于开江前完成整座码头的拆除工作。

有鉴于此，本署立即通知戊通航业公司停止拆除工作，优先清理废弃石料。然而，戊通航业公司并无可用于清理废弃石料的资金，而市面上的货车又皆被即将前往齐齐哈尔的士兵所征用，商人们一时难以找到合适的货车。道尹兼海关监督与商会商议后，迅速达成共识，决定由商人出具抗议书，保证海关可征用到一切可运输石料的货车，并在车上悬挂海关旗帜，以求尽快完成石料清理工作。之后，商人中最有实力的两位立即开始行动。一次，几辆货车被军方拦下，但还未经海关出面干涉，仅凭商会的抗议书，军方便将车辆释放。最终，本欲前往齐齐哈尔的士兵均未能按时出发，废弃石料的清理和运输工作得以迅速完成。所有废弃石料均已于 4 月底冰面破裂之前被运走。此外，码头最远区域已有一半拆除完毕，另一半也已完全加固，目前已无需担忧港口会被石料填满。本署已向海关监督致函说明情况，并请求于秋季封江后继续开展码头剩余部分的拆除工作。

遗憾的是，今年未能于航运季开始之前完全拆除该码头。尽管目前码头面积已缩小不少，对港口的危害也已降到最低，但若无其他问题，码头剩余部分还应于秋季予以拆除。

随呈附上本署与海关监督之间关于此事的往来信函抄件（附件 1）。附件 2 所示为码头初建平面草图，码头于 1921 年改建后的平面草图，以及码头目前状态的平面草图。

此抄件发送至巡工司。

您忠诚的仆人

包安济（G. Boezi）

瑷珲关署理税务司

4. 为协商挖掘新河道及通过增加江捐税率支付改建费用之提议事

Harbour Improvement: negotiations in connection
with digging of new channel for, reporting on.
Taoyin's proposal that same be paid for from
increased River Dues Tariff, submitting.

311.
I.G.

311.
I.G.

Aigun   18th April, 1927.

Sir,

        With reference to my telegram of the 16th

March, 1927:

        Conditions favour and require immediate
dredging of channel across spit in
harbour for less than $2,000 while
river bed is frozen. Aigun despatch
No. 99. May I proceed with idea and
report Taoyin to find money:

and to your reply of the 18th March, 1927:

        Your telegram of 16th March: As no
aids money available you may only
proceed ? with improvement if Taoyin
willing provide funds from local source
which must be in hand before work is
begun. Report action taken by despatch:

I now have to report on my negotiations in
connection with this project. Before going into
details as to what has been done, however, it

might

Officiating Inspector General of Customs,

Peking.

might be well to relate the causes that have

brought about the necessity for such a channel.

In the winter of 1919/20 the Wutung

Steamship Company built a jetty some 275 feet in

length extending into the river at the upper part

of the harbour to serve as a protection for their

steamers against floating ice. This jetty was built

without the permission of the Customs and without

expert advice. It soon became apparent that the

current, which naturally flowed through the Taheiho

harbour, was being deflected to the other side of

the river and that the harbour was silting up.

This state of affairs was reported in Harbin

despatch No. 2309 to I. G.; and in I. G. despatch

No. 2477/82,629 in reply the Inspector General records

the opinion that the jetty should be removed. Aigun

despatch No. 118 reports the removal of the outer

half of the offending jetty though the sketch plan

enclosed did not show that there still remained a

height of some three or four feet of the original

structure

structure resting on the bottom of the river, to
continue the silting process in a lesser degree.
I. G. despatch No. 129/94,536 contains the Inspector
General's congratulations on the successful removal
of the jetty. I now enclose a sketch showing
the original plan of the jetty, and its dimensions
after its partial removal which might well be
compared to the plan just referred to.

Aigun despatch No. 99 reported that a
survey of the harbour had been made and a copy of
this survey was enclosed. From an examination of
that chart it can be seen to what an extent
silting up had occurred at the time the survey was
made - 5 years ago. This process had been
accelerated by the construction of the Wutung jetty
in the winter of 1919/20 and continued rapidly
until its removal during the winter of 1921/22 when
the survey was made. No complete survey of the
harbour has been made since but it has been
ascertained that on the removal of the jetty the

main

main current of the river did not resume its old
course and the spit has been growing steadily until
the future of the harbour has now become a matter
of grave concern. The worst sufferers have been
the Wutung Company themselves (now known as the
Tungpei Company) the approach to their wharf having
shoaled to an extent that, whereas their steamers
originally came alongside, they must now lie some
200 feet out in the stream access being had to
the wharf by a long gangway.

On my return to this port I again took
up the matter of improvement of the harbour and
had obtained estimates as to what it would cost
to dredge a channel across the spit using the
mining dredge that now lies idle in the harbour.
At the very least these operations would cost some
$5,000 which seemed a large sum to raise in this
poverty stricken port. It was obvious, however,
that further postponement of action would only mean
greater expense and that something would have to be

done

done when the Technical Adviser to the Aids Commission hit on the expedient of digging the channel by manual labour while the river bed was still frozen. As this could be done at much smaller expense and as there was very little time to spare before the ice broke up I at once submitted the project to the Taoyin/Superintendent explaining that it was the very minimum of work demanded. On his agreeing in principle to the work being undertaken, at a cost already estimated at from $1,500 to $2,000, I wired you in the sense quoted above. Copy of my despatch to him in this connection is enclosed.

On the receipt of your reply I again consulted the Taoyin, informing him of its nature, and asking him how he could raise the money locally. His idea was to pay for the work out of Aids funds, where there is a small surplus of about the required amount over the estimates of 1927, but I took the position that the expenditures

concerned

concerned this port only and that, moreover, the

repayment of advances already received from the

Sungari Aids took precedence over anything else. It

might be remarked at this point that the relative

authority of the Taoyin and the Commissioner over

the administration of the Aids funds has never been

clearly defined and I shall refer the question to

you again at some future time.

On the 2nd instant the Taoyin called a

meeting at his office to consider the question of

funds and invited the Chairman of the Chamber of

Commerce, the Manager of the Bank of China, the

Manager of the Tungpei Steamship Company, the

Technical Adviser to the Amur Aids and myself to

be present. When the Taoyin asked my plan for

raising funds for the new channel I told him that

I thought the simplest and most fair system would

be to put a local surtax of 5% on the existing

River Dues Tariff. Last year the collection from

this source was some $20,000. This would give a

revenue

revenue of $1,000 and in two years a loan of
$2,000, which might be raised from the Bank of
China, could be repaid.

I found, however, that the Taoyin had
worked up a much more ambitious program and after
relating how the Aids Commission had not paid its
way and was in debt to the Sungari Aids (a fact
I had often reminded him of) he announced that he
was in receipt of instructions from the Provincial
authorities to the effect that the River Dues Tariff
should be increased. With this increase he proposed
to pay for the digging of the new channel and to
gradually repay the advances from the Sungari Aids.

When the Taoyin asked my opinion of this
proposal I said I could say nothing definite until
I had referred the matter to you but that I was
sympathetic with his ideas and would recommend them
to your favourable consideration. At the same time
the others present all approved the plan.

In approving the Taoyin's suggestion and

agreeing

agreeing to recommend it to you it might appear
that I had receded from my original position that
the digging of the channel should be paid for
locally. However I had read into the first phrase
of your telegram - "As no Aids money available" -
that were such funds on hand they could be used
for this purpose. Further I concluded that, from
the fact that the President of the Chamber of
Commerce was present at the conference, the Taoyin
wished primarily to get the sanction of that body
to the increase in the River Dues Tariff and were
it to be arranged that the present improvement of
the harbour was to be paid for from such an
increase, and not to be a local surtax, the
Chamber of Commerce would the more readily agree.
As the President of this organization had already
approved the Taoyin's proposal, as noted above, I
felt that if I still held out that the digging
of the channel should be paid for locally I
would be "putting a spoke in the Taoyin's wheel"

and

and the repayment of the Sungari advances, involving a much larger sum, might be indefinitely postponed. It is extremely doubtful if we will have another Taoyin who is so punctillious in such matters.

Pending the final settlement of the question I asked for an advance of $2,000 to be raised by a loan with the Bank of China. This request was referred to the Manager of the Bank of China, who was present as stated above. He at first demurred to making a loan without my signature in support of the Taoyin's but soon agreed to accept the latter's signature only.

The extent by which the River Dues Tariff was to be raised was then discussed and it was agreed that the Taoyin should address me officially in the matter giving general instructions as to the increase and that the details should be worked out with the Chamber of Commerce. I have since received the necessary despatch and enclose a copy. I have made a rough estimate that the

increased

increased collection will amount to some $10,000 per

year, but will address you further on the subject

as soon as the matter can be gone into thoroughly.

The next day the Taoyin and the Manager of

the Bank of China left suddenly for Harbin and I

was nervous for fear the loan could not be arranged.

However I managed to get it through after considerabl

difficulty but the Bank would give the Taoyin a no

more favourable rate than $1\frac{1}{3}\%$ per month. As time

was so pressing I advised the Acting Taoyin to

accept these terms and the money was duly handed

over to me. The loan was made for only one month,

however, on account of the exorbitant interest rate

(the local Bank of China as now managed is anything

but a public-spirited organization) and I have the

honour to recommend that, if the Taoyin's proposal

that the cost of the new channel be paid out of

the increased River Dues collection meets with your

approval, you authorize me to repay this loan at

once from Aids funds, where there is an available

balance

balance at present, and pending the introduction of the new tariff on the opening of navigation this spring. The loan was dated 7th April. I should add that the Taoyin made the point that in the future other harbours along the Amur, where there is no harbour organization, would also be helped, as required, from Aids funds.

The digging of the channel has since been taken in hand and is being rapidly pushed to completion. I will forward in due course a full report of the work done and the expenditure incurred in this connection. At the same time I shall report the successful effort on my part to have the Tungpei Company remove that part of their jetty reported above as remaining on the bottom of the river, after the outer half of the jetty was all supposed to have been taken away. This improvement was necessary in order to accelerate the flow of water through the new channel.

The Chinese correspondence exchanged during

the

the month of March, in the above connection, is
being forwarded in March Non-Urgent Chinese
Correspondence.

I have the honour to be,

Sir,

Your obedient Servant,

Acting Commissioner.

REFERENCE.

From I. G.   To I. G.

2477/82,629 to Harbin   Harbin No.2309.
129/94,536 to Aigun   Aigun No.99.
                          "   " 118.

350
I.G.

INSPECTORATE GENERAL OF CUSTOMS,

Aigun   No. 112,642.

PEKING,   18th May 1927.

Sir,

 I have to acknowledge receipt of your

Despatch No. 311 :

  reporting, in connection with the
necessity for the immediate dredging
of a channel across the spit in
the harbour which has continued to
expand during recent years, that the
Technical Advisor to the Aids Commission
had suggested, in the interests of
economy, that the channel be excavated
by manual labour while the river bed
was frozen, at a cost estimated
between $ 1,500 and $ 2,000; stating
that the Taoyin, in order to meet
this expenditure and to provide for
repayment of the advances received by
the Amur Aids to Navigation Account
from the Sungari Aids Account, had
announced that he was in receipt of
instructions from the provincial
      authorities

Commissioner of Customs,

 A I G U N.

authorities to arrange for an increase
of the River Dues Tariff, to come
into force as from the opening of
navigation this Spring, and that the
Chairman of the Chamber of Commerce,
the Manager of the Bank of China and
the Manager of the Tungpei Steamship
Company had accepted this proposal;
and adding that a loan of $ 2,000.00
to carry out the proposed work of
excavation had been made by the
Taoyin with the Bank of China, on
which interest @ 1 1/5 % per month
was charged, and asking that my
authority be given for the immediate
repayment of this loan from the
balance of funds in your Amur Aids
Account on the understanding that this
sum will be recovered from surplus Aids
receipts as a result of an increased
tariff :

and, in reply, to say that, in view of the

understanding which has now been reached with the

Taoyin in regard to the proposed increase of the

River Dues Tariff, I have to authorise you to repay

to the Bank of China the loan contracted in the

                                         name

name of the Taoyin, for the purpose of this

harbour improvement work, from your Amur Aids

Account.   I have, however, to point out

that you should have been guided more literally

by the actual wording of my telegram of 18th

March 1927, which informed you that there were no

Aids funds available for the purpose of this

harbour improvement, and that you should only

consider proceeding with the work after the Taoyin

had actually provided you with the necessary funds

from local sources.   The funds now remaining

in your Aids Account were specially advanced from

Sungari Aids Account to meet a clearly defined

programme of Aids work on the Amur; and if these

funds are not required for the purpose for which

they were allocated, they should properly be

returned to the Sungari Aids Account.

In this connection, I have to request you

to observe that no arrangements are to be made

for the collection of increased dues until the

Shui-wu

Shui-wu Ch'u's authority for the introduction of the revised tariff has been received.   You should, therefore, request the Taoyin to lose no time in submitting his proposals in this regard, and as it is advisable that I should be aware of what is being recommended, you should forward, for my information, a copy of the further correspondence exchanged on this subject.

You are also requested to send a copy of Aigun Despatch No. 311 to the Harbin Commissioner for his information.

I am,

Sir,

Your obedient Servant,

Officiating Inspector General.

呈海关总税务司署 <u>311</u> 号文　　　　　　　　瑷珲关 1927 年 4 月 18 日

尊敬的代理海关总税务司（北京）：

根据瑷珲关 1927 年 3 月 16 日电呈：

"航务顾问建议在河床冻结的情况下，最好迅速疏通港口沙嘴的河道，并能将费用控制在 2000 银圆以内。瑷珲关第 99 号呈：瑷珲关可否疏通河道并呈请道尹筹款。"

及海关总税务司署 1927 年 3 月 18 日复电：

"贵署 3 月 16 日电呈：当前没有可用的黑龙江航路标志专款，但只要道尹同意从地方财政拨款，且资金能够在工程开始前到位，瑷珲关或可以修缮港口河道。请呈文报告已采取的措施。"

兹呈报该工程的相关协商事宜。首先说明亟须改造河道之原因，而后将详述已采取的措施。

1919-1920 年冬季，为避免轮船撞上浮冰，戊通航业公司修筑了长约 275 英尺的码头，一直延伸至港口上部的江中。但该码头的修筑既未得到海关批准，也未咨询专家意见，弊端很快便显露无遗：大黑河港口的水流本该顺流而下，却因受阻而流向河道另一侧，以致港口被淤泥堵塞。哈尔滨关致海关总税务司署第 2309 号呈汇报了上述情况；海关总税务司署第 2477/82629 号令批复应拆除该码头。瑷珲关第 118 号呈汇报，该码头外部已被拆除，但该呈所附草图并未显示剩余三四英尺的水下部分。在海关总税务司署第 129/94536 号令中，总税务司对瑷珲关成功拆除码头表示祝贺。兹附码头原图，并标明其水下剩余部分，不妨将该草图与瑷珲关第 118 号呈所附草图比较查看。

瑷珲关致海关总税务司署第 99 号呈曾上报一份港口测量数据，并附测量数据副本。通过测量图可以看出五年前测量时港口的淤塞程度。1919-1920 年冬季，戊通码头修筑后，淤塞程度每况愈下，直至 1921-1922 年冬季测量期间，码头才得以拆除。虽然，此后海关一直未进行全面的港口测量，但可以明确的是，码头拆除后，江水主流并未沿原河道流过，且沙嘴外扩速度稳定，直至目前港口之未来成为备受关注之事。受此影响最为严重的是戊通航业公司（现为东北航路局），通往码头的水域变浅，以致本可以并排行驶的轮船现在必须停在 200 英尺开外的河流中，再通过一条长长的跳板到达码头。

本署返回该口岸后即刻重新着手处理港口改建问题，目前港口有闲置挖泥船，若用其疏通沙嘴处河道，费用预计约 5000 银圆，但就港口目前的经济状况而言，难以筹集如此大额之款项。然而延期动工势必会产生更多费用。此时,航务专门顾问想到可趁河床冻结之时通过人工挖掘来疏浚河道,如此便可大大减少费用。但距离冰面融化的时日已不多,该行动刻不容缓,本署遂立即将此情况上报道尹兼海关监督。道尹兼海关监督基本同意该措施,并表示应将费用控制在1500银圆到2000银圆之间。本署已将上述内容电呈贵署。随函附上本署致道尹兼海关监督的呈文副本。

收到贵署的批复后,本署再次与道尹洽谈,告知此事利害,并询问其如何在当地筹款。因1927年预算仍有少量结余,故道尹有意从黑龙江航路标志资金拨款。但本署认为,此开支仅与本口岸有关,且偿还松花江航路标志账户的垫付款优先于一切。就此,可以看出道尹与税务司各自对黑龙江航路标志专款管理的权限从未明确,将来本署会就该问题向贵署专门呈报。

本月2日,道尹在黑河道尹公署召开会议,邀请商会主席、中国银行经理、东北航路局经理、黑龙江航务专门顾问及本署一同探讨筹款问题。道尹问及本署新河道筹款之方案时,本署回复在当前江捐税率的基础上加5%的地方附加税乃最简单、最公平之方案。去年征收江捐约20000银圆,若在当前江捐税率的基础上加5%的地方附加税,预计税款可增加1000银圆,两年内即可偿还中国银行的2000银圆贷款。

但本署知晓,道尹已制定出一个更加大胆的计划。道尹说明黑龙江水道委员会如何资不抵债,如何欠下松花江航路标志账户大量债款(本署经常提醒其此事)之后,宣布已收到省政府增加江捐税率之指示。道尹提议,用增加的税款支付疏浚河道的费用,再逐步偿还松花江航路标志账户的垫付款。

道尹询问本署对此提议的看法时,本署回复需将此事提交至总税务司公署之后,才能予以确切答复。事实上,本署十分赞同道尹之提议,望贵署酌情考虑。其他与会人员亦同意此方案。

本署最初表示该河道疏浚费用应由地方承担,现又赞成道尹之提议并荐予贵署,看似有所偏离,但贵署电令前半句“当前没有可用的黑龙江航路标志资金”是否可理解为若有资金便可用于此事。本署从商会主席出席会议一事进一步推断,道尹主要希望得到商会的支持,以此增加江捐税率。如果当前港口改建费用取自增加的江捐税收,而非地方附加税,商会定会欣然接受。如上文所述,商会主席已赞同道尹之提议,若本署坚持由地方承担疏浚河道的费用,势必会破坏道尹之计划,而且偿还松花江航路标志账户垫付款一事也会无限期推迟。道尹处事一丝不苟,实为难得。

在等待最终解决方案之时,本署请求从中国银行贷款2000银圆。如上所述,中国银行经理亦出席了此次会议，本署已向其提出贷款请求，其最初表示，若无本署签字，便不予提供贷款，但很快又同意只需道尹签字即可。

之后会议探讨了江捐税率的增幅问题，商定由道尹向本署正式致函下达增税指示，具体细节需与商会协商制定。本署已收悉该函并于此附上其副本。本署粗略估算每年税收将增加 1000 银圆左右。若有进展，本署将向贵署报告。

次日，道尹及中国银行经理突然动身前往哈尔滨，本署担忧贷款之事难成，幸而纵有重重困难，终将此事解决。但银行提供给道尹的最低优惠贷款利率为每月 1.2%，鉴于时间紧迫，本署建议署理道尹接受，钱款亦适时交予本署。由于利率过高，且贷款期限仅为一个月（现在黑河的中国银行绝非公益组织），兹提议，若贵署同意道尹之提议，用增加的江捐税款支付疏浚河道的费用，那么可授权本署在等待今春开航引入新税率之际，即刻用黑龙江航路标志资金的可用余额偿还该贷款。贷款日期为 4 月 7 日。另外，道尹还指出，将来黑龙江沿岸其他没有港务组织机构的港口，也会按需从黑龙江航路标志资金得到拨款。

目前河道疏浚工作已经开始，并将加速完工。本署将适时向贵署汇报完工情况及相关支出情况。兹报告，鉴于码头外部已全部拆除，本署已成功让东北航路局拆除码头水下部分。为加速新河道的水流速度，该项改建工程十分必要。

有关上述问题的中文往来通信已于 3 月在中国非紧急信件中呈交贵署。

您忠诚的仆人

铎博赉（R. M. Talbot）

署理税务司

致瑷珲关第 <u>350/112642</u> 号令　　　　海关总税务司署（北京）1927 年 5 月 18 日

尊敬的瑷珲关税务司：

　　第 311 号呈收悉：

　　　　"近年来港口沙嘴不断扩大，疏浚水道变得十分必要。兹报告，黑龙江水道委员会技术顾问出于成本考虑，建议在河床冻结时，可用人力疏浚水道，预计开销为 1500 银圆至 2000 银圆；为支付此开支，且需偿还松花江标志账户拨给黑龙江航路标志账户的预支款，道尹奉省政府指令声明，安排提高江捐税率事宜，自今年春天航季伊始生效，商会主席、中国银行经理以及戊通航业公司经理均已接受此提议；道尹已向中国银行贷款 2000.00 银圆，用于开展疏浚水道工作，借款利息为每月 1.2%。并且，道尹要求我署授权，如果黑龙江航路标志账户因提高江捐税率而有盈余，则用来偿还此次贷款。"

　　现批复如下，兹告知：鉴于提议提高江捐税率事宜已达成共识，现授权贵署用黑龙江航路标志账户的盈余偿还道尹在中国银行的贷款，以开展港口改建工作。但是，我须强调，贵署应完全遵照 1927 年 3 月 18 日的电报行事，其中已告知贵署，航路标志账户没有可用的资金用来改建港口。所以，必须在收到道尹的地方经费后，方可考虑开展疏浚水道工作。现黑龙江标志账户余额应为松花江标志账户专项预支款，用以支付黑龙江上航路标志工作明确规定的项目；如果此资金不用于规定目的，则应返还至松花江航路标志账户。

　　对此，要求贵署注意，只有税务处正式授权修改税率，方可安排增税事宜。因此，贵署须请道尹立即提交此事的建议书。鉴于我需了解此事项，请贵署提交此事的往来信件副本，以供我参考。

　　敬请抄送瑷珲关第 311 号呈至哈尔滨关税务司，供其参考。

您忠诚的仆人

易纨士（A. H. F. Edwardes）

代理总税务司

5. 为大黑河港口前滩筑堤事

BUNDING OF HARBOUR FORESHORE, TAHEIHO: completion of
major portion of, from Aids funds, reporting.

439.

I. G.   Registered.

Aigun   12th July, 1929.
                                        5th August, 1929.

Sir,

Appendix No. 1.

1.   I have the honour to append a copy
of a letter received from the Provisional Mayor
(formerly Taoyin), President of the Chinese Aids
Commission, dated the 9th April, 1929, in which
he states that he is in receipt of a report
from the Technical Adviser to the Amur Aids
Commission recommending that an appropriation
of $2,000 be made from Aids funds for the
purpose of strengthening the foreshore which had
been greatly weakened (by last year's flood),
and that a sum of $406.63, advanced from Aids
account last year, be regarded as a charge on
Aids and directing that these two amounts be
paid; also copy of a second letter of the
same date in which the Mayor directs that the

Appendix No. 2.

appropriation be increased to $5,000 which sum
is to include the $406.63 expended last year.

2.   In my semi-official letter No.106 of the
20th April, 1929, I report that I had received
the above instructions and asked that I be
informed by wire if they should be put into
                                                effect.

THE INSPECTOR GENERAL OF CUSTOMS,

    SHANGHAI.

effect. Your telegram of the 4th May in reply
was to the effect that you had no objection to
the proposed bunding scheme provided that the
Amur did not suffer thereby and the Sungari
Aids Commission did not demand immediate refund
of the advances made.

3.   The scheme of bunding, as proposed by
the Technical Adviser to the Mayor, and
provisionally sanctioned by yourself, has now been
practically completed. As it is a work of great
importance to Taheiho and as further work of the
same nature, though not so extensive, may have
to be taken in hand, I consider that it would
be well to place on record an account of what
has been done toward improving the foreshore
during the past few years, and of the present
project.

4.   The question of conserving the foreshore
was taken up by myself in 1921 when Aigun was
a sub-office of Harbin and I was Assistant-in-
Charge here. At that time it could be seen
that the bund was being eroded away and that it
was important that steps be taken at once if
it was to be preserved at a good width. I
accordingly drew up a scheme for bunding that
included the foreshore from the lower end of the
Wu Tung (now Tungpei) Steamship Company's property
to the Public Park, a distance of 450 chang, at
a rough cost of $15,000, not including provision
for metalling and future upkeep. The improvement
was to be paid for by a system of wharfage

Dues

Dues, the scheme in its entirety being submitted to the Taoyin for discussion with the local merchants. I left the port shortly afterwards and though the question of bund conservation has remained a live issue, that of paying for it by the assessment of Wharfage Dues seems to have been dropped.

5.   The first attempt at bunding the foreshore, aside from the work done privately by the Wutung Steamship Company, was by the Customs in 1923. Aigun despatch No.121 of that year reports that the erosion of the bund was continuing and that, pending the drawing up of a general bunding scheme for the whole foreshore, the stretch immediately in front of the Custom House was being improved at a cost of $250 and asking sanction for the payment of that amount. The expenditure was authorized in I. G. despatch No. 133/94,724, to be charged to A/c. A : 4/1. Later in the same year and early in 1924 an adjoining stretch of foreshore in front of the Bank of Communications and extending a short distance up-river was bunded to reinforce the bit in front of the Custom House. The cost of this additional work was $500 which was paid for out of Aids funds, apparently on the authority of the Taoyin only. Altogether some 360 feet of the foreshore were included in these two projects.

6.   The following method of bunding was employed. The face of the bund, from the top

to

to the water's edge, was levelled off at an
angle of some 45°. Wooden stakes about 3' 6"
long were then driven in by rows, each stake
about 2' 6" from the next one, the rows being
about 4' apart and crossing each other diagonally.
About 8" of each stake was left above the
surface of the bund and long willows were then
woven out and in between them forming diagonal
pockets 4' on each side and 8" high. These
pockets were filled with stones that had been
broken up into small pieces. Holes were next
made by forcing a crowbar through the stones and
into the ground underneath at fairly close
intervals, and into these holes were inserted
short lengths of willow which were watered
regularly and subsequently began to grow. After a
lapse of 6 years the face of that part bunded
has been completely covered with a growth of
willows the roots of which firmly bind the whole
surfacing together. This form of bunding has
stood the test of time admirably and the width
and condition of the Customs bund is now in
marked contrast to that of the rest of the
foreshore. The enclosure to this despatch shows
a diagram illustrating what I have just tried to
describe.

7.   The great flood of last year which rose
to the top of the bund at the beginning of
August, did not effect our section but made great
inroads at other points and it was easily to be
                                              seen

seen that another such rise would erode the bund
back to the building line in some places,
destroying its continuity and usefulness and
endangering the structures along it. Had a strong
north wind set in during the height of last year's
flood this would have happened then.

8.　　　　Under these circumstances steps had to be
taken at once to guard against any further erosion
and in September of last year the Taoyin asked
the Technical Adviser and myself to consult with
him about the matter. It was then decided that
a short stretch of foreshore some 472 feet in
length beginning at the Winter Road Office and
extending along the frontage of the Kwang Hsing
Bank, Taoyin's yamen and Tidesurveyor's Bungalow
should be taken in hand. The Taoyin authorized
an advance from Aids funds for the work and it
was carried out under the supervision of the
Technical Adviser at a cost of $406.63, the sum
spoken of in the Taoyin's letter at the beginning
of this despatch. The method of bunding employed
was the same as that described above.

9.　　　　For the balance of the bunding I suggested
that a system of Wharfage Dues be introduced, as
I had proposed in 1921, but the Taoyin demurred
pointing out that the local merchants already paid
River Dues and the trade of the port was at such
a low ebb that it would not stand any further
taxation. He maintained that the expenditure should

and

and could come from River Dues and instructed the Technical Adviser to draw up a report with his recommendations. It was of course explained to, and understood by, the Mayor that the improvement contemplated was a local one whereas Aids funds were derived from dues collected on cargo and passengers between all places on the Amur and Ussuri.

10.   The Technical Adviser went into the matter thoroughly and recommended that the stretch from that part of the bunding completed in front of the Bank of Communications in 1923/1924 to just below the Tungpei Wharf, a length of 2,677 feet, be taken in hand employing the same surfacing as hitherto found to be so satisfactory. The Taoyin thereupon instructed me as reported above. In directing that $5,000 be appropriated (to include $406.63 already expended) he had not understood the Technical Adviser's estimate correctly the latter having considered that an outlay of some $7,000 would be required. However by carefully watching each item of expenditure the projected scheme has practically been completed at an outlay of $5,837.60 which includes the $406.63 already expended and another item of $28.55 for minor repairs on the old bunding. The work was carried on under the careful supervision of the Technical Adviser who has had considerable experience of a similar kind.

11.   I append several photographs showing the foreshore as it now appears.   I regret that

Appendix No. 3:

one

one wasn't taken before the work commenced to show
the contrast. Before the project was undertaken I
took the position that all buildings must be
cleared from the bund and all street drains
emptying under it put in order. The Military,
Police and merchants cooperated wholeheartedly in
the undertaking with the result that, with the
exception of two small military guard houses, all
buildings, old or new, along the stretch to be
improved were removed and drains renewed (by the
Chamber of Commerce) where required. The road along
the bund is now well metalled and drained, a row
of trees has been set out its entire length, a
raised path has been constructed and benches set
up at convenient distances. The result is that
what was before a neglected, uneven and unused
thoroughfare has now become the most travelled and
popular place in the town. Notices have been put
up by the police that no refuse shall be dumped
along the bund nor nuisances committed.

12.   The cost of the improvement has been met
from a small surplus in Aids funds. I pointed out
to the Taoyin that the Sungari Aids had a prior
claim on all surplus for the repayment of the
$15,000 advanced to the Amur Aids. He acknowledged
this but in the present instance held that the
emergency of the work required justified a further
postponement of the repayment of this loan.

13.   A statement of the expenditure incurred is
appended. There is still a stretch of 150 yards
                                              to

Appendix No.4

to be bunded commencing where the bunding finished
in front of the Tidesurveyor's Bungalow and extending
in front of the property belonging to General Pa
Ying-ngao (巴英额). Heavy surfacing will not be
required there and the estimate for the work should
be around $2,500. If this is undertaken it will
not be until some time later.

14.   I further enclose, under separate cover, a
rough sketch prepared by the Technical Adviser's
office showing the bunding of 1923/24, the present
bunding and that contemplated.

15.   Since writing the above the Amur has again
had a tremendous rise reaching a height of 426.35
feet above sea level on the 7th July approximating
the record of 427.1 feet on the 31st July last
year which was the highest since 1876. Fortunately
the bunding project was completed. Had it not been
the damage would have been irreparable. The new
bunding has thus been subjected to a very severe
test at the beginning and that it came through
intact speaks well for the system employed. The
heavy rains, however, showed that the drainage
paving of the road along the bund, were ina'
and on the Mayor's instructions, later to be
in writing by him, another $1,000 was spent
remedying these defects.

          I have the honour to be,
               Sir,
          Your obedient Servant,

              Acting Commissioner.

                    Appendix.

Appendix No. 4.

Statement of expenditure incurred in bunding the Taheiho
Harbour foreshore from Custom House and including frontage
of Miyasaki, Kwang Hsing Bank, Taoyin's yamen and Tidesurveyor's
Bungalow (completed in 1928), and the foreshore from Ta Tung
Street to just below Tungpei Navigation Bureau's wharf.

(Vide I.G. despatches Nos.90,055 & 92.051 and I.G.
telegram of 3rd May, 1929)

	Currency ($150	Hk. Tls. Hk.Tls.10
Wages: Foreman: 52½ days @ 3.00	157.50	
" 3 " @ 2.00	6.00	
Carpenter: 29 " @ 3.00	87.00	
" 6 " @ 2.50	15.00	
" 41 " @ 2.00	82.00	
Labourers:126½ " @ 1.50	189.75	
" 1,371 " @ 1.25	1713.75	
Cartage: Double carts: 176 days @ 4.00	704.00	
Single carts: 153 " @ 3.00	459.00	
Stones: 50 Cubic sajens @ 10.00	500.00	
Willows: Labour for cutting and cartage	287.00	
Timber: Beams: 52½ pieces @ various prices	111.85	
Planks: 784 " " "	631.74	
Poles: 2,075 " " "	400.34	
Rough Planks: 82 " " "	14.00	
Sundries: Nails, various assortments	153.99	
Axes 3 pieces	15.90	
1 Smooth file	.65	
2 Saws	4.25	
Bolts	2.00	
Hinges	.90	
Ropes	7.59	
Screws	.50	
Carried forward:	5,544.71	

	Currency ($150	Hk. Tls. =Hk.Tls.100
Brought forward:	5,544.71	
Sundries: 2 Spades @ 0.80	1.60	
1 Whetstone	1.00	
1 Measuring stick	1.40	
1 Watering can	1.70	
8 Hammers of various sizes	20.65	
Chinese knives	.60	
Oil Varnish	1.26	
Pitch	77.71	
Kerosene Oil 1 tin	4.60	
Felt	2.25	
Benzine. 2 cases	52.00	
Paint and Oil	16.73	
Repairs to Mattock and crowbars and other implements	13.30	
Medical fee for 1 workman	3.50	
Painting of notice boards	3.00	
Cost of removing old Police shed	12.00	
Grates for drains	17.50	
Draining work	5.00	
6 Brooms	2.25	
98 Poplars (including labour of planting and watering)	74.84	
TOTAL COST	5,837.60	
Less: (1) Advanced in Dec. Qr.1928: vide A/c.D, Sch.6, Vr. No. 17.:$435.18*		
(2) Advanced in Mar. Qr.,1929:vide A/c.D.Sch.6, Vr.No. 21 : $255.80	690.98	
	5,146.62	3,431.08

* Made up as follows;
New bunding $406.63
Repairs to old..... 28.55
$435.18

Acting Commissioner.

CUSTOM HOUSE,
Aigun/Taheiho, 12th July, 1929.

[A.—27d]

No. 485   COMMRS.

Aigun   No. 123,791

SHANGHAI OFFICE OF THE
INSPECTORATE GENERAL OF CUSTOMS,

SHANGHAI, 19th September, 1929.

SIR,

I am directed by the Inspector General to acknowledge receipt of your despatch No. 439:

> reporting upon the completion of the major portion of the bunding work undertaken on the harbour foreshore at Taheiho;

and, in reply, to say that you are to be congratulated on the successful completion of what is apparently a fine piece of public work.

At the same time it must not be overlooked that the carrying-out of this public utility, which benefits Aigun only, has in reality been done at the expense of the Sungari Aids Commission to whom the Amur Aids Commission is in debt. As the chairman of this latter Commission is also the Mayor (formerly taoyin), and the leading local authority, and as he understands the situation and accepts full responsibility for this use of Amur Aids money, the matter need not be pressed in such a way as to cause friction and unpleasantness. The debt, however, should not be lost sight of.

I am,

Sir,

Your obedient Servant,

Chief Secretary.

The Commissioner of Customs,
AIGUN.

呈海关总税务司署 439 号文　　　　　　　　　瑷珲关 1929 年 7 月 12 日

尊敬的海关总税务司（上海）：

　　1. 兹附暂代黑河市政筹备处处长（前道尹）兼中国水道委员会委员长于 1929 年 4 月 9 日来函副本（附件 1）。函中说明其已收悉黑龙江航务专门顾问之报告，建议从航路标志资金拨款 2000 银圆，用以加固港口前滩堤岸（因去年洪水已变得很不牢固），同时将去年从航路标志账户预支的 406.63 银圆记作航路标志费用，并指示支付这两笔费用；兹附暂代黑河市政筹备处处长同日第二封来函副本，函中说明港口前滩筑堤拨款增至 5000 银圆（附件 2）。

　　2. 本署于 1929 年 4 月 20 日瑷珲关第 106 号半官函中汇报已收悉上述指示，但提出需要收到电报通知，方能执行。海关总税务司署 5 月 4 日电令回复，只要该筑堤方案不会影响黑龙江航路标志工作，且松花江水道委员会不要求立即还款，即无反对意见。

　　3. 由航务专门顾问向暂代黑河市政筹备处处长提议的筑堤方案，经暂行批准，现已基本完工。鉴于该工程对大黑河极为重要，且将来还会开展类似工作（规模或许不至于此），本署认为将过去几年的前滩堤岸修缮工作以及该工程记录在案，必有益处。

　　4. 本署于 1921 年开始处理前滩堤岸维护工作，当时瑷珲关仍为哈尔滨关之分关，本人任署理税务司。当时堤岸逐渐被损毁，若要保留堤岸宽度，必须马上采取措施。本署随即草拟筑堤方案，修筑范围从下游前滩、戊通（现东北）航业公司关产前的前滩到公园，长 450 英尺，成本约 15000 银圆，其中不包括碎石铺砌及后续维护工作之费用。修缮费用使用码头税捐进行支付，该筑堤方案已全部交于道尹，以供其与当地商人讨论。不久之后本人离开口岸，尽管筑堤问题尚在讨论中，但似乎已放弃使用码头税捐进行支付。

　　5. 海关于 1923 年首次尝试在前滩筑堤，戊通航业公司私下所做不包括在内。1923 年瑷珲关第 121 号呈汇报堤岸持续受损，在等待整个前滩的筑堤总方案期间，已修缮海关前方堤岸，花费 250 银圆，请求批准拨款。海关总税务司署第 133/94724 号令批准该项支出由账户 A：4/1 支付。1923 年末至 1924 年初，为加固海关前方堤岸，在与之相邻的交通银行及其上游一小段前滩筑堤，花费 500 银圆，由航路标志资金支付，经由道尹批准。两项工程所涉前滩共计 360 英尺。

　　6. 筑堤方法：首先保证堤岸侧面从顶面至水缘呈 45° 角平行，然后成排插入长约 3 英尺 6 英寸的木桩，两根木桩间距约为 2 英尺 6 英寸，两排木桩间距约为 4 英尺，呈对角线交叉。堤岸上面每根木桩留出 8 英寸长,用长柳编织成网,每边形成 4 英尺斜槽,高 8 英寸。用碎石填充斜槽。然后用铁撬棍砸穿石头直至地面底下(间距很近),在砸出的洞中插入短柳,定期浇灌,柳树便可生长。六年后,修筑的堤面已经完全改变,柳树长大,其根部把整个堤面牢牢固定在一起。以此法筑堤经得起时间的考验,现海关前方堤岸无论是宽度还是状况都与其他前滩堤岸形成鲜明对比。兹附图解说明筑堤方法。

7. 去年大洪水于 8 月初涨至堤岸顶面,海关前方堤岸未受影响,但其他河段堤岸却受到严重侵蚀。如此大洪水若再次来袭,有些堤岸必会受损,甚至退至建筑红线,无法继续使用,同时也会殃及沿线建筑。去年大洪水高峰期若再遇强劲北风,这些堤岸当时便会受损至此。

8. 因此必须立即采取行动,以防侵蚀范围扩大。去年 9 月道尹邀航务专门顾问及本署共同商议此事,并协定从海关冬令过江检查处起,沿广信银行(Kwang Hsing Bank)、道尹公署至监察长平房正面的前滩筑堤,长约 472 英尺。道尹批准由航路标志资金支付此项费用 406.63 银圆(即此呈开篇道尹函件所述金额),同时由航务专门顾问监督该项工程。筑堤方法同上文所述。

9. 本署建议使用码头税捐支付筑堤费用(1921 年本署亦有此提议),但道尹反对,并指出当地商人已付江捐,且口岸贸易也处在低潮期,恐怕无法再负担其他税捐。道尹坚持认为应使用江捐支付,遂命航务专门顾问按其建议草拟报告。本署已向黑河市政筹备处处长说明修缮计划属地方性质,而航路标志资金源于黑龙江及乌苏里江航道所有货运及客运之税收,其表示理解。

10. 航务专门顾问彻底探究此事后,建议鉴于上述筑堤方法效果良好,遂继续使用该方法从 1923-1924 年完工的交通银行前方堤岸至东北码头下方开始筑堤,全长约 2677 英尺。道尹随即通知所需经费约为 7000 银圆。但航务专门顾问经验丰富,仔细监管该工程及其各项支出,完工后实际费用为 5837.60 银圆,其中包括已支出的 406.63 银圆以及另外一小笔堤岸修缮费用 28.55 银圆。

11. 兹附几张堤岸现状照片。未能于开工前拍下照片以作对比之用,深表遗憾。开工前,本署主张移除堤岸上的所有建筑物,排空堤岸下方所有排水管并将其有序排列。军方、警方以及商人都为此全力合作,最后除了两个军方小警卫房以外,沿线所有建筑,无论新旧,均被移除,并在必要的地方更换排水管(商会所做)。堤岸沿线道路现已用碎石铺好、沥干,路边栽种一排树,在适当的距离摆放长椅。这条路以前疏于保养,以致路面崎岖、闲置无用,而今已经成为城内人们最喜欢去的地方。警方已张贴标识,严禁在堤岸沿线丢弃垃圾及其他损害行为（附件3）。

12. 已使用航路标志资金的少量结余支付该项修缮费用。本署向道尹指出,黑龙江航路标志的全部结余应优先偿还从松花江航路标志资金预支的15000银圆借款。道尹认同,但坚持认为目前此项工程实属紧急,不得不推迟还款。

13. 兹附支出报表。此外,从监察长平房前方完工堤岸至巴英额将军住宅前方河段需要筑堤,全长150码。该段堤岸不需要很多铺面材料,预算约2500银圆。此项工程得以批准后,将于晚些时候动工（附件4）。

14. 另函寄航务专门顾问办事处所制草图,包括1923-1924年所筑堤岸,现今堤岸以及预计修筑的堤岸（另函附件1）。

15.7月7日黑龙江水位再次上涨至海平面以上426.35英尺,接近去年7月31日427.1英尺的记录（1876年以来最高纪录）。所幸堤岸已完工,否则损失将无法弥补。新堤岸刚完工就经受住了严峻考验,由此也证明筑堤方法确实有效。同时大雨也验证了堤岸沿线道路的排水系统及路面仍有不足之处,按照黑河市政筹备处处长指示,另支出1000银圆用于修补工作,之后呈文说明。

您忠诚的仆人

铎博赉（R. M. Talbot）

瑷珲关署理税务司

附件 4

大黑河港口海关关产前滩筑堤工程支出报表

包括宫崎（Miyasaki）医院、广信银行（Kwang Hsing Bank）、道尹公署和监察长平房

（1928 年完工）前方前滩以及大东街（Ta Tung Street）至东北航政局码头下游

前滩的筑堤工程

（参阅海关总税务司署第 90055 号和 92051 号令及 1929 年 5 月 3 日电令）

	银圆 150　＝	海关两 100
薪俸：工头：52.5 天，每天 3.00 银圆	157.50 银圆	
工头：3 天，每天 2.00 银圆	6.00	
木匠：29 天，每天 3.00 银圆	87.00	
木匠：6 天，每天 2.50 银圆	15.00	
木匠：41 天，每天 2.00 银圆	82.00	
工人：126.5 天，每天 1.50 银圆	189.75	
工人：1371 天，每天 1.25 银圆	1713.75	
货车：双轮车：176 天，每天 4.00 银圆	704.00	
单轮车：153 天，每天 3.00 银圆	459.00	
石头：50 立方俄丈，每立方俄丈 10.00 银圆	500.00	
柳树：伐木及运输劳工	287.00	
木料：方木：62.5 块，每块价格不同	111.85	
木板：784 块，每块价格不同	631.74	
桅杆：2075 根，每根价格不同	400.34	
糙木板：82 块，每块价格不同	14.00	
杂项：铁钉：各式	153.99	
斧头：3 个	15.90	
细锉：1 个	0.65	
锯：2 个	4.25	

续表

	银圆 150　　=	海关两 100
螺栓	2.00	
铰链	0.90	
绳子	7.59	
螺丝钉	0.50	
结转：	5544.71	
承前页：	5544.71	
杂项：2个铁锹，每个0.80银圆	1.60	
1个魔石	1.00	
1根量尺	1.40	
1个洒水壶	1.70	
8个不同尺寸的铁锤	20.65	
中国刀	0.60	
油质清漆	1.26	
沥青	77.71	
煤油：1罐	4.60	
毛毡	2.25	
汽油：2箱	32.00	
油漆及油画颜料	16.73	
维修鹤嘴锄头、铁锹棍及其他工具	13.30	
1名工人医疗费	3.50	
公告板涂漆	3.00	
拆除废旧警棚费用	12.00	
排水管格栅板	17.50	
排水工作	5.00	
6把扫帚	2.25	
98棵杨树（包括栽种及浇灌劳工）	74.84	
费用共计	5837.60	

续表

	银圆 150 =	海关两 100
扣除:(1)1928 年第四季度预支费用: 　　参阅 D 账户,第 6 项费用,传票字号 17: 　　435.18 银圆	690.98	
(2)1929 年第一季度预支费用: 　　参阅 D 账户,第 6 项费用,传票字号 21: 　　255.80 银圆		
	5146.62	3431.08
明细： 新筑堤岸　　406.63 银圆		
修缮旧堤　　28.55 银圆		
435.18 银圆		

铎博赉（R. M. Talbot）

瑷珲关署理税务司

瑷珲关 / 大黑河, 1929 年 7 月 12 日

此副本抄送至海务巡工司

录事：黎彭寿 二等同文供事中班

致瑷珲关第 485/123791 号令　　　　海关总税务司署（上海）1929 年 9 月 19 日

尊敬的瑷珲关税务司：

第 439 号呈收悉：

"兹报告，大黑河港口海滩的堤岸工程重要项目完工。"

奉总税务司命令，现批复如下，祝贺瑷珲关完成此工程，相信此公共工程一定十分壮观。

同时，开展此项公共事业，仅仅有利于瑷珲关发展，因为这实际上是以牺牲向黑龙江水道委员会举债的松花江水道委员会为代价的，此点不容忽略。鉴于黑龙江水道委员会主席亦为大黑河市政筹备处处长（前道尹）兼地方长官，对当前状况表示理解，并对使用黑龙江航路标志账款承担全部责任。因此，无须催促黑龙江水道委员会主席，以免造成摩擦与不愉快。但是，不得忽略此笔贷款。

您忠诚的仆人

华善（P. R. Walsham）

总务科税务司

6. 为建议分开管理海关港务事务和航路标志工作及申请批准开设 C 账户事

HARBOUR DEPARTMENT: desirability of keeping Harbour matters
distinct from Amur Aids, submitted; authority to open A/c
C and apply for special Inspectorate Grant of Hk. Tls. 150.00
for this purpose, requested

547

547
I G

I.G.   A I G U N   31st March 1931.

Sir,

1.   With reference to Aigun despatch No. 330 :

          requesting authority for an expenditure of

          Hk. Tls. 25.64 for moving meteorological

          instruments to the New Customs Site :

to I. G. despatch No. 367/114,251 :

          stating that the sum expended in connection

          with the meteorological instruments is a proper

          charge on the Amur River Dues Account :

to Audit Secretary's S/O Memorandum of the 21st August,

1928 :

          instructing that the cost of lighting the

          harbour buoy, and of gloves for the Boatmen

          removing stones in the harbour, brought to

          account in Account <u>A</u> for the December Quarter

          1927, Schedule 7/5, Voucher No. 14, should have

          been charged to the River Dues Account :

to Section XI of Enclosure No. 2 to Aigun despatch

No. 452 :

          explaining that the cost of moving the

          meteorological instruments had been kept in

          Suspense Account :

to Aigun despatch No. 492 :

          reporting the proposal of the Provisional

          Mayor that the River Dues Collection, less

          one-tenth for Customs cost of collection, be

                                                    turned

The Inspector General of Customs,

S H A N G H A I.

turned over to him monthly; and outlining
                briefly the Commissioner's position in Aids
                matters since their inception :

and to your despatch No. 569/132,077 :

                instructing, _inter alia_, that there is no
                objection to handing over to the Mayor at
                the close of each month the Dues collected,
                minus one-tenth for Customs cost of collection:

it is now necessary for me to seek your further
instructions regarding the sum expended in moving the
meteorological instruments, and concerning the Accounts
treatment to be accorded in future to certain recurring
expenses connected with the Taheiho Harbour.

2.   From the instructions contained in I. G. despatch
No. 367/114,251, and in Audit Secretary's S/O Memoranda
of the 21st August 1928, and the 24th October 1930,
it would appear that there has been a tendency in the
past to regard the relative positions of the Amur Aids
Commission and the Aigun Customs in much the same
light as those of the Sungari Aids Commission and the
Harbin Customs and that, in consequence, an attempt
has been made to co-ordinate the activities and finances
of two separate and distinct institutions. In point
of fact, the constitution and control of the two
Commissions are entirely dissimilar and, as explained
by my predecessor in his despatch No. 492, the Aigun
Commissioner's control of Aids funds has always been
restricted and subordinate to that of the Taoyin, now
the Mayor. I venture to submit that the policy so
far followed will ultimately tend to weaken Customs
control of the Taheiho Harbour by indirectly empowering
the Amur Aids Commission to claim a joint interest in
harbour matters, and I would place on record my
support of the view expressed in Aigun S/O letter No.

                97

97 that Customs' and Aids' questions should be kept apart. This conception of the relative functions of both organisations would seem to be upheld by the contents of I. G. despatches Nos. 2477/82,629 (to Harbin) and 93/92,051, in which it is stated that the Customs will attend to harbour control and the provision of the necessary harbour aids to navigation, and that it is not the Customs but the Aids Commission which controls Aids expenditure. From the second of these two despatches it would also seem that the inclusion of the name of the Technical Adviser on Amur Aids to Navigation in the Service List was the first of a series of anomalies arising from a misconception of the status of the Amur Aids Commission.

3.   I now have the honour to recommend that I be authorised to open an Account C in my Service Accounts, to apply for a special Inspectorate Grant of Hk. Tls. 150.00 for this purpose, and to meet the cost of moving the meteorological instruments, of lighting the harbour buoy, of removing stones brought down by the ice, of repairs to river gauges, etc., from this account. A grant of Hk. Tls. 150.00 should suffice for three or four years.

I have the honour to be

Sir,

Your obedient Servant,

(Signed) C. B. Joly

(C. H. B. Joly)

Acting Commissioner.

呈海关总税务司署 <u>547</u> 号文　　　　　　瑷珲关 1931 年 3 月 31 日

尊敬的海关总税务司（上海）：

　　1. 根据瑷珲关第 330 号呈：

　　　　"申请支出 25.64 海关两用以将气象仪迁至新海关关址。"

及海关总税务司署第 367/114231 号令：

　　　　"迁移气象仪相关费用可记入黑龙江江捐账户。"

及 1928 年 8 月 21 日会计科税务司机要通令：

　　　　"此前记入 A 账户（第四季度，费用项目 7/5，传票字号 14）的港口浮标装灯费
　　　　用及水手手套（为清理港口石块）费用，应记入江捐账户。"

及瑷珲关第 452 号呈（附件 2 第二部分）：

　　　　"迁移气象仪之费用已记入暂付款账。"

及瑷珲关第 492 号呈：

　　　　"汇报暂代黑河市政筹备处处长提议，瑷珲关每月扣除 10% 海关征税佣金后向
　　　　其上交江捐税收；简要说明自水道委员会成立以来，瑷珲关税务司之处境。"

及海关总税务司署第 569/132077 号令：

　　　　"关于瑷珲关每月扣除 10% 海关征税佣金后，将江捐税收上交至暂代黑河市市
　　　　政筹备处处长一事，无反对意见。"

　　有关迁移气象仪所产生的费用，以及大黑河港口经常性支出的入账办法，请予以进一
步指示。

　　2. 从海关总税务司署第 367/114231 号令及 1928 年 8 月 21 日和 1930 年 10 月 24 日
会计科税务司机要通令中可以看出，黑龙江水道委员会和瑷珲关之间的关系曾一度被认
为与松花江水道委员会和滨江关之间的关系相同，这两个独立且不同的机构亦曾因此而
被要求在工作和财务上相互配合。但实际上，两个委员会的管理和构成全然不同，正如前
任瑷珲关税务司于瑷珲关第 492 号呈中所述，瑷珲关税务司对航路标志资金的支配一直受
制于道尹（现为黑河市市政筹备处处长）。兹认为，当前政策已然是在间接赋予黑龙江水
道委员会参与港口事务之权，如此一来，海关对大黑河港口的管控权终将被削弱。瑷珲关
第 97 号半官函曾提出，海关事务应与航路标志工作分开管理，对此，本署表示赞同。

　　此外，海关总税务司署致滨江关第 2477/82629 号令及致瑷珲关第 93/92051 号令中
曾说明海关应致力于港口管理工作，于港口内竖立必要的航路标志，而航路标志资金则

应由水道委员会负责管理。于此,两个机构的职能似乎已然明了,然海关总税务司署第93/92051 号令却将黑龙江航务专门顾问之姓名列于《海关职员录》中,如此似乎与黑龙江水道委员会的职能不符,且自此之后,此类情况又多次出现。

3. 兹申请于瑷珲关账户项下开设 C 账户,用以支付搬运气象仪,为港口浮标装灯,清理港口被浮冰击落的石块,以及修复河道计量器等费用; 为此特申请拨发海关总税务司署专项经费 150.00 海关两,该笔款项可满足三到四年之需。

您忠诚的仆人

周骊（C. H. B. Joly）

瑷珲关署理税务司

录事： 陈培因三等二级税务员

专题四

船只管理

1. 为拟议中国船只航行于黑龙江之暂行办法事

No.1879. Commrs.   INSPECTORATE GENERAL OF CUSTOMS,

Harbin, No.70,042   PEKING, 30th July, 1918.

        Sir,

1.   In connection with the opening of the River Amur to navigation by vessels under the Chinese flag, the Heilungchiang Tuchün has requested that an inspection of the river from the mouth of the Sungari to Mo Ho T'ing (漠河廳) should be undertaken by the Maritime Customs with a view more especially to obtaining and recording particulars of the aids to navigation established by the Russian Government.

2.   In the unavoidable absence of the Coast Inspector on special duty elsewhere, I have selected the Yangtze River Inspector, Mr. H.G. Garden, as the Officer most competent to undertake this delicate work and he has already been transferred to Harbin to be placed at your disposal.

3.   Having learned from you that the Revenue Launch "Heilung" is the most suitable vessel with which to undertake this inspection and that she can be spared, and also that you have communicated through the Tao-yin with the Heilungchiang Tuchün and that such arrangements as are possible in present conditions have been made with the Russian Authorities, I have to instruct you as follows:-

                                The "Heilung"

P. Grevedon, Esquire,

        Commissioner of Customs,

            H A R B I N.

The "Heilung" is to be placed at Mr. Garden's
disposal and is to be despatched as soon as
possible to the Amur in charge of a competent
pilot. On arrival at Lahasusu and before quitting
the Sungari, Mr. Garden will communicate with the
Assistant in charge and together they will make
such dispositions as are necessary to ensure that
the vessel will not be molested or obstructed by
the Russian guardship stationed at the confluence
of the two rivers. Having entered the Amur, Mr.
Garden will keep so far as navigation permits to
Chinese waters and will proceed to Aigun where he
will report to the Assistant in charge and get
into communication with you by telegraph in case
you have any instructions for him. Assuming that
Mr Garden has provided himself with a chart of
the Amur, he is to keep a careful log of
each day's progress and is to note on the chart
the position of all aids to navigation passed
whether ashore or afloat. Those which are in
Chinese waters or on Chinese territory are to
be inspected closely and a full description of
each is to be recorded. Mr Garden, drawing on
his own experience, is to estimate as closely as
he can the first cost of such aids and the
cost of their maintenance according to Service
standards. As regards the aids in Russian waters
and on Russian territory, Mr. Garden must use his
discretion. As much information as possible about
them is desired but no risks are to be run,
more especially in the matter of landing on
Russian soil. Mr Garden is to understand that
the Chinese

"the Chinese Government proposes to make itself
responsible for half the expenditure incurred in
maintaining Amur River Aids /and desires to have some
first hand and independent information concerning
them. But it is not yet known whether China
will undertake the actual administration of the
Aids in Chinese territoty. On arrival at Aigun
Mr. Garden will have to consider carefully how
much further he can go in the direction of Mo
Ho T'ing, having regard to the closing of the
river and his return in good time to Harbin.
It is not known here how far the Aids extend
and it is not necessary to go beyond them.

4.   You are to provide Mr. Garden with a
qualified interpreter and are to see that he has
sufficient funds. It is not, however, desirable
that he should carry a very large sum of money
with him: no doubt you can arrange for him to
obtain funds at Aigun. The expenses of this
inspection, including Mr. Garden's salary and
allowances while stationed at Harbin, are to be
advanced by you and will ultimately be recorered
from Revenue Account. I do not know what
arrangements Mr. Garden has made about his family,
but, if he has brought them to Harbin, you are
authorised to apply for a Rent Allowance for him.
Mr Garden may draw his salary in whole or in part
in Shanghai Taels or Roubles at the salary-paying
rate for the month as he may prefer.

5.   I must leave it to your discretion
to decide whether to send a Chinese Guard with
the Heilung or not. If you consider it desirable,
you are

you are to apply to the Taoyin for the
necessary men who should be under the control
of reliable officer.

     I am,

      Sir,

     Your obedient Servant,

     (signed) F. A. Aglen

       Inspector General.

True copy

_____ Unclassed Assistant.

No. 2111   Commrs.   INSPECTORATE GENERAL OF CUSTOMS,

Harbin   No. 74,778   PEKING, 29th August, 1919.

Sir,

1.   As you are aware Article No. 1 of the Treaty
of Aigun of 1858, between Russia and China, restricted
navigation of the Rivers Amur, Sungari and Ussuri to
Russian and Chinese vessels and this stipulation was
specially confirmed by Article No. 18 of the 1881
Treaty of St. Petersburg. China's rights of navigation
on the Amur and Ussuri have, until recently, not been
asserted, in so far at any rate as steam vessels are
concerned, either because such assertion would have
been considered impolitic or because it would have been
actively resisted. Circumstances, however, have now
made it possible for the Chinese Government to claim
the exercise of her rights of navigation and informal
negotiations have taken place between the Heilungchiang and local Russian Authorities on the one hand ,
and on the other hand between the Russian Legation
and the Wai-chiao Pu. These negotiations have now
crystallized to the extent that both sides feel it
desirable that some provisional arrangement should
be made under which Chinese vessels shall be able at
least to enjoy the same facilities of navigation on
the Amur as Russian vessels enjoy on the Sungari.
The arrangement can only be provisional seeing that
there is no recognised Russian Government competent
to conclude an agreement, and it must necessarily take
into account accomplished facts arising from the sole
control on the Amur hitherto maintained by Russia :-
such are, the existence of a complete system of aids

to

to navigation established on both sides of the river, Russian Navigational Regulations, Pilotage Regulations and so forth, in which China has hitherto had no say.

2.

Despatches Nos. 1058,1081,1205 and 1321 from:-Letter No. 910 and Despatch No. 191 to:-Shui-wu Ch'u.

I append copy of correspondence with the Shui-wu Ch'u dealing with the proposed discussion for a temporary procedure for Chinese navigation on the Amur from which you will see that I have been requested to instruct you to associate yourself with the Harbin and HeiHo Taoyin in these negotiations, the delegates on the Russian side being the Consul General Mr. Popoff and two technical advisers. You will also observe that I have suggested the procuring of a copy of the Russian Regulations referred to in Ch'u despatch No. 1081 and have recommended the appointment of Mr. W. F. Tyler as an additional delegate on the Chinese side.

3.

For your further information I send you a brief resumé in English of all my correspondence with the Shui-wu Ch'u on the Amur River question. You will see that the question of China's participation in the Amur Aids to Navigation has been settled in principle - the Chinese Government agreeing to pay a share of the cost and to leave the administration in Russian hands. A cognate question, that of the Aigun Harbour, is also treated and you have already received instructions in this connection.

4.

I think you will do well to postpone negotiation until the arrival of Mr. Tyler, with whom I have discussed the question and who knows my views, and, as the matter is largely a technical one, to leave the

negotiation

negotiation mainly in his hands. How far the two
Taoyin will be prepared to go in concluding a provisional agreement without referring to Peking I do
not know, but, if reference is necessary, you are to
refer to me before putting your signature to the
document. I can only give you very general instructions at this stage. The object of the Chinese
delegation should be to secure the maximum of conces-
sion and as equal a position as possible for China.
Discussion will reveal how far the Russians are
prepared to go and it may be expedient to accept the
Minimum, in order not to delay matters, while putting
on record and reserving for future discussion all that
China claims under treaty and as a neighbouring
independent Power.

I have to request that you will keep me
informed of the progress made and of any difficulties
that may unexpectedly arise.

I am,

Sir,

Your obedient Servant,

(signed) A. F. Aglen
Inspector General.

APPENDIX.

APPENDIX No. 2.

AMUR RIVER NAVIGATION.

D. No.663 from Ch'u. Proposed employment of Chinese steamers:Heilung-
23 April 1918.　　chiang Governor requests that Customs may sup-
　　　　　　　　　ply estimate of amount expended by Russian
　　　　　　　　　authorities in dredging and establishing lights,
　　　　　　　　　etc., also that Harbin Harbour Master may lend
　　　　　　　　　assistance to Chinese steamers and that Harbin
　　　　　　　　　Commissioner may request Russian Customs to
　　　　　　　　　let them ply.

D.No.711 from Ch'u. Heilungchiang Governor wishes Harbin Commission-
29 April 1918.　　er to despatch launch to pilot Chinese mail
　　　　　　　　　steamer Ch'ing Lan.

D. No.89 to Ch'u. Harbin launches are fully occupied on Sungari,
3 May 1918.　　　conditions on the Amur are dangerous, and
　　　　　　　　　Harbin Harbour Master has no experience of
　　　　　　　　　Amur navigation: to despatch Harbin launch is
　　　　　　　　　therefore inexpedient.

L. No.588 from Ch'u. Enquiring if instructions (desp.No.663) have
3 May 1918.　　　been issued to Harbin Commissioner.

L. No.883 to Ch'u. Despatch No. 663: instructions have not been
9 May 1918.　　　issued to Harbin Commissioner.

D.No.1413 From Ch'u. Proposed Customs barrier at confluence of Amur
15 August 1918.　　and Sungari: Harbin Commissioner to report as
　　　　　　　　　to suitability of site proposed.

D.No.179 to Ch'u. Proposed Customs barrier at confluence of Amur
22 August 1918.　　and Sungari: I.G. cannot submit report till
　　　　　　　　　after return of River Inspector from his tour
　　　　　　　　　of inspection of Amur aids to navigation.

No.1464

D. No.1464 from Ch'u. 21 August 1918.	Amur River Aids to Navigation: I.G. to propose a procedure for control and maintenance by Harbin Customs.
D.No.183 to Ch'u. 2 Sept. 1918.	Amur River Aids to Navigation: I.G. must await report of River Inspector before making proposals.
L.No.634 from Ch'u. 2 October 1918.	Survey of Amur: I. G. to report results for consultation with various departments concerned. Meanwhile River Inspector Mr. Garden May return to his original post.
D. No.1943 from Ch'u. 26 October 1918.	A special Harbour Master Customs to take in hand promptly to Aigun Customs to take in hand prompt -ly the necessary arrangements and negotiations in reference to navigation by Chinese vessels on opening of river next spring.
D.No.2219 from Ch'u. 6 Dec. 1918.	Appointment of Harbour Master at Aigun: urgency of case: reply to No.1943 requested.
D. No.166 from Ch'u. 4 Feb. 1919.	Amur River Aids to Navigation: proposed control of along the Chinese bank: pressing for I. G.'s report on.
D.No.35 to Ch'u. 6 Feb. 1919.	Mr. Garden has reported on his investigations, but charts have not been completed.
D.No.529 from Ch'u. 11 April 1919.	Pressing for I.G's reply to proposed appoint- ment of Harbour Master to Heiho.
D.No.82 to Ch'u. 22 April 1919.	Mr. Garden's English report of survey with charts and Chinese précis of report forwarded. I.G. deals with three questions: (1) Aids to navigation: Mr. Garden pronounces that a double administration is not feasible. The

The only way in which China can secure
representation is by arranging with Russian
Government to contribute part of the initial
cost and maintenance charges. As regards
the amount that China should contribute, the
figures given by Mr. Garden in his report
can only be considered very approximate,
but they furnish a basis for discussion.

(2) The proposal to establish a Customs barrier
at the confluence of the Amur and Sungari
Rivers. This concerns military or police
authority. As Customs have a station at
Lahasusu, there is no necessity for another
barrier for Customs purposes.

(3) The Question of confiscation of steamers
that have been sold by Russians to Chinese
by order of General Horwath. This does not
concern Customs.

The I.G. does not see that at this stage the
placing of a Harbour Master at Aigun (Taheiho)
would be of much assistance in the solving of
any of the above questions, but he will send
Mr. Garden to Aigun for a few months as it may
be of assistance to have a technical man to
refer to.

D. No.884 from Ch'u. 5 June 1919.	Harbour Master's Office: proposed establishment of at Aigun: Mr. River Inspector Garden to be instructed to assist Heiho Taoyin in arranging for
D.No.134 to Ch'u. 14 June 1919. In reply to No. 884.	Proposed Harbour control at Aigun: River Inspector Garden instructed to arrange with Heiho Taoyin and Aigun Assistant-in-charge.

Question

Question of aids must wait until Chinese
Government has settled question of principle
with some recognised Russian authority. Copy
of telegram dated 7th June to Harbin Commissioner forwarded.

D. No.952 from
Ch'u.
16 June 1919.

Proposed establishment of Harbour Office at
Aigun: the Wai Chiao Pu has duly received copy
of Mr. Garden's report, etc.. The Heilungchiang
Governor and Chiao-t'ung Pu have written to
Wai Chiao Pu requesting early establishment of
Harbour Office at Aigun. As the Wai Chiao Pu
has already declared to the Russian Minister
China's willingness to share half the cost of
aids on the Amur and the Russian Minister has w
wired to General Horwath to deal with Chinese
merchants direct as regards Chinese steamers
navigating the Amur, establishment of a sub-
Harbour Master's Office at Aigun is all the
more urgent. The I.G. is therefore requested
to instruct Mr. Garden to co-operate with the
Tuchün and the Taoyin in the matter.

D. No.1024 from
Ch'u.
26 June 1919.

Cost of aids on Amur: as regards cost of aids
on Amur, the Wai Chiao Pu has been variously
informed. The Russian Minister estimates
China's share at 43 millions (? roubles). The
Investigating Officer of the Ts'an Mou Pen Pu
(参謀本部) at Blagovestchensk estimates amount
spent by Russia at 500,000 roubles. Mr.Garden
estimates

estimates cost of aids on Chinese bank at
about 100,000 roubles. The Wai Chiao Pu requires an estimate of the initial cost and
cost of annual maintenance spent by the
Russians. The SHui-wu Ch'u requests that
Mr. Garden be instructed to assist the Taoyin
and the Mou T'ung s.s. Company in arriving
at such an estimate.

D. No.1058 from
Ch'u.
1 July 1919.

Temporary procedure for Chinese navigation on
the Amur: The Russian Minister refuses to
enter into negotiation as regards China's
right of navigation on the Amur pending
establishment of a formal Government. Mean-
while he has wired to General Harwath to deal
with Chinese merchants direct. The Wai Chiao
Pu has also instructed Minister Liu at
Vladivostock to open negotiation with General
Horwath. The Minister has suggested at the
instance of General Horwath to conclude a
temporary procedure for Chinese shipping on
the Amur to be revised when the question of
the aids on the Chinese bank is settled.
The Wai Chiao Pu desires that the Harbin
Commissioner should assist the Hei Ho Taoyin
in the matter of negotiating this temporary
procedure.

D. No. 1081 from
Ch'u.
7 July 1919.

Temporary procedure for Chinese navigation:
the Chiao-t'ung Pu has received a report from
Minister Liu stating that General Horwath
proposes that until China is able to establish her own aids to navigation, Chinese
steamers had better run under the Russian

Regulations

Regulations and that a temporary procedure
for such navigation may be agreed upon. The
Chiao-t'ung Pu requests the I.G. to instruct
the Harbin Commissioner and Mr. Garden to
assist the Harbin and the Heiho Taoyin in
the Matter of negotiating such procedure.

D. No.1091 from Ch'u. 8 July 1919.	Proposed establishment of Harbour Office at Aigun: The I.G's telegram to Harbin of the 7th June (vide I.G. despatch No.134) has been transmitted to the Wai Chiao Pu and the Chiao-t'ung Pu. As regards the question of aids, the Chiao-t'ung Pu does not think it necessary to wait till there is a formal representative of Russian Government since General Horwath is prepared to deal with the Mou T'ung S.S. Company. The Chiao-t'ung Pu thinks that the question of the aids should be taken up at once. The Shui-wu Ch'u requests the I.G. to instruct the Harbin Commissioner, the Assistant-in-Charge of the Aigun Customs and Mr. Garden accordingly.
L. No. 910 to Ch'u. 10 July 1919.	Temporary procedure for Chinese navigation on the Amur: Ch'u despatch No. 1081 refers to certain "Russian Regulations". The I.G. suggests that Minister Liu be requested to apply to General Horwath for copy of such "Russian Regulations".
D. No.1205 from Ch'u. 2 August 1919.	Temporary procedure for Chinese navigation on the Amur: The Wai Chioa Pu is in receipt of letter from the Russian Minister saying that he has received a telegram from General Horwath

Horwath to the effect that it has already
been arranged with the Omsk Government that
Mr. Popoff, Acting Consul-General at Harbin
will negotiate with Chinese delegates and
Mr. K'o Li Ning（柯利宵）Chief of Amur
Waterways Bureau（黑龍江一帶水道局局長　）and
Mr. Hsieh Li Chieh To Fu（謝立捷多福　），
Superintendent of Navigation（航業監督　）
will also be present at the meeting in their
capacity as technical experts. The above
is to be transmitted to the Harbin Commissioner,
etc. for their information.

D. No.191 to Ch'u.
4 August 1919.
In reply to no.1205.

Amur River: temporary procedure for navigation
of by Chinese steamers to be arranged for
with representative at Harbin: the River
Inspector Mr. Garden is ill with typhoid
fever and will be unable to assist the
Commissioner. Nevertheless there should be
some one on the Chinese side competent to
advise from a technical point of view. The
matter concerns communication and navigation
and the I.G. thinks that the technical adviser
to the Chiao-t'ung Pu, and Admiralty - Mr.
Tyler - should also be requested to go to
Harbin to co-operate.

致哈尔滨关第 <u>1879/70042</u> 号令　　　海关总税务司署（北京）1918 年 7 月 30 日

尊敬的哈尔滨关税务司：

1. 关于中国船只在黑龙江开通航运一事，黑龙江督军要求，海关巡察黑龙江从松花江河口至漠河廷（Mo Ho T'ing）之河道，以便记录由俄国政府所建的航路标志之相关细节。

2. 鉴于特殊公事需求，巡工司无空监管此事，现命扬子江巡江工司贾登（H.G.Garden）先生任巡江工司（黑龙江处），其最有能力胜任上述细致工作，遂现已将其调至哈尔滨关，听从差遣。

3. 从贵署处得知，贵署已通过道尹与黑龙江督军商议过配备巡艇一事，鉴于与俄国政府的当前形势，巡艇"黑龙"（Heilung）号是最为合适，且尚有出巡时间，故现作如下指示：巡艇"黑龙"号由贾登先生任意支配，并急派一名有能力的领港将该巡艇驶至黑龙江。在巡艇刚到达拉哈苏苏且尚未离开松花江时，贾登先生需立即与哈尔滨关代理税务司商议并共同做出必要部署，以确保巡艇在两河汇流处不受俄国哨舰干扰。巡艇驶入黑龙江时，贾登先生将一直持有中国河道航行许可，并在将进入瑷珲分关时，通过电报向哈尔滨关代理税务司汇报工作并请求指令。若贾登先生本人已有黑龙江航图，则只需每日记录详细的航海日志并在航图上标出经过之处所观察到的所有航路标志的位置（无论是在岸上还是在黑龙江上）。凡在中国水上和陆地上的航路标志皆需靠近观察，并对每一航路标志完整描述并记录。请贾登先生根据其自身经验及海关经费标准，将尽可能预估类似航路标志的收购及维修成本。对俄国水上及陆地上的航路标志必须谨慎处理，虽然希望获得尽可能多的相关信息但不必冒风险而为之，尤其是关于在俄国土地靠岸一事上。贾登先生需理解，中国政府建议自行承担一半修护黑龙江航路标志之支出并渴望获得第一手关于航路标志的独立信息之举。但尚未了解中国是否将承担实际管理中国领域的航路标志之工作。鉴于河道的关闭及适时返回哈尔滨关，贾登先生一到达瑷珲分关，将不得不仔细考虑如何能朝漠河廷方向继续前进一事。

4. 此次巡察，需为贾登先生配备一名合格译员。资金方面，其所持现金需足够但不宜过多，由瑷珲分关支出，巡查经费，包括其在哈尔滨关就职的薪俸与津贴，将先由哈尔滨关预支，最终由税收账户支付。本署尚不清楚贾登先生如何安置家人，但若其携家人一同至哈尔滨，请为其发放房租津贴。其薪俸可由其个人意愿，按当月薪俸标准提取全部金额或部分上海两或卢布。

5.关于是否为"黑龙"号巡艇安排一名中国卫兵一事，交由贵署处理；若有安排之意，可向道尹申请委派一名可靠关员。

您忠诚的仆人

（签字）安格联（F. A. Aglen）

总税务司

该抄件内容真实有效,特此证明：

录事：罗作福（T. M. Rozoff）未列等帮办

致哈尔滨关第 2111/74778 号令　　　海关总税务司署（北京）1919 年 8 月 29 日

尊敬的哈尔滨关税务司：

1. 中俄《瑷珲条约》（1858 年）第 1 条，唯有中俄两国船只可在黑龙江、松花江、乌苏里江上航行，并且在《圣彼得堡条约》（1881 年）第 18 条中又特别明确此项规定。至今，至少在蒸汽船方面，仍未主张维护中国在黑龙江和乌苏里江的航行权，不仅因为此主张不是很明智，还因为该主张将会遭到强烈抵制。然而鉴于当前局势有利于中国主张维护航海权利和进行黑龙江与当地俄国政府双方半官方谈判及进行俄国领事与外交部双方的半官式谈判。这些谈判涉及，中国船只在黑龙江行船与俄国船只在松花江行船应该享有相同的便利条件下，明确一些双方共同希望之章程安排。因无法与俄国政府达成协议，此章程现仅定为临时章程，并考虑到黑龙江受俄国单独控制这一事实：例如俄国持有中俄两岸建设航路标志的完整体制《俄国航行章程》及《引水章程》等，在这些方面中国至今没有发言权。

2. 关于拟议中国船只航行于黑龙江之暂行办法一事，兹附本署与税务处往来信函抄件，请与哈尔滨关道尹和黑河道尹一同参与相关协商会议，俄国参会代表为总领事博勃福（P.Popoff）先生与两名技术顾问。请获取税务处第 1081 号令中关于俄国章程之抄件，并任命戴理尔（W.F.Tyler）先生作为另一华方代表。

3. 关于黑龙江相关事宜，兹附与税务处往来函件之摘要，以供参考。从中可知，中国代表在黑龙江航路标志方面提出的问题，在原则上已经解决——中国政府同意承担一定比例的经费并将管理权交由俄国。瑷珲港港务类似问题处理方式同上并现已下达相关指令。

4. 因本署已与戴理尔（W.F.Tyler）先生商议过此事，且其了解本署观点，同时此事内容大部分涉及技术知识，故将此次协商主要交由戴理尔先生负责，遂在其到达前请推迟会议时间。本署尚不清楚两位道尹将达成什么程度的临时协议并且是否涉及北京，但若有必要涉及北京，在签署文件之前须向本署请示。现阶段本署仅下达基本指令。我方代表的目的是确保中国与俄国地位尽可能持平同时确保最多的特权。讨论中将清楚俄方准备达成何程度之临时协议及其能接受之最少特权，以免延误事宜，请保留好相关记录，作为未来讨论中国在条约和邻国独立主权下所主张的一切的依据。

请汇报谈判进程及可能出现的任何困难。

您忠诚的仆人

（签字）安格联（F. A. Aglen）

总税务司

附录 2

黑龙江航务

1918 年 4 月 23 日税务处第 663 号令：

　　"提议使用中国汽艇：请黑龙江省省长命令海关提供俄国官方疏浚河道、修建灯塔等事宜之经费预算，并命令哈尔滨理船厅援助中国邮船，同时命哈尔滨关税务司向俄国海关提出允许此船在俄国水域航行之申请。"

1918 年 4 月 29 日税务处第 711 号令：

　　"黑龙江政府希望哈尔滨关税务司派汽艇为中国邮船"镜兰"（Ch'ing Lan）号引航。"

1918 年 5 月 3 日致税务处第 89 号呈：

　　"哈尔滨关汽艇全部在松花江上，暂无空闲汽艇，并且黑龙江上航运状况恶劣，哈尔滨理船厅又无在黑龙江上行船之经验：故派哈尔滨汽艇前去引航实属不妥。"

1918 年 5 月 3 日税务处来函第 588 号：

　　"询问指令（税务处第 663 号令）是否已发给哈尔滨关税务司。"

1918 年 5 月 9 日税务处去函第 883 号：

　　"税务处第 663 号令：指令尚未发给哈尔滨关税务司。"

1918 年 8 月 15 日税务处第 1413 号令：

　　"提议于黑龙江与松花江汇流处开设海关关卡：请哈尔滨关税务司详细报告所推荐关址适宜之理由。"

1918 年 8 月 22 日致税务处第 179 号呈：

　　"提议于黑龙江与松花江汇流处开设海关关卡：在巡江工司完成巡察黑龙江航路标志返回前，本署无法提交报告。"

1918 年 8 月 21 日税务处第 1464 号令：

　　"黑龙江航务：关于哈尔滨关管理及维护黑龙江航路标志一事，请海关总税务司署提交方案。"

1918 年 9 月 2 日致税务处第 183 号呈：

　　"黑龙江航务：本署须在收到巡江工司巡察报告后，方可制定方案。"

1918 年 10 月 2 日税务处来函第 634 号：

"黑龙江调查报告：请海关总税务司署汇报与相关各部门协商之结果，同时汇报巡江工司贾登（H.G.Garden）先生是否会返回原职位。"

1918 年 10 月 26 日税务处第 1943 号令：

"关于明年春天航运季开通一事，请专门理船厅至瑷珲分关立即接管中国船只航运事宜。"

1918 年 12 月 6 日税务处第 2219 号令：

"任命瑷珲口岸理船厅：紧急事件：请速回复税务处第 1943 号令。"

1919 年 2 月 4 日税务处第 166 号令：

"黑龙江航务：提议管理中国沿岸航路标志：催促海关总税务司署提交相关报告。"

1919 年 2 月 6 日致税务处第 35 号呈：

"贾登（H.G.Garden）先生已上交其调查报告，但航图尚未完成。"

1919 年 4 月 11 日税务处第 529 号令：

"速请海关总税务司署回复任命黑河理船厅之提议。"

1919 年 4 月 22 日致税务处第 82 号呈：

"呈送贾登（H.G.Garden）先生英文调查报告附航图及报告中文摘要。本署对以下三个问题之处理措施：

（1）航路标志：贾登先生认为中俄双方共同管理航路标志不可行。只有俄国政府承担部分初始费用及维修费用，中国方能确保提议。关于中国承担之费用，贾登先生在报告中提议之数目虽仅可被视为非常接近，但该数目为讨论费用提供了参照。

（2）提议于黑龙江与松花江汇流处开设海关关卡一事，涉及军事或警方权利，并且因海关已在拉哈苏苏设立海关分卡，故没有必要再开设另一海关关卡。

（3）奉霍尔瓦特（Horwath）长官命令，已没收由俄国卖给中国的邮船之事，与海关无关。

海关总税务司署不清楚当下为瑷珲口岸（大黑河）安排一名理船厅是否将会有助于处理以上问题，但本署将派贾登先生前往瑷珲口岸，担任几个月技术顾问，以协助处理上述问题。"

1919 年 6 月 5 日税务处第 884 号令：

"于瑷珲口岸拟建港务课：请巡江工司贾登（H.G.Garden）先生协助黑河道尹

安排建造事宜。"

1919年6月14日致税务处第134号呈（回复税务处第884号令）：

"拟议瑷珲口岸港务管理办法：由巡江工司贾登（H.G.Garden）先生奉命与黑河道尹及瑷珲分关代理税务司一同商定。航路标志事宜须待中国政府与公认的俄国官方解决原则问题后，再予以处理；呈送6月7日电报抄件至哈尔滨关税务司。"

1919年6月16日税务处第952号令：

"于瑷珲口岸拟建港务课：外交部已及时收到贾登（H.G.Garden）先生报告之抄件等相关资料。黑龙江政府与交通部已向外交部致信，申请尽早在瑷珲口岸建造港务课。因外交部已告知俄国部长中国愿意承担一半黑龙江航路标志之经费，且俄国部长已电令霍尔瓦特（Horwath）长官直接与中国商人讨论处理中国船只在黑龙江行船之事宜，故在瑷珲口岸建造港务课之事十分紧急，遂请海关总税务司署指派贾登（H.G.Garden）先生前往与督军和道尹共同处理此事。"

1919年6月26日税务处第1024号令：

"黑龙江航路标志经费：关于黑龙江航路标志一事，外交部已告知各方，俄国部长估计中国需承担之费用为4300万（？卢布）。布拉戈维申斯克（Blagovestchensk）参谋本部调查股估算俄国需承担之费用为50万卢布。贾登（H.G.Garden）先生估算在中国沿岸航路标志之费用约为10万卢布。外交部需要一份俄国需承担的初始费用和年维修费用之报价。请贾登先生协助道尹及戊通航业公司制作报价。"

1919年7月1日税务处第1058号令：

"中国船只于黑龙江航行之暂定办法：俄国部长拒绝，在中国正式成立港务课前，协商中国在黑龙江的航行权一事，同时其电告霍尔瓦特（Horwath）长官直接与中国商人协商处理。外交部也已命驻符拉迪沃斯托克的部长刘先生与霍尔瓦特长官进行公开协商。部长刘先生提议，根据霍尔瓦特长官要求草拟中国船只在黑龙江航行之暂行办法，待中国沿岸航路标志问题解决后，再行修订。外交部希望哈尔滨关可帮助黑河道尹与俄方协商暂行办法。"

1919年7月7日税务处第1081号令：

"中国航务之暂行办法：交通部已收到部长刘先生的报告，获知霍尔瓦特（Horwath）长官提议，在中国有能力建造自己的航路标志前，中国船只最好遵守《俄国章程》航行，并且可能会同意类似航务的暂行办法。外交部向海关总税务司署申请,请哈尔滨关税务司及贾登（H.G.Garden）先生一同协助哈尔滨关及黑河道尹,与俄方协商此类航务的暂行办法。"

1919 年 7 月 8 日税务处第 1091 号令:

"于瑷珲口岸拟建港务课:已将 6 月 7 日海关总税务司署致哈尔滨关电报(参阅海关总税务司署致税务处第 134 号呈)转送至外交部及交通部。关于航路标志问题,交通部认为没有必要等待一名俄国政府的正式代表到来,因为霍尔瓦特（Horwath）长官已经准备与戊通航业公司进行协商。交通部认为此事应立即着手处理,遂请贵署向哈尔滨关税务司、瑷珲分关代理税务司及贾登（H.G.Garden）先生下达相关指令。"

1919 年 7 月 10 日致税务处第 910 号呈:

"中国船只于黑龙江航行之暂行办法:税务处第 1081 号令中涉及某些之内容。本署建议请部长刘先生向霍尔瓦特（Horwath）长官索要相关《俄国章程》之抄件。"

1919 年 8 月 2 日税务处第 1205 号令:

"中国船只于黑龙江航行之暂行办法:外交部收到俄国部长之来信,从中可知,俄国部长已收到霍尔瓦特（Horwath）长官之电报,并已经安排鄂木斯克（Omsk）政府驻哈尔滨的署理总领事博勃福（P.Popoff）先生与中国代表共同协商此事(黑龙江一带水道局局长柯利宁先生与航业监督谢立捷多福先生也将会作为技术专家参与此会议)。请将上述内容转送至哈尔滨关税务司,以供参考。"

1919 年 8 月 4 日致税务处第 191 号呈(回复税务处第 1205 号令):

"黑龙江:关于中国船只于黑龙江航行之暂行办法一事,将安排与俄国驻哈尔滨的代表进行协商会议:虽然巡江工司贾登（H.G.Garden）先生因病将无法协助哈尔滨关税务司,但华方仍有一些技术方面人员在场,此事涉及外交与航务方面,本署提议请交通部兼海军部技术顾问戴理尔（Tyler）先生共同参与协商会议。"

2. 为批准黑河商人使用煤油引擎轮船于黑龙江松花江一带往来行驶事

~~Amur and Sungari~~ Motor Boat:
proposed running of, by Heiho merchants,
THE INSPECTOR GENERAL to HARBIN COMMISSIONER.
on Amur and Sungari Rivers. Report
No. 2463.　Commrs.　*on ~~~~ requested*

———————————————

Harbin.　No. 82,268.　　　　PEKING, 17th January, 1921.

　　　　　　　　Sir,

　　　　　　　　　　I append, for your information and
guidance, copy of Shui-wu Ch'u despatch No. 1668,
from which you will see that the merchants at
Heiho propose to purchase a motor boat to ply on
the Sungari and Amur, and the Heiho Chamber of
Commerce has been requested to find out if this
enterprise will be permitted.　The Shui-wu Ch'u
desires a report from you if there will be any
objection to the proposed running of a motor boat
on the Amur and Sungari from the Customs point of
view.

　　　　　　　　　　You are accordingly requested to submit a
report as requested by the Ch'u with a Chinese
version in duplicate.

　　　　　　　　　　　　　　I am, etc.,

　　　　　　　　　　　　(Signed)　F. A. AGLEN,

　　　　　　　　　　　　　　　Inspector General.

True copy:

　　2nd Clerk: C.

I.G. Despatch No. 2463 to Harbin

Append No. 1.

税務處令

據黑河商會代理會長丁官堂呈稱據本鎮商人李萬臣稱竊商等擬組織一煤油引

擎機器輪船於黑龍江松花江一帶往來行駛營業因觀黑龍松花兩江之輪船概係蒸汽

機器而此等機器佔用地位甚多兼之重量更大照煤油引擎機器同一馬力比較能差

十分之八第未識以煤油引擎機器裝製輪船於海關理船廳章程是否相合能否照唯

行駛懇祈呈請稅務處所擬是否有當與准予行駛之處請鑒核准予轉請施行等情據

此查近年松黑兩江每苦水少輪船吃水稍深即難行駛該商等組織煤油引擎機器輪船重

量既輕吃水自淺苟遇江水消乏之時仍可行駛自如事心實業不無見地本會為提倡企業起

見自應極予贊助以期仰副政府鼓舞實業之至意惟此項機器向無如此辦法是否與理船

廳章程相符理合呈請鑒核量予維持賜以辦法手續並祈將理船廳章程抄賜一分尤

所禱感等情前來究竟可否准予行駛之處相應令行代理總稅務司查照來呈所稱各節

轉令理船廳查酌聲復以憑辦理此令 中華民國九年十一月十一日

第一六六八號

<u>Copy.</u>

No. 2549.   COMMRS.

——————   ——————

Harbin,   No. 83,847.

INSPECTORATE GENERAL OF CUSTOMS,

Peking, 29th April, 1921.

Sir,

      With reference to your despatch No.2363

(in reply to I. G. despatch No.2463/82,268):

           reporting that there is no objection from

the Customs point of view to the proposed

running of a motor boat by Heiho merchants

on the Amur and Sungari Rivers, provided

this boat complies with the Amur and

Sungari Regulations:

      I append, for your information and guidance, copy

of Shui-wu Ch'u despatch No.580, from which you

will see that the proposed running of this motor

boat is sanctioned.

      You are requested to see that all

Regulations applicable are duly complied with.

                    I am,

True copy:

                            Sir,

C.S.Giobe

Unclassed Assistant.

                    Your obedient Servant,

                    (signed) F. A. Aglen,

                    Inspector General.

The Commissioner of Customs,

      H A R B I N .

税务处令第五八〇号 中华民国十年四月二十七日

案据黑河商会代理会长丁宦堂呈据本镇商人李万臣等拟组织一煤油引擎机器轮船于黑龙江

松花江一带往来行驶营业未谂於海关理船厅章程是否相合能否照准行驶据情转请鉴

核量子维持赐以办法等情前来当经本处令行代理总税务司查照来呈转令理船厅查酌呈

复以凭办理在案现据总税务司呈复称奉令当即令行滨江关税务司转令理船厅查酌呈

复去后现据该商所拟组织煤油引擎机器轮船行驶松黑两江除应领

有交通部执照外如遵守松花江现行航规暨爱珲分关章程似无不合各情形备文呈

复前来理合将滨江关税务司原呈附请酌夺示遵等情到处查商人李万臣等拟组

织煤油引擎机器轮船於松黑两江一带往来行驶营业既据查明尚无不合自可准子

照办除批复黑河商会并咨行交通部暨令滨江关监督查照外相应令行总税务

司转令滨江关税务司知照可也此令

枬春 同校
赵学谦

Enclosure.
(In duplicate)

2363.

MOTOR BOAT: proposed running
of, on Amur and Sungari
Rivers. No objection from
the Customs point of view,
reporting.

I. G.

HARBIN, 11th April, 1921.

SIR,

15 JUN 1923.

I have the honour to acknowledge receipt

of your Despatch No. 2463/82,268:

forwarding for my information and

guidance copy of Shui-wu Ch'u

Despatch No. 1668 in which the Board

desires a report from me if there

will be any objection to the

proposed running of a motor boat

by Heiho merchants on the Amur and

Sungari from the Customs point of

view:

and, in reply, to report that there is no objection

from the Customs point of view to the proposed

running of a motor boat on the Amur and Sungari

Rivers, provided this boat complies on the Sungari

with the Sungari and Customs regulations now in

force, and on the Amur with the Aigun Customs

regulations, and is covered by a Chiaotung Pu

Chihchao.

From information received from the Assistant in

Charge

THE INSPECTOR GENERAL OF CUSTOMS,

PEKING.

Charge at 'Aigun the object of the enterprise is to trade along the Amur for some 300 li from Taheiho; the length of the boat is to be 60', breadth 12', depth 8' and draft 2' and she is to be equipped with a motor engine bought from a Japanese firm in Dairen. Its hull will be procured either at Harbin or Taheiho.

A Chinese version, in duplicate, of this despatch is enclosed.

I have the honour to be,

Sir,

Your obedient Servant,

(Signed) René d'Anjou,

Commissioner.

True Copy:

Chief Asst. Sp. List.

[K.—21]

Harbin ....Despatch No. 2363 to I. G.

Enclosure.

呈為遵查黑河商人擬組織之煤油引擎機器輪船行駛於松黑兩江於關章尚無不合應准組織

惟頃遵守一切關章各情形據實呈復事稿奉第一四六三號

鈞令內開奉

稅務處令開據黑河商會代理會長丁宦壹呈稱據本鎮商人李萬臣稱竊商等擬組織一煤

油引擎機器輪船於黑龍江松花江一帶往來行駛營業同觀黑松花兩江之輪船概係蒸汽

機器而此等機器係用地位甚多兼之重量更大照煤油引擎手機器同一馬力比較能差十之八

第未識以煤油引擎機器裝製輪船於海關理船廳章程是否相合能否照准行駛祈呈

請稅務處所擬是否有當與准予行駛之處請鑒核施行等情據此查近年

松黑兩江每苦水少輪船吃水稍深即難行駛該商等組織煤油引擎機器輪船重量既輕吃水

自淺苟遇江水淺之時仍可行駛有如果心實業不無見地本會為提倡企業起見應

概予贊助以期仰副政府鼓舞實業之至意惟此項機船向無如此辦法是否與理船廳章

程相符理合呈請鑒核量予維持賜以辦法乎續並祈將理船廳章程抄賜一分允所感據等情前

[K.—21]

来究竟可否准予行驶之处相应令行代理总税务司查核来呈所称各节转令理船厅查酌肇复以

凭办理等因奉此相应令行咨甯澜关税务司转令理船厅查酌呈复以便转呈等因奉此当经饬由

理船厅详查该商所组织之煤油引擎机器轮船行驶於松黑两江并无不合且与关章亦无抵触之处

本关对於此案并无异议惟该轮除应领有交通部执照外其行驶松花江特须遵守松花江现行

之航规并海关章程其行驶黑龙江时须遵守爱珲分关章程复据爱珲分关主任佥呈报吉该商

此次组织煤油引擎机器轮船志在於黑龙江距黑河三百华里内往来行驶营业船身长懂六

十英尺宽十二英尺高八英尺吃水量三英尺其所雇配之引擎机器係雇自大连月商者而其船壳

则在哈埠平武黑河配置之所有呈复本关对於黑河商人拟组织之煤油引擎机器轮船行驶於松

黑两江无异议各缘由理合备文呈请

鉴核施行谨呈

总税务司 安　中华民国十年四月十一日

True Copy:

Chief Asst. Sp. Dist.

致哈尔滨关第 <u>2463/82268</u> 号令 　　　海关总税务司署（北京）1921 年 1 月 17 日

尊敬的哈尔滨关税务司：

　　兹附税务处第 1668 号令抄件，以供参考。内称黑河商人欲组织煤油引擎机器装置轮船于黑龙江及松花江一带往来行驶营业，并请黑河商会代为询问此项实业能否获准。税务处要求海关呈交关于此事的意见。

　　请按照要求呈交报告，并附中文译本，一式两份。

　　　　　　　　　　　　　　　　　　您忠诚的仆人

　　　　　　　　　　　　　　　　　（签字）安格联（F. A. Aglen）

　　　　　　　　　　　　　　　　　　总税务司

该抄件内容真实有效，特此证明：

录事：方骏良二等同文供事正后班

致哈尔滨关第 <u>2549/83847</u> 号令　　　　　海关总税务司署（北京）1921 年 4 月 29 日

尊敬的哈尔滨关税务司：

根据哈尔滨关第 2363 号呈（为回复海关总税务司署第 2463/82268 号令）：

"关于黑河商人拟组织煤油引擎机器轮船于黑龙江松花江一带往来行驶营业一

事，只要该船遵守松花江现行航规及瑷珲分关章程，于海关便无不合之处；"

兹附上税务处第 580 号令抄件，以供参考。从中可知，该商人拟组织煤油引擎机器轮

船于黑龙江松花江一带往来行驶营业之事已获批准。

务必要求该船照章行驶。

您忠诚的仆人

（签字）安格联（F. A. Aglen）

总税务司

该抄件内容真实有效，特此证明：

录事：吉补思（C. S. Gibbes）未列等帮办

呈海关总税务司署 <u>2363</u> 号文　　　　哈尔滨关 1921 年 4 月 11 日

尊敬的海关总税务司（北京）：

　　海关总税务司署第 2463/82268 号令收悉：

　　　"兹附税务处第 1668 号令抄件以供参考，内称税务处要求海关呈交关于黑河
　　商人欲组织煤油引擎机器装置轮船于黑龙江及松花江一带往来行驶营业事的意见
　　报告。"

　　查该商所组织之煤油引擎机器轮船行驶于松黑两江并无不合且与关章无抵触之处，
唯该轮除应领有交通部执照外，其行驶松花江时，须遵守松花江现行之航规及海关章程，
其行驶黑龙江时，须遵守瑷珲分关章程。

　　复据瑷珲分关代理税务司报告，该商此次组织煤油引擎机器轮船，志在于黑龙江距大
黑河 300 里内往来行驶营业，船身长 60 英尺、宽 12 英尺、高 8 英尺，吃水量 2 英尺，其所装
配之引擎机器系购自大连日商者，而其船壳则在哈尔滨或大黑河配置之。

　　兹附上本呈汉文版，一式两份。

您忠诚的仆人

覃书（R. C. L. d' Anjou）

哈尔滨关税务司

该抄件内容真实有效，特此证明：

录事：司丹博（J. Steinberg）超等帮办特班

3. 为建议于航运季开始时检查轮船及锅炉事

a.

b.   Aigun / Taheiho 8th April, 1922.

Sir,

1.   I have the honour to report that many
Steamers winter here, and undergo repairs both to
the hull and the boilers. - Until now, such
Steamers have been allowed to leave Port at the
opening of Navigation, without a proper inspection;
this is dangerous to passengers, and is indicative
of a lack of control on the part of the Customs.

2.   I therefore have the honour to propose that
we start from this very year an inspection to the
hull and boilers, as it is done in Harbin, charging
a fee on the same scale as Harbin, which I am
going to ascertain.

3.   In Harbin the Engineer is entrusted with
the inspection of the boilers; here, as we have no
                                        Engineer,

The Inspector General of Customs,
          P E K I N G.

ngineer, I propose to ihre the services of Mr. B. E. Sperk, who supervised the building of the Liang-chiat'un Office, and is an expert in the matter, at a cost not to exceed the amount of fees collected.

4. The Superintendent has been approached in the matter, and he agrees with me in the advisability of enforcing the inspection, in accordance with international practice, and in order to strengthen our control of the shipping in every way.

5. As the opening of the Navigation is fast approaching, I would be obliged by your telegraphic instructions, if my suggestion meets with your approval.

                    I have the honour to be,

                         Sir,

                    Your obedient Servant,

                    Acting Commissioner.

呈海关总税务司署 42 号文 　　　　　　　　璦珲关／大黑河 1922 年 4 月 8 日

尊敬的海关总税务司（北京）：

1. 兹汇报，冬季有很多轮船停泊于大黑河口岸，同时进行维修，包括船体及锅炉。然而，迄今为止，每年航运开通后，此类轮船未经适当检查便可获准离港；如此不但危及乘客的人身安全，亦显示海关的管理尚有不足之处。

2. 因此本署提议，自今年起，开始按照哈尔滨关之办法检查船体和锅炉，收费标准亦与哈尔滨关保持一致（但本署须确认其收费标准）。

3. 哈尔滨关检查锅炉之工作由营造司负责，但璦珲关尚无营造司，遂建议雇用该方面的专业人士施佩克（B.E.Sperk）先生，其曾经监督过梁家屯分卡的房屋建造工事，费用不会超出收费金额。

4. 本署已向海关监督提及此事，其表示同意本署按照国际惯例执行检查事宜，以加强璦珲关对船运工作的全面管理。

5. 鉴于航运即将开始，如蒙贵署电令批准该建议，本署将不胜感激。

您忠诚的仆人

包安济（G. Boezi）

璦珲关署理税务司

4. 为商议按照马力收取查验费用事

43

COMMRS.

Inspectorate General of Customs.

Aigun   No. 89,181   *PEKING,*   2nd May,   *19*22.

SIR,

I am directed by the Inspector General to
acknowledge receipt of your Despatch No. 42 :

> Inspection of Steamers on Opening of
> Navigation : suggesting, and appointment
> of Mr. B. E. Sperk for temporary duty
> in inspecting boilers, recommending;

and, in reply, to say that your proposal requires
further ventilation before it can be sanctioned,
especially in view of the fact that you propose
to charge fees on the same scale as at Harbin
where fees are charged according to horse-power.

You should report, therefore, more fully
on the general conditions regarding steamers at your
port, and for your guidance copies of Harbin
despatches Nos. 2297 and 2345 together with their
enclosures and "C.I's comments" and of I.G.despatch
No.2496/82,968 are appended.

Your

THE COMMISSIONER OF CUSTOMS,

AIGUN.

Your attention is specially called to the latter part of § 1 of I.G. despatch No. 2496/82,968 to Harbin which reads as follows :

"The authority for inspecting Chinese vessels periodically, in order to ensure the safety of passengers and crew, rests at present with the Customs .... .Compulsory inspection must therefore be confined to steamers under the Chinese flag, but if there is no objection on the part of the owners or agents of Russian steamers to their being inspected by Customs Officers and to paying the same fees as Chinese steamers pay they may also be inspected."

A copy of this despatch is being sent to the Coast Inspector, to whom you are requested to send a copy of your despatch under reply, as well as a copy of your reply to this despatch.

I am,

Sir,

Your obedient Servant,

Cecil A. V. Brown,

Chief Secretary.

Appendix.

The Harbin Commissioner to the Inspector General.
────────

No. 2297.   Custom House,
I. G.   Harbin, 11th January, 1921.

Sir,

         Steamers plying on the Sungari River are
governed by Inland Waters Steam Navigation Regulations.
The Inspection of engines and boilers was started
for the first time last year at the beginning of
the navigation season and in collecting fees for
such inspection this Office followed the scale
indicated in I.G. Circular No. 2366. The Harbour
Master thinks that, owing to the special types of
vessels plying on the Sungari, the scale of fees
is out of proportion to the use these vessels are
put to. He suggests that, instead of charging
according to tonnage, a charge according to Horse
Power be inaugurated this season. In contention of
this proposal the Harbour Master points out that the
greater proportion of vessels plying on the River
are not used as carriers of cargo but as tugs,
towing from 1 to 4 barges. Those employed as tugs
are greater profit earners and pay a lesser fee
than larger vessels with less Horse Power and less
cargo space. Another argument in favour of the
levy of fees according to horse power is that no
tonnage dues are paid by vessels navigating the

                                        Sungari

Sungari but river dues are, according to quantity
of cargo carried. Furthermore the question of
measuring vessels for tonnage has been set aside
for many years; we do not possess accurate figures
concerning the tonnage of vessels and it would take
a considerable time and would be a waste of time
to measure all the vessels registered at our River
Customs Office.   On the other side it would take
an inconsiderable time to ascertain the horse power
of any vessel coming for inspection.

The Harbour Master suggests that the fee
per horse power should be fixed at Hk.Tls.0.4.0.0.
This figure is arrived at by taking 49 steamers of
all types and calculating the fees that would be
collected according to tonnage and according to
horse power.

The Harbour Master's proposal appears to
me sound, simple and fair and if the Inspectorate
will consider the proposal in that light the new
system of levy of fees on engines and boilers
could be inaugurated at the beginning of this
season.

A copy of this despatch is being forwarded
to the Coast Inspector.

I have the honour to be,

Sir,

Your obedient Servant,

(Signed) R. C. L. d'Anjou,

Commissioner.

Sub-Appendix

Sub-Appendix No.1.

M E M O R A N D U M.

Owing to the special types of vessels plying on the Sungari the present scale of fees charged for inspection of boilers and engines of steamers running under Inland Waters Regulations seems out of proportion.

Some vessels are in reality but tugs only, and seldom if ever enter or clear without 1 to 4 Barges in tow, whilst, they are fitted with heavy machinery they only register a comparatively small tonnage, other crafts have, owing to the larger amount of space devoted to passenger accommodation, a heavy tonnage but at the same time having comparatively small engine power as they do not as a rule tow.

The consequence is that a vessel with 400 H.P. Engines, i.e. S.S. " San Shui" pays under the existing system of collection of inspection fees, a fee of Hk.Tls.30 - whilst the S.S. " Lung Chiang " with only 120 H.P. Engines pays Hk.Tls.100.

It is the Engines and Boilers that are inspected and not the Hulls, hence I venture to suggest that a system of fees be based not upon tonnage, but, on per H.P.

I append herewith a list of Chinese vessels running under Inland Waters Regulations, their comparative H.P. and tonnage fees they paid in 1920 and what they would pay under the rule now suggested.

A

A special arrangement could be made for Motor
Boats and other crafts (say up to 10 H.P.) engaged
in commercial traffic in and about the Harbour ,
these would pay a minimum fee of Hk.Tls.10.

As River Dues are charged in lieu of tonnage
dues the question of measuring vessels for tonnage
has been set aside for years, besides newly built
vessels, others have been altered in various ways,
which would mean that a large number of the crafts
would have to be measured and/or remeasured, for no
other reason but to ascertain the fee to be charged
for inspection, such " measuring" would require more
time and staff than the actual "inspection", the
Horse Power of an Engine can however be accurately
calculated in a few minutes by the Inspecting
Engineer and thus delays by subjecting the vessels
to clearing out the Holds for measuring tonnage
would be avoided.

The present system of measuring steamers to
obtain the tonnage for Trade Returns purpose
gives misleading results, in as much as Barges which
constitutes more tonnage than actual steamers, have
not been measured since 1910.

The appended list represents 49 steamers of
all types on the Sungari and may be considered
sufficient material to obtain the average.

The Horse Power divided into Total Fees
gives Hk.Tls.0.3.5.1. per Horse Power, as a round
figure I consider Hk.Tls.0.4.0.0 would be a just
charge to all parties concerned, i.e. the Customs
and/or Launch Inspector as well as the owners, and

would

would in aggregate only slightly exceed the sum as
charged under the present system.

(Signed) H. Abrahamsen,

Harbour Master.

Sub-Appendix

Sub-Appendix No.2.

LIST OF CHINESE STEAMERS PLYING ON THE SUNGARI RIVER 1920.

Table Showing Tonnage, Hk.Tls. Fee Collected, Horse Power, etc.

Vessel.	Net Registered Tons	Gross Tons	Hk.Tls Fee 1920	Horse Power	Fee @ Hk.Tls. 0.4.0.0.	Difference More	Difference Less
"...ng Chow"	86	231	40	300	120	80	...
"...iang Ao"	8	18	20	36	14	...	6
"...iang Fu"	9	21	20	86	34	14	...
"...iang Chin"	49	213	20	100	40	20	...
"...iang Ning"	177	425	75	400	160	85	...
"...i Hung"	100	199	50	100	40	...	10
"...i Wei"	258	451	100	150	60	...	40
"...'i Yang"	359	605	125	300	120	...	5
"...'ih Chow"	352	516	125	240	106	...	19
"...ih Yang"	290	369	100	105	42	...	58
"...ing Lan"	628	796	125	280	112	...	13
"...ing Po"	306	554	100	182	73	...	27
"...ing Shan"	351	505	125	180	72	...	53
"...ing Yuen"	98	251	40	225	90	50	...
"...An"	97	203	40	20	8	...	32
"...Po"	47	133	20	25	10	...	10
"...Shan"	149	259	50	100	40	...	10
"...ai Ch'eng"	832	1307	125	650	260	135	...
"...angchow"	227	441	75	200	80	5	...
"...sin Yüan"	90	153	40	120	68	28	...
"...sien Yu"	190	295	75	45	18	...	57
"...ua Tai"	243	387	75	40	16	...	59
"...I Hsing"	687	944	125	330	132	7	...
"...uang Chi"	185	421	75	300	120	45	...
"...uang Chow"	229	360	75	140	56	...	19
"...uang Li"	378	610	125	250	100	...	25
"...ung Chi"	48	111	20	50	20	...	...
"...aichow"	128	281	50	225	100	50	...
"...Li Yuan"	111	285	50	400	160	110	...
"...Lung Chiang"	310	401	100	120	48	...	52
"...Ming Shan"	74	157	30	140	56	26	...
"...an Hsiang"	266	528	100	400	160	60	...
"...Po Ho"	101	163	50	40	16	...	34
"...an Chiang"	374	496	125	120	48	...	77
"...an Shui"	58	199	30	400	160	130	...
"...Shao Hsing"	686	1080	125	250	100	...	25
"...Shanghai"	702	1057	125	240	96	...	29
"...Shen Yang"	225	362	75	130	52	...	23
"...ung Chiang"	52	94	30	30	12	...	18
"...Ta Hsing"	239	405	75	240	96	21	...
"...ai Ping"	153	242	75	82	33	...	42
"...ien Li"	62	152	30	45	18	...	12
"...ung Chiang"	80	293	40	400	160	120	...
"...'ung Shan"	308	447	100	115	46	...	54
"...ung Yuan"	108	194	50	40	16	...	34
"...u Chin"	109	325	50	500	200	150	...
"...u Hsing"	204	484	75	500	200	125	...
"...ang Hu"	145	349	50	300	120	70	...
"...u Hua"	41	136	20	110	44	24	...
Total	11,009	18,898	3,440	9,781	3,952		

(Signed) H. Abrahamsen,
Harbour Master.

Coast Inspector's Comments on Harbin No.2297, I.G.

Mr. Abrahamsen's suggestion to charge fees on horse power instead of on tonnage for steamers plying on the Sungari River is a good one, and as such a ruling would not affect any other section of China, there would seem to be no harm in introducing it tentatively. It should be noted that while it is pointed out that the earning powers of a high powered steamer employed as a tug are greater than those of a low powered steamer that cannot tow, it is not stated whether the tow is charged river dues. It would seem that if river dues are charged on tows as well as on the steamer towing them matters are equalized. Nevertheless Mr. Abrahamsen's suggestion is a good one, when there is no orthodox means of ascertaining the tonnage of steamers.

(Signed) T. J. Eldridge,
Coast Inspector.

Coast Inspector's Office,
    Shanghai, 19th January, 1921.

The

The Inspector General to the Harbin Commissioner.

_____

Inspectorate General of Customs,

Peking, 5th March, 1921.

No.2496   Commrs.

Harbin   No.82,968

Sir,

I am directed by the Inspector General to acknowledge receipt of your despatch No.2297:

recommending that the fees charged for the inspection of boilers and machinery of steamers plying on the Sungari should be at the rate of Hk.Tls.0.4.0.0. per horse power instead of the tonnage scale laid down in Circular No. 2366;

and, in reply, to say that it is presumed with reference to your opening remark in dealing with this question, namely, "Steamers plying on the Sungari River are governed by I.W.S.N. Regulations" that this remark applies only to Chinese steamers in certain respects, e.g. issue of certificate, etc., as one of the points in which the present Sungari Regulations differ from those of 1909 was that the I.W.S.N.Regulations became no longer applicable to the River Sungari(see § 5(a) of I.G. despatch No. 544/32,980.) The authority for inspecting Chinese vessels periodically, in order to ensure the safety of passengers and crew, rests at present with the Customs and when foreign vessels ply in inland waters elsewhere in China we have also the right to require a Survey Certificate

issued

issued by a national authority to be produced before
we issue or renew an Inland Certificate. On the
Sungari, however, agreements preclude us from exercising
this right and in normal times, no doubt,
periodical inspection of Russian vessels would be
carried out by Russian authorities. Compulsory
inspection must therefore be confined to steamers
under the Chinese flag, but if there is no
objection on the part of the owners or agents of
Russian steamers to their being inspected by
Customs officers and to paying the same fees as
Chinese steamers pay, they may also be inspected.

2.   In regard to your proposal to charge
fees for the inspection of boilers and machinery
at the rate of Hk.Tls.0.4.0.0. per horse power. I
am to authorise you to adopt this system provisionally.   I am at the same time to inquire which
officer or officers will be detailed to undertake
inspection, and to request you to submit through
the Coast Inspector your opinion whether any
proportion of the fee received should be paid
to the inspecting officer or not, and if you
think that the nature of the work calls for
payment of part fee to state what proportion.

3.   As you have made no comments on the
Harbour Master's suggestion that a special
arrangement could be made for motor boats and
other craft (say up to 10 H.P.) engaged in
commercial traffic in and about the Harbour, by
which they would pay a minimum fee of Hk.Tls.10
it is presumed that you do not approve of it and
it seems better that the rate should be uniform

for

for all vessels, but all vessels under the Chinese flag, large or small, whatever their business, should be inspected.

4.   I am further to draw your attention to the instructions of § 4 of I.G. Circular No. 2620 which require the inspection of hulls as well as of boilers and machinery. Present conditions at Harbin may make it better not to insist on this requirement but it should be borne in mind and given effect to when feasible. The inspection of hulls will not imply increase of the inspection fee but it may mean the payment of a proportion or larger proportion of it to the inspecting officer.

5.   A copy of this despatch is being sent to the Coast Inspector.

                I am,

                    Sir,

                      Your obedient Servant,

                        (Signed) C.A.V.Bowra,

                        Chief Secretary.

                                  The

The Harbin Commissioner to the Inspector General.

N° 2345.

I. G.

Custom House,

Harbin, 22nd March, 1921.

Sir,

I have the honour to acknowledge receipt of your despatch No. 2496/82,968 (in reply to Harbin despatch No. 2297):

authorising this office to adopt provisionally the system of charging for the inspection of boilers and machinery on Chinese steamers plying under the Inland Waters Steam Navigation Regulations on the Sungari at the rate of Hk.Tls.0.4.0.0 per Horse Power, but that this procedure is not applicable to steamers under the Russian flag unless with the consent of the owners or agents; drawing my attention to the instructions of Circular No. 2620 concerning the inspection of Hulls which should be given effect to when feasible; and calling for certain information regarding the inspection fee to be charged on motor boats and other commercial craft plying in and about the Harbour, Staff to be employed on inspection of boilers, etc., and proportion of fee payable to this Staff.

In reply, I beg to report that the Officer detailed to undertake the inspection of boilers, machinery and hulls will be Mr. Stoyanoff, who has recently been appointed Harbin District Launch Inspector and who

is

is fully qualified for that work. As Mr.
Stoyanoff's time is fully employed in supervising
the repairs, etc., to the Revenue and Aids to
Navigation craft on the Sungari and as the
inspection will concern steamers for the most part
and not launches and entail a good deal of extra
work it would be reasonable to issue to the
inspecting officer a certain percentage of the
fee, which I recommend to be 2/10ths.

With regard to the Harbour Master's
suggestion (on which I did not comment) that
a special arrangement could be made for motor-boats
and other craft (say up to 10 H.P.) engaged in
commercial traffic in and about the Harbour
by which they would pay a minimum fee of Hk.Tls.
10 my personal opinion and recommendation is that
the fee should be uniform for all vessels.

As regards the inspection of Hulls I
do not foresee any difficulty in carrying
this out so far as the Chinese vessels are
concerned. The inspection of Hulls can be
undertaken at the same as that of the Boilers
and machinery and although it will necessitate
some additional work I do not recommend the
issue of a greater proportion of the inspecting
fee.

I have the honour to be,

Sir,

Your obedient Servant,

(Signed) R.C.L.d'Anjou,

Commissioner.

True copies :

H. Farbes

ting Assistant Secretary.

致瑷珲关第 <u>43/89181</u> 号令　　　　　海关总税务司署（北京）1922 年 5 月 2 日

尊敬的瑷珲关税务司：

　　第 42 号呈收悉：

　　　　"提议开航时查验轮船；建议委派斯波克（B. E. Sperk）先生暂时负责查验汽炉
　　工作。"

奉总税务司命令，现批复如下：兹告知，在批准贵署提议前，特别是考虑到贵署提议与哈
尔滨关同样按照马力收取查验费，仍需进一步公开讨论。

　　因此，贵署应详细报告贵口岸轮船的整体情况，兹附哈尔滨关第 2297 号与 2345 号
呈及附件、"超等总巡的意见"以及海关总税务司署第 2496/82968 号令副本，供贵署参照
执行。

　　特请贵署注意海关总税务司署致哈尔滨关第 2496/82968 号令第 1 条后半部分，如下
所示：

　　　　"定期查验中国船只以保障乘客与船员安全，该权限目前属于海关……因此，强
　　制性查验必须只针对悬挂中国旗帜的船只，但如果俄罗斯轮船的船主或代理不反
　　对海关关员查验，同意付费标准与中国轮船相同，海关也可以对俄罗斯轮船进行查
　　验。"

　　同时，此令副本已抄送给巡工司，请贵署将呈文副本与复此令呈文副本抄送给巡
工司。

　　　　　　　　　　　　　　　　　　　　　　您忠诚的仆人

　　　　　　　　　　　　　　　　　　　　　　包罗（C. A. V. Bowra）

　　　　　　　　　　　　　　　　　　　　　　总务科税务司

附件

呈海关总税务司署 <u>2297</u> 号文　　　　　　**哈尔滨关 1921 年 1 月 11 日**

　　往返于松花江的轮船由《内港轮船航行章程》管理。哈尔滨关去年航季季初开始对往来松花江的轮船的引擎和锅炉进行查验，收费标准依照海关总税务司署第 2366 号通令执行。理船厅认为，有特殊类型的船只往返于松花江上，现行收费标准已不再适用。理船厅建议，不再根据船只吨位收费，本航季改为按照马力收费。为证明自己的提议，理船厅指出绝大部分往返于江上船只都不是运货船，而是拖着 1 到 4 条驳船的拖船。这些拖船利润高，缴费却比小马力小货运量的大船少。另一个支持按马力收费的原因是，松花江上航行的船只不缴船钞（船舶吨税），但按货运量缴江捐。此外，船只吨位的测量问题已历经多年未得到解决；我们无法得知船只吨位的准确数字，而若要测量完所有在本江关注册船只的吨位，无疑要耗费大量时间。另外，确定待查验船只的马力数所需时间很短。

　　理船厅建议收费标准定为每马力 0.4 海关两。这个数字是综合 49 艘各型轮船，计算按吨位收费和按马力收费两种情况所得。

　　在我看来，理船厅的提议公平合理，简单易行，若海关总税务司署考虑此提议，新的引擎汽炉收费制度可在本航季季初开始实行。

　　同时，此令副本已抄送给巡工司。

您忠诚的仆人

（签字）贾韦（R. C. L. d' Anjou）

哈尔滨关税务司

子附件 1

备忘录

　　因有特殊类型船只往返于松花江，根据《内港章程》制定的现行轮船汽炉与引擎查验收费标准已不再适用。

　　有些船只实际上只做拖船使用，在往返于松花江时总会拖着 1 到 4 条驳船，虽然这些船的机械设备很重，但注册吨位相对较小。其他船只因满足乘客膳宿需求，需要更大空间，故注册吨位较大，但由于不用作拖船，引擎相对较小。

　　结果导致，引擎足足有 400 马力的船只（如"三水"号）在现行查验收费制度下只交付 30 海关两，而"龙江"号的引擎只有 120 马力，却要交付 100 海关两。

　　查验部位为引擎与汽炉，而非船体。因此我大胆提议一种新的收费制度，根据马力收费，而非根据吨位收费。

　　随函附上中国船只 1920 年根据《内港章程》按吨位付费标准下所缴费用与现在提议的按马力付费标准应缴费用的对比表。

　　进出港口从事商运的摩托艇和其他船只（比如说不超过 10 马力）予以特殊处理，最低收取 10 海关两的费用。

　　因已用征收江捐替代船钞，测量船只吨位的问题已经搁置多年，除了新造船只，其他船只都因各种原因而有所变化，这就意味着因为要确定查验应收费用，就要测量或重新测量许多船只。这样的"测量"需要的时间和人手甚至比"查验"本身还要多。但仅需数分钟，查验机师便可精确查出引擎的马力，避免船只因吨位测量导致延迟离港。

　　现行轮船测量体系在计算贸易利润吨位时常常得出令人误解的结果，比如驳船，吨位实际上大过轮船，但自 1910 年起就未再进行吨位测量。

　　附表中已列出松花江上 49 艘各类船只，提供的资料足以计算得出平均值。

　　总费用按马力均分，单价为每马力 0.351 海关两，我认为取整设定单价为每马力 0.4 海关两，对各方（海关与 / 或小轮公司以及船主）来讲都很合理，所收总费用与现行收费制度相比仅有轻微上涨。

（签字）阿布兰森（H. Abrahamsen）

理船厅

子附件2

1920年往返于松花江中国轮船名单

表中给出了吨位、马力、按海关两计算的收费等

船只	净登记吨位	长吨	1920年按吨位收费（海关两）	马力	按每马力0.4海关两收费	差价 多	差价 少
"常州"号（Chiang Chow）	86	231	40	300	120	80	…
"蒋鹜"号（Chiang Ao）	8	18	20	36	14	…	6
"江凫"号（Chiang Fu）	9	21	20	86	34	14	…
"蒋靳"号（Chiang Chin）	49	213	20	100	40	20	…
"蒋宁"号（Chiang Ning）	177	425	75	400	160	85	…
"吉宏"号（Chi Hung）	100	199	50	100	40	…	10
"吉威"号（Chi Wei）	258	451	100	150	60	…	40
"赤阳"号（Ch'i Yang）	359	605	125	300	120	…	5
"池州"号	352	516	125	240	106	…	19
"揭阳"号（Chih Yang）	290	369	100	105	42	…	58
"庆澜"号（Ching Lan）	628	796	125	280	112	…	13
"庆浦"号（Chih Po）	306	554	100	182	73	…	27
"庆山"号（Ching Shan）	351	505	125	180	72	…	53
"庆远"号（Ching Yuen）	98	251	40	225	90	50	…
"富安"号（Fu An）	97	203	40	20	8	…	32
"富浦"号（Fu Po）	47	133	20	25	10	…	10
"釜山"号（Fu Shan）	149	259	50	100	40	…	10
"海城"号（Hai Ch'eng）	832	1307	125	650	260	135	…
"杭州"号（Hangchow）	227	441	75	200	80	5	…
"鑫源"号（Hsin Yuan）	90	153	40	120	68	28	…
"贤宇"号（Hsien Yu）	190	295	75	45	18	…	57
"华泰"号（Hua Tai）	243	387	75	40	16	…	59
"义兴"号（I Hsing）	687	944	125	330	132	7	…
"广济"号（Kuang Chi）	185	421	75	300	120	45	…
"广州"号（Kuang Chow）	229	360	75	140	56	…	19

续表

船只	净登记吨位	长吨	1920年按吨位收费（海关两）	马力	按每马力0.4海关两收费	差价	
						多	少
"广利"号（Kuang Li）	378	610	125	250	100	…	25
"公济"号（Kung Chi）	48	111	20	50	20	…	…
"莱州"号（Laichow）	128	281	50	225	100	50	…
"漓源"号（Li Yuan）	111	285	50	400	160	110	…
"龙江"号（Lung Chiang）	310	401	100	120	48	…	52
"茗山"号（Ming Shan）	74	157	30	140	56	26	…
"南兴"号（Nan Hsiang）	266	528	100	400	160	60	…
"博贺"号（Po Ho）	101	163	50	40	16	…	34
"三江"号（San Chiang）	374	496	125	120	48	…	77
"三水"号（San Shui）	58	199	30	400	160	130	…
"绍兴"号（Shao Hsing）	686	1080	125	250	100	…	25
"上海"号（Shanghai）	702	1057	125	240	96	…	29
"沈阳"号（Shen Yang）	225	362	75	130	52	…	23
"松江"号（Sung Chiang）	52	94	30	30	12	…	18
"大兴"号（Ta Hsing）	239	405	75	240	96	21	…
"太平"号（Tai Ping）	153	242	75	82	33	…	42
"天利"号（Tien Li）	62	152	30	45	18	…	12
"同江"号（Tung Chiang）	80	293	40	400	160	120	…
"铜山"号（T'ung Shan）	308	447	100	115	46	…	54
"东远"号（Tung Yuan）	108	194	50	40	16	…	34
"乌金"号（Wu Chin）	109	325	50	500	200	150	…
"武兴"号（Wu Hsing）	204	484	75	500	200	125	…
"洋湖"号（Yang Hu）	145	349	50	300	120	70	…
"玉华"号（Yu Hua）	41	136	20	110	44	24	…
总计	11009	18898	3440	9781	3952		

（签字）阿布兰森（H. Abrahamsen）

理船厅

巡工司对哈尔滨关致海关总税务司署

第 2297 号呈的意见

阿布兰森（H. Abrahamsen）先生关于对往返于松花江的轮船按马力收费而不按吨位收费的提议很有道理。这样的规定不会影响中国其他地区，试验性引进此种收费方式似乎没有任何害处。须注意的一点是，虽然现已发现，大马力轮船用作拖船的赚钱能力比无法拖船的小马力轮船的赚钱能力强，但是否对被拖的船征收江捐尚未确定。恐怕要对拖动其他船只的轮船与被拖船只都征收江捐，才会显得公平。阿布兰森（Abrahamsen）先生的提议非常有道理，普通方法无法确定轮船吨位。

（签字）额得志（T. J. Eldridge）

巡工司

巡工事务局

上海，1921 年 1 月 19 日

总税务司致哈尔滨关税务司函

致哈尔滨关第 <u>2496/82968</u> 号令　　　　海关总税务司署（北京）1921 年 3 月 5 日

第 2297 号呈收悉：

　　"关于往返于松花江轮船的机械设备和汽炉查验费用，建议从第 2366 号通令规定的按吨位收费改为按马力收费，费率为每马力 0.4 海关两。"

奉总税务司命令，现批复如下：根据贵署开篇有关"往返于松花江的轮船由《内港轮船航行章程》管辖"的注解，现推测此项注解仅在特定情况下适用于中国轮船，如开具内港航行专照等。现行《松花江章程》与 1909 年版本之间不同的一个要点为，《内港轮船航行章程》已不再适用于松花江（参见海关总税务司署第 544/32980 号令第 5（a）条）定期查验中国船只以保障乘客与船员安全，该权限目前属于海关。对于往返于于中国其他内河的洋船，在为其开具或更换新内港专照之前，海关同样有权要求其出示由国家政府签发的船舶检查证书。然而在松花江上，海关受制于协议规定，无法行使此项权利。毋庸置疑，平常对于俄罗斯船只的定期查验由俄罗斯政府负责执行。因此，强制性查验必须只针对悬挂中国旗帜的船只，但如果俄罗斯轮船的船主或代理不反对海关关员查验，同意付费标准与中国轮船相同，海关也可以对俄罗斯轮船进行查验。

　　2. 贵署关于将汽炉和机械设备查验费用定为每马力 0.4 海关两的建议，兹授权贵署暂时采用此方法。与此同时，请贵署回复，查验工作由哪一位或哪几位关员负责，此外，请贵署通过巡工司转达是否应给予查验关员提成的意见。若贵署认为此项工作的性质需要给查验关员提成，请说明提成比例。

　　3. 因贵署对理船厅关于"进出港口从事商运的摩托艇和其他船只（比如说不超过 10 马力）予以特殊处理，最低收取 10 海关两的费用"的建议未置评论，故假定贵署对此持反对意见，费率最好应对所有船只一视同仁，但是凡悬挂中国旗帜的船只，无论大小，无论用途，都应进行查验。

　　4. 贵署还应进一步注意海关总税务司署第 2620 号通令第 4 条的指示，指示要求在查验汽炉与机械设备时也要对船体进行查验。哈尔滨关目前的情况可能无法落实此项要求，但请牢记，一旦情况允许立即贯彻落实。对船体的查验并不会增加查验费用，但给查验关员的提成比例可以有所提高。

5. 同时,此令副本已抄送至巡工司。

您忠诚的仆人

（签字）包罗（C. A. V. Bowra）

总务科税务司

哈尔滨关税务司致海关总税务司

呈海关总税务司署 2345 号文　　　　　哈尔滨关 1921 年 3 月 22 日

第 2496/82968 号令（复哈尔滨关第 2297 号呈）收悉：

"授权哈尔滨关暂时对松花江上受《内港轮船航行章程》约束的中国轮船实行新汽炉与机械设备查验收费制度，按每马力 0.4 海关两的费率收费，但除非得到俄罗斯船主或代理的同意，否则本办法对悬挂俄罗斯旗帜的轮船不适用；提请哈尔滨关注意第 2620 号通令指示，等到情况允许，应立即落实船体查验；需要关于进出港口的摩托艇和其他商业船只查验费用、查验汽炉等项目的雇员情况以及员工查验提成的具体信息。"

兹报告，为负责查验汽炉、机械设备以及船体所选派的关员为近期任命为哈尔滨关就地小轮工司，斯托亚诺夫（Stoyanoff）先生，其完全有资格胜任此工作。因监督松花江上征税船只和航务船只的修理等工作已占用斯托亚诺夫（Stoyanoff）先生大量时间，而查验工作主要针对轮船，不是汽艇，将会使他负担大量额外工作，故向查验关员发放一定比例的提成很合理，我建议按两成的比例发放提成。

至于本署未予置评的理船厅建议，即进出港口从事商运的摩托艇和其他船只（比如说不超过 10 马力）予以特殊处理，最低收取 10 海关两的费用，我个人意见与建议是，对所有船只统一收费标准。

本署认为，若只考虑中国船只，对船体检查的贯彻落实不会有任何问题。对船体的查验可以与汽炉和机械设备同时进行，尽管这样确实必会增加额外工作，但不建议增加提成比例。

您忠诚的仆人

（签字）贾韦（R. C. L. d'Anjou）

哈尔滨关税务司

此副本内容真实有效，特此证明。

确认人签字：福贝士（A. H. Forbes）

代理总务科副税务司

5. 为购入大黑河港口所需之摩托艇事

Aigun / Taheiho 8th April, 1922.

Sir,

1.   Previous to the Summer of 1918, China's rights to navigate on the Amur was not admitted by the Russian Government, and control of steamers by the Chinese Customs commenced only after the vessel had tied up at the foreshore, no boarding of vessels in the stream being tolerated by the Russian Authorities; accordingly, the Aigun Customs was unprovided with any sort of craft, unlike other River Stations of the Harbin District.

    One of the first steps taken to establish our control, when the River opened to Navigation in 1920, was that of boarding and searching on arrival - and clearing on departure - in middle stream Russian and Chinese vessels calling at this Port. However, no craft was procured, notwithstanding

repreated

Inspector General of Customs,

PEKING

repeated applications by the Senior Assistants in charge of Aigun/Taheiho; we have now only an old, small, clumsy two oared gig, which cannot be used in a current varying from 3 to 6 knots, nor with a boarding party. We are therefore obliged to use the Steamers' own rowing boats for boarding on arrival and leaving after clearance - i. e. for enforcing our own rules. This state of affairs not only entails considerable loss of time, but is quite irregular and not dignified: should one of the steamers refuse to lend her own gig, we would be unable to board her.

2.   I have therefore the honour to requisition for one four oared gig for the Taheiho Harbour, for boarding and general work; the gig can be built here, on plans prepared in Shanghai or locally, at a cost not exceeding $ 400. Four boatmen, @ Hk. Tls. 11 per month, are required in addition to the present Staff.

        The movements of Steamers at Aigun are not very important; vessels are allowed to come directly to their moorings, and the practise can continue

for

for some time, until Harbour Limits, Moorings and
Landing Stages have been fixed (vide Aigun despatch
No. 40, § 9).

3.   In addition, it would be urgent to check
up-river rafts which now, notwithstanding our best
efforts, come into Harbour helter-skelter, endangering
shipping and making control difficult; quarantine
vessels, and vessels carrying explosives or inflamm-
bles should be boarded and cleared outside the
Lower Harbour limits; it would be most important
to watch the contraband which is going on outside
Harbour limits, not far from town, and occasionally
farther away. - There is thus a distance of nearly
15 verst from Upper Blagovestchensk to the mouth
of the Zea, the two chief points for smuggling above
and below Harbour, to be patrolled, with an occa-
sional visit to Aigun, 55 verst down river; there
is besides the Survey of the Harbour to take in
hand.

4.   To secure these ends I have the honour
to apply for a Motor Boat or Motor Launch of
sufficient power to make a maximum of 11 knots in
still waters, and capable of making a cruise of

about

about 100 miles. The purchase of a launch has already been recommended, in case of promulgation of the Harbour Regulations, by the Harbin Commissioner in his despatch No. 2344.

5.   The Boat could be purchased in Harbin or here, or built locally.

A ready-built Motor Boat is for sale here for $ 4.000; it has only run from June to October 1921, and is practically new; it would suit our requirements fairly well, and has the advantage of being ready as soon as the purchase is sanctioned. Its characteristics are given below :

MOTOR: Gray Marine Motor, new, four cycle 25 H.P. Steward Carburetor. Burns either Benzine or Kerosene; consumes in 2 ½ hours steady running at full speed one-gallon tin of oil (benzine, gasoline or kerosene) The Motor is all oiled from the base, and there is a gauge to indicate amount of oil in base, also glass to see if oil is circulating.

MAGNETO : Bosch.

HULL : Built in Summer 1921; finished in oak with brass fixtures - 25 ft long over all, and 5 feet beam. - Seating capacity 12 people; auto steering gear with all controls at driver's seat. Auto top which can be folded at stern when not is use. One extra brass propeller.

SPEED : 15 verst in still water.

It is also possible to build a good hull about 25 ft. long here, from plans drawn at Shanghai or locally, at a cost of 800 - 1000 dollars. The engine may be either purchased in Shanghai, or

chosen

chosen amongst a few which are offered locally for

sale, the approximate price for engine and hull

being as follows :-

> For a 28 ft. launch, opened, with Marine Engine
> FERRO, 16 H.P., running on Benzine and Kerosene,
> 2-cylinders, electric spark, Magneto BOSCH
> $ 3,000-

> For the same launch equipped with a STUDE-
> BAKER Engine (Motor Car), 30 H.P., 6 cylinders,
> Magneto BOSCH
> $ 3,750-

> For the same launch equipped with a CADILLAC
> Motor Car Engine, Model 57, 8 cylinders, 40 H.P.,
> with self-starter and electric lighting
> Delco system
> $ 4,000-

6.   As regards Staff, a Mechanic would be

necessary for the launch. A **good** Russian Mechanic,

competent in motors and capable occasionally to make

installations and repairs in the way of telephones,

electric light and bells, etc, can be engaged here

at the pay of a Chinese Mechanic in Harbin, i. e.

Hk. Tls. 50 a month.

7.   As a Customs Pontoon and Landing Stage I

would propose either to buy a small junk, or to

make a log pontoon fitting it up with the neces-

sary upper structures, the total estimated cost

for which from start to finish would not exceed

Hk. Tls. 100.

      I would add that the provision of a

launch

launch and Gig for the Taheiho Harbour would ensure
sufficient control, which is at present far from
satisfactory, of all shipping, would permit of search
parties being properly organised and efficient search
carried out, both day and night, and would bring
port practice at Taheiho into line with that at
other ports in China, including Harbin.

8.　　　In my opinion however, control should not
be confined to the Harbour, but extend gradually
to the whole River in Chinese Waters. The proposed
New Customs Regulations (Aigun desp. No. 37) provide
for control of trade on the frontier generally, and
for boarding of vessels <u>en route</u>; the eventual
levy of Duty on Amur Traffic (Aigun desp. No. 38)
makes it necessary to occasionally check Manifests
of Vessels and Vessels' movements at places other
than the Customs Stations. - For long cruises, for
patrolling different parts of the River and for raids
on smugglers, the Customs require a rapid shallow-
draft vessel with a cruising radius of 250 to 300
miles, and sleeping accomodation for 2, possibly 3,
foreigners, besides the crew.

9. There

9.　　　There are two alternative crafts :

　　a) a specially built steam launch, preferably consuming firewood; the cruising radius however is limited by the space required for firewood;

　　b) an Hydro-glider, of the Commercial type D. R., Motor B. D. S., recently experimented on the Yangtse and Tang Kiang; if this craft lives up to descriptions, it should be prove an ideal one for the Amur

　　a) because it is rather economical;

　　b) on account of the speed (30 to 40 miles an hour) which allows of long cruises on the River (about 1650 verst from Moho to Lahasusu) being made in a reasonable time, and renders surprises on smuggling possible;

　　c) because the shallow draft makes navigation easy anywhere and at any time.

　　The last two qualities are also a good protection against the Hunghutze, and the smugglers which are a difficult lot to deal with.

　　The need for this craft is not absolutely urgent yet, but one will be required at no distant time, if we must seriously control Trade on the River; and, if China takes her share in the Aids-to-Navigation (which question is likely to be discussed soon) it will be most useful. I therefore would

like

like the Coast Inspector to enquire into the
possibilities of an hydro-glider for service on the
Amur. The following prices of different fuels here
during the Navigation Season will be useful in this
connection :

    Coal, Fushun, about $ 34 per ton;
    Coal, other qualities, from $ 27 to $ 31 per ton;
    Firewood, $ 12 to 13 per cubic sajen;
    Benzine, $ 22 per 10 gallons probable reduction for
                                  wholesale purchase,
    Kerosene,$ 11 " " "   about 10 %.

        As to Staff, one Russian Mechanic, helped by
an Assistant Mechanic (chinese) to be procured from
Harbin @ 25 to 30 Taels per month, could attend to
both the hydro-glider and the motor launch. - For a
Steam launch, an Engineer and Fireman would be
required.

        Copy of this despatch is sent to the
Coast Inspector.

                    I have the honour to be,
                    Sir,
                    Your obedient Servant,

                    Acting Commissioner.

2 2 MAY 1922

COAST INSPECTOR'S COMMENTS ON AIGUN/TAHEIHO DESPATCH
NO.41, I. G.

It would seem desirable to recommend that both the four-oared gig and the 25 ft. motor launch suggested be authorised, the former to be built locally, designed to suit the conditions of the port, and for use in the harbour. The latter, for preventive work and other revenue work outside the harbour, is not expensive if in good condition and well built at a cost of $4,000.00.

With regard to the above and other requirements, the following Shanghai prices are given:-

Teak wood hull for motor boat 25 ft. long:

Cost, Shanghai Taels 1,600.00.

Kelvin Motor 12 H.P. for above hull: Cost £260.

Speed of launch with 12 H.P. motor about 6 miles per hour.

Kelvin Motor 26 H.P. for above hull: Cost £490.

Speed of launch with 26 H.P. motor about 8.5 knots.

Hydro-

Hydro-glider, Italian type, 40 ft. long: Cost about

Shanghai Taels 12,000.00.

Speed 50 miles per hour; consumption about 20

gallons gasolene per hour costing $44.00 at Aigun.

Hydro-glider, French type, 35 ft. long: Cost about

Shanghai Taels 12,000.00

Speed 27 miles per hour; consumption about 10

gallons gasolene per hour costing $22.00 at Aigun.

(Signed) T. J. Eldridge,

Coast Inspector.

Coast Inspector's Office,

Shanghai, 3rd May, 1922.

True copy.

Supervisor.

No. 45

COMMRS.

Aigun No. 89,487

Inspectorate General of Customs,

PEKING, 22nd May, 19 22.

SIR,

I am directed by the Inspector General to acknowledge receipt of your Despatch No. 41 :

requesting authority for the purchase of a four-oared gig for boarding and general work in the Taheiho Harbour; for the engagement of four boatmen with pay at the rate of Hk.Tls.11.00 each a month; also for the provision of a motor boat or launch; stating that a ready built motor boat is for sale at Taheiho for $4,000.00, that it has only run from June to October, 1921, and is practically new, that it would suit our requirements fairly well and has the advantage of being ready as soon as the purchase is sanctioned;

and, in reply, to approve of the provision of a four-oared gig for the Taheiho Harbour. This gig is to be built locally from locally prepared plans, the cost - which is not to exceed $400.00 - is to be charged to your Account A : 5/1.

The

THE COMMISSIONER OF CUSTOMS,

A I G U N.

The engagement of four boatmen at Hk.Tls. 11.00 each a month is also approved. These men are to be medically examined and suitably secured.

With regard to the motor boat for general supervision work, the Inspector General thinks that the provision of such a boat will probably be advisable; but, before sanctioning any expenditure in this connection, he would like to know :

1. In what manner you propose to satisfy yourself that the motor boat you refer to as being available locally is in a perfectly sound state of repair and in good working order generally.

2. Who is the present owner ? and

3. If you would be able to secure a reliable guarantee for so many months satisfactory running.

I am to add that our experience of second-hand motor craft has hitherto been disastrous, and, before sanctioning purchase, the Inspector General will have to be satisfied that we are not taking over a craft that in a short time will be

condemned

condemned as useless, or that will have to be

re-engined.

I am,

Sir,

Your obedient Servant,

Cecil a. v. Bowra

Chief Secretary.

呈海关总税务司署 <u>41</u> 号文　　　　　　　瑷珲关 / 大黑河 1922 年 4 月 8 日

尊敬的海关总税务司（北京）：

1. 1918 年夏天以前，俄国政府不准许中国船只航行于黑龙江航道上，亦不允许中国海关于江中登船检查，只能管辖停泊靠岸的船只；因此瑷珲关未能如哈尔滨关辖区其他分关一样配备船只。

1920 年航道开通后，凡停靠于大黑河口岸的中俄船只，无论到港、结关离港抑或停于江中，皆由瑷珲海关登船检查。鉴于此，当时的瑷珲分关 / 大黑河超等帮办（总办）多次提出配备船只之申请，但未能如愿；如今，瑷珲关仅有一艘粗陋陈旧的双桨小船，无法载人，且当江水流速从 3 节变到 6 节时，便无法行驶，因此海关关员若要对到港和结关离港的轮船进行登船检查，则只能借用这些轮船自带的划艇。如此行事不仅耗费时间，亦不合乎规则，有损海关尊严；此外，若有轮船拒绝借出划艇，海关关员则无法完成登船检查。

2. 兹请求为大黑河港口配备一艘四桨船，以便完成登船检查及日常工作；关于此船，可于当地建造，由上海或当地设计，费用不超过 400 银圆。人员方面，除现有职员之外，仍需 4 名水手，每月薪俸 11 海关两。

瑷珲口岸方面，轮船于港口内如何行驶并不重要，可直接驶入其停泊地点，在确定港口界限、泊地及浮码头之前，可继续按此惯例执行（参阅瑷珲关第 40 号呈第 9 项）。

3. 此外，海关亟待开展之工作包括：检查自上游而来的木筏，木筏入港时速度极快，易对其他船只造成危险，亦难以管理；于港口下流停泊界限以外对检疫船只及携带易燃易爆物的船只进行登船检查，办理结关手续；于港口界限以外监管走私，通常不会到离镇子太远之处，仅偶尔会远些。布拉戈维申斯克（Blagovestchensk）上游及结雅河口是大黑河港口上游和下游两个主要走私地点，两地距离约 15 俄里，海关关员需要往来巡查，偶尔亦需行至大黑河港口下游 35 俄里处的瑷珲口岸进行巡查，此外还需完成港口测量等事务。

4. 鉴于此，兹申请一艘摩托艇或汽艇，动力充足，于静水中航速可达 11 节，巡航 100 英里。哈尔滨关税务司于哈尔滨关第 2342 号呈中颁布《理船章程》时，已提出购买摩托艇之申请。

5. 摩托艇可于哈尔滨或当地购入，或者于当地建造。

大黑河目前有一艘建好的摩托艇，售价 4000 银圆，仅在 1921 年 6 月至 10 月行驶过，因此几乎是全新的；该摩托艇完全符合瑷珲关之要求，且批准购买后，便可即刻投入使用。该摩托艇各项信息如下：

发动机：格雷（Gray）船用发动机，全新，四冲程循环，25 马力，斯图尔德（Steward）化油器；燃烧轻汽油或煤油；全速稳定行驶 2.5 小时消耗 5 加仑油（轻汽油、汽油或煤油）。发动机均从底部加油，底部有油量指示计量器，可透过玻璃看到油的循环。

永磁电机：博世（Bosch）

船体：建造于 1921 年夏；用铜架固定橡木而成；长 25 英尺，宽 5 英尺；可容纳 12人；自动操舵装置，均于驾驶员座椅处操控。自动船篷，不用时可折叠置于船尾。一个备用铜制螺旋桨。

航速：静水航速 15 俄里。

但亦可于当地建造一艘新船，长约 25 英尺，由上海或当地设计，费用为 800 到 1000 银圆。发动机可在上海购买或于当地挑选，发动机及船体价格约为：

船体 28 英尺长，选用费罗（FERRO）船用发动机，16 马力，燃烧轻汽油和煤油，2 个气缸，电火花加工，博世永磁电机。

3000 银圆

船体 28 英尺长，选用斯图贝克（STUDEBAKER）汽车发动机，30 马力，6 个气缸，博世永磁电机。

3750 银圆

船体 28 英尺长，选用卡迪拉克（CADILLAC）汽车发动机，57 型号，8 个气缸，40 马力，配备自动启动器及德科（Delco）电力照明系统。

4000 银圆

6. 职员方面，需要一名匠董。兹建议，雇用一名优秀的俄国匠董，除具备与发动机相关的专业技术资格外，间或还可以安装维修电话、电灯、警铃等，薪俸与哈尔滨关的华籍匠董一样，每月 50 海关两。

7. 关于港口浮码头和栈桥的管理，兹建议，购置一艘小型民船，或者建造一艘木制趸船，趸船上可搭建必要架构，费用预计不会超出 100 海关两。

若可为瑷珲关配备摩托艇和四桨小船，一方面可确保港口船运工作得到充分管理，毕竟目前管理效果不尽如人意；另一方面可允许海关适当调配搜查人员，有效展开日夜搜查，以使大黑河港口与中国其他港口（包括哈尔滨关）齐头并进。

8. 但同时，本署认为管理工作不应仅限于港口，还应逐渐拓展至中国境内的所有水道。瑷珲关所拟的《新章程》（参阅瑷珲关第 37 号呈）对管辖边境贸易和沿途登船检查事项做出了相应的规定；此外,鉴于瑷珲关已开始向黑龙江航道上的货物运输进行征税(参阅瑷珲关第38号呈),因此关员则须抽查船只的舱口单以及于海关分关以外的航行情况。海关关员巡缉航道各处或搜捕走私者时,往往需要远程巡航,故需要一艘航速较快的浅吃水船,巡航半径可达250到300英里,舱内宿舍可供船员及2名或3名洋籍人员居住。

9. 关于此船,兹提议两种方案：

(1)专门建造汽艇,适宜燃烧木桦；但因木桦需要空间,巡航半径受到限制；

(2)水上滑翔机,D.R. 商务型；B.D.S. 发动机；该款水上滑翔机近期已于长江及钱塘江试航,若与描述相符,应非常适合于黑龙江上航行,原因如下：

① 非常经济；

② 航速可达每小时30到40英里,远程巡航(如从漠河至拉哈苏苏约1650俄里)所耗时间合理,亦可突袭走私；

③ 浅吃水,适合随时随地航行。

基于最后两项特性,该滑翔机亦适于对抗土匪(红胡子)和走私者。

虽然目前并不急需此船,但若欲严管航道沿线贸易,不久亦需将其购入,而且,若中国开始承担其分内的航路标志工作,此船将会极有助益。因此本署希望,巡工司可查究水上滑翔机能否用于黑龙江航道之上。兹列举航运季期间各燃料价格,以供参考：

煤(抚顺),每吨约34银圆；

煤(其他品级),每吨约27到31银圆；

木桦,每立方俄丈12到13银圆；

轻汽油,每10加仑22银圆；

煤油,11银圆

(大批购买可能减价约10%)

职员方面,有关水上滑翔机及摩托艇的维修等事,需要一名俄国匠董,薪俸为每月25到30海关两,并为其于哈尔滨寻一名副机匠(华籍)；关于汽艇的维修等事,需要一名机师和一名火夫。

此抄件发送至巡工司。

您忠诚的仆人

包安济(G. Boezi)

瑷珲关署理税务司

关于瑷珲关致海关总税务司署第 41 号呈的意见

兹认为,关于瑷珲关提出购入四桨船及 25 英尺摩托艇的申请,可予以批准；四桨船可于当地建造,按照口岸具体情况设计,于港口内使用。25 英尺摩托艇可用于港口外的防护及征税工作,若摩托艇状况良好,建造精良,那么 4000 银圆的价格实属合理。

上海方面的相应价格如下：

25 英尺长摩托艇,柚木船体：价格为上海 1600 海关两。

凯尔文（Kelvin）发动机,12 马力,可供上述船体使用；价格为 260 英镑。

配备 12 马力发动机的摩托艇,航速约每小时 8 英里。

凯尔文发动机,26 马力,可供上述船体使用；价格为 490 英镑。

配备 26 马力发动机的摩托艇,航速约 8.5 节。

水上滑翔机,意大利式,40 英尺长；价格约为上海 12000 海关两。

航速每小时 50 英里；时耗 20 加仑汽油,于瑷珲关购买 20 加仑汽油的费用为 44 银圆。

水上滑翔机,法式,35 英尺长：价格约为上海 12000 海关两。

航速每小时 27 英里；时耗 10 加仑汽油,于瑷珲关购买 10 加仑汽油的费用为 22 银圆。

（签字）额得志（T. J. Eldridge）

巡工司

1922 年 5 月 3 日,江海关巡工事务局

此抄件内容真实有效,特此证明

录事：劳德迩（H. G. Lowder）监事员

致瑷珲关第 45/89487 号令　　　　海关总税务司署（北京）1922 年 5 月 22 日

尊敬的瑷珲关税务司：

第 41 号呈收悉：

"请示：购买一艘四桨船，用于大黑河港口靠拢船只及日常工作；雇用四名船员，每月薪俸 11 海关两；装备一艘摩托艇或汽艇；并说明大黑河有一艘造好的摩托艇正在出售，售价 4000 银圆，仅在 1921 年 6 月至 10 月期间使用过，几乎全新，它十分符合本关要求，只要批准购买，即可交付使用。"

奉总税务司命令，现批复如下：批准为大黑河港口装备一艘四桨船。该四桨船可按照当地设计图在当地打造，成本不得超过 400 银圆，从贵署账户 A：5/1 支出。

批准雇用四名水手，每月薪俸 11 海关两。这些水手均应参加体检，提交适当的担保证明。

关于用于日常管理工作的摩托艇，总税务司认为装备这样一艘摩托艇的要求合理；但是，批准相应经费之前，总税务司需要了解以下情况：

1. 贵署提到可在当地购买的摩托艇，如何保证其保养得当，运转良好。

2. 现在的船主是谁？

3. 贵署是否能得到船主的可靠保证，确保船只长时间正常运作。

依据我们之前的经验，迄今为止，二手摩托艇经常出各种事故，结果令人不快；批准购买之前，总税务司必须事先确认，将要接手的这艘船会不会很快就失去使用价值，或面临改造。

您忠诚的仆人

包罗（C. A. V. Bowra）

总务科税务司

6. 为往来于黑龙江航道的俄国船只之管理办法事

58.

Aigun / Taheiho 23rd June, 1922.

Sir,

　　I have the honour to acknowledge the receipt of your telegram of 20th instant :

> "What flag do russian vessels plying on
> Amur and reporting at Aigun fly ? Far
> Eastern Republic flag or old Russian
> national flag ? If they fly Far Eastern
> Republic flag, what Customs treatment has
> been applied by you or do you propose
> to apply pending official recognition of
> Far Eastern Republic by China ?"

to confirm my telegram of 21st instant :

> "your telegram of yesterday Since 1920
> Russian vessels plying on the Amur have
> been flying red flag, later Far Eastern
> Republic flag and have been allowed to
> report at Aigun without hindrance as
> before. I would propose to make no change
> in existing arrangements except to
> demand deposit of Ship Papers and pay-
> ment of fees like non-Treaty Power
> vessels

Inspector General of Customs,

　　P E K I N G.

vessels. Despatch follows"

and, in addition, to explain that the reason why
no objection was ever made to the use of a non-
recognised flag is, that the waters of the Amur have
in the past, and until Russia's collapse, been claimed
by that Power as being under her exclusive jurisdiction
The change from this arbitrary regime to one of
international equity, and of recognition of China's
Treaty rights, has been gradual, every step being gained
by China by the favour of circumstances, not by
virtue of any formal arrangement : chinese steamers
entered - and traded on - the Amur, the Customs took
over control of the Aigun and Taheihe Harbours, local
agreements have been made regarding the navigation
of the River and the Aids to Navigation. But the
process is still in the making, and there has been
no sharp change; thus it has happened that the
revolutionary flag and the flag of the Far Eastern
Republic have been hoisted on Russian steamers, before
China's position was definite enough to warrant a
formal protest by the Customs. It has also happened
that russian vessels have continued to trade at all

places

places on the Chinese side of the Amur other than
Aigun and Taheiho, without control , without a counterpart for Chinese steamers on the Russian side. There
are still Russian steamers plying between Taheiho and
Ch'ikot'e, between Taheiho and Humaho or Moho exclusively.

2.   As to the question of the Russian Flag, I
am of opinion that things should be allowed to go on
as before, until recognition of the F. E. R. by China.
Circumstances have sanctioned in fact the right of
the Far Eastern Republic flag to enter Chinese Ports
on the Amur; if now we raise a question on this
point, there will be great difficulties with the Russians
and it is not sure that, in return for other concessions, they may not grant Japan or other Powers
right of navigation on the Amur, thus putting China
in a very awkward position. While I hear that China
is anxious to reserve right of Navigation on the
Amur to herself and Russia only; but this she can
do by a tactful de facto recognition of the Russian
Authorities, implying the validity of the former
Treaties on this point ; the Treaties have been

denounced,

denounced, but the Russians still act more or less
in accordance with their spirit, especially on this
point. - This feeling should not be hurt by unnecessary unfriendly measures, such as would appear a protest against the use of the F.E.R. flag, which has
been admitted for a long time.

3.   However, the Customs may slowly bring things
in line with general practice and Regulations; there
is no reason why Russian Steamers should not deposit
their Papers with us, while so far Ship's Papers
have been inspected on board by the Boarding Officer,
very summarily at that. It has happened, although very
seldom, that steamers, generally out of ignorance of
our rules, have left for Blagovestchensk without regular Clearance. They have been caught on their return,
however, and it may be said that, if the Russian
Authorities connive, a steamer may leave without her
Papers, and have new ones made out ; but in most
cases our control will be strengthened by having the
Papers in our hands. - As to the usual fee (Circ.
No. 456) I would propose to fix it at a moderate
sum, say Hk. Tls. 2.00 - in the same way and for the

                                                        same

same reasons that Special Permit Fees have been made specially low in the Harbin District. - I must add that the Russians do not demand deposit of Ship's Papers, but they have more forcible means at their disposal : they would open fire on any vessels leaving without permission. - As to the deposit of Ship's Papers on the Sungari, I would ask the advice of the Harbin Commissioner; nor would I advocate the depositing of Ship's Papers by Chinese Steamers, on which we have sufficient hold already.

4.   With regard to the freedom accorded Russian vessels of calling and trading at intermediate places on the Chinese shore between Taheiho and Lahasusu, I would propose to approach the Russian Navigation Office, and ask, in return for this facility, the same treatment to Chinese Steamers on the Russian shore. So far, Chinese Steamers have only dared call at Blagovestchensk and, very seldom, Ekaterino-Nikolsk, as far as I know; but they would welcome a chance of trading at other Russian points, if duly assured against confiscation, requisition and other dangers. - Should the Russians refuse, we may force their Steamers either

to

to take out Inland Waters Certificates, as enforced
on the Sungari, or to run under certain special Regulations to be framed later on, or, as a last step,
to call only at Lahasusu, Aigun and Tsaike, with right
to stop at other places only for taking firewood -
without landing or taking on board passengers or
cargo. -

This question, however, is not exclusively
within Customs jurisdiction, and is rather delicate,
bearing on the general policy of China towards the
Far Eastern Republic; I will only therefore offer
my suggestions, and take no action, nor change anything
to existing practice, without your specifical instructions.

Copy of this despatch is being forwarded to
the Harbin Commissioner.

I have the honour to be,

Sir,

Your obedient Servant,

Acting Commissioner.

呈海关总税务司署 <u>58</u> 号文　　　　　　瑷珲关 / 大黑河 1922 年 6 月 23 日

尊敬的海关总税务司（北京）:

1. 根据海关总税务司署 6 月 20 日电报:

"目前往来黑龙江航道且于瑷珲关报关的俄国船只悬挂何种旗帜？远东共和国旗帜还是俄国旧国旗？对于悬挂远东共和国旗帜之船只，瑷珲关目前如何处置？在中国政府官方承认远东共和国之前，对于此等船只，瑷珲关有何处置建议？"

及瑷珲关 6 月 21 日电报:

"回复海关总税务司署 6 月 20 日电令: 1920 年以来往来黑龙江航道的俄国船只一直悬挂红旗，而后悬挂远东共和国旗帜；对于此等船只，瑷珲关如之前一样允许其报关，不予阻碍。兹提议延续此惯例，但要求此类船只与非合约国船只一样抵押牌照并缴纳费用。随后将呈文详细说明。"

特此说明，对于悬挂非认可旗帜之船只，瑷珲关一直未予阻碍之原因在于，俄国分裂前一直宣称黑龙江所有航道均受其专属管辖。但随后此专制政权逐渐演变成一个国际公正之政权，一个认可中国合约权利之政权；而中国的每一步收益均得益于此形势之变化，而非任何正式协议之签署。目前，中国轮船已进入黑龙江航道航行，并可于黑龙江上进行贸易；海关亦接管了瑷珲口岸和大黑河口岸，并签订了与黑龙江航道航运及航路标志相关的地方协议。然而，一切仍在进行之中，并未有任何骤然之变动；因此在中国政府立场足够明确，愿意为海关提出正式抗议保驾护航之前，海关将无法对俄国轮船悬挂革命旗帜和远东共和国旗帜一事提出反对。此外，除了瑷珲口岸及大黑河口岸，俄国船只依然行至黑龙江航道华岸各地进行贸易，不受管制，但中国轮船却不允许在黑龙江航道俄岸如此行事。另有一些俄国轮船往来于大黑河与奇克特之间，以及大黑河与呼玛河或漠河之间。

2. 关于俄国旗帜问题，兹认为，在中国政府承认远东共和国之前，可允许如此前一样行事。事实上，实际情况已经默认悬挂远东共和国旗帜之船只有权进入黑龙江航道上的中国口岸；若现在对此提出疑问，实难应对俄方，且亦不确定俄方为求华方做出其他让步，是否会不再允许日本或其他国家在黑龙江上航行，致使中国陷入窘境。据悉，中国政府只希望保留中俄两国在黑龙江上航行之权利；实际上，只要中国政府可以婉转地承认俄国政府，暗示与此相关的先前条约有效，便可达此目的；虽然条约已被废止，但俄方或多或少依然遵循条约精神，尤其在此事方面。兹认为，不应采取不必要的强制措施，破坏两国关系，比如对一直允许使用的远东共和国旗帜提出反对之举。

3. 但海关可以逐渐依照惯例和章程办事；虽然迄今为止皆由轮船检查员登船检查牌照，但俄国轮船亦无理由不向中国海关抵押牌照。此外，亦有少数轮船因不知海关规定而未至海关结关便前往布拉戈维申斯克（Blagovestchensk），但会在返程时被发现。可以说如果俄国政府默许，那么轮船离港时可不带牌照，而后再行开具新的牌照；但多数情况下，海关若能手握牌照，必有助于加强管理。至于手续费（海关总税务司署第456号通令），兹建议，不宜过多，比如2.00海关两——哈尔滨关地区规定的特别执照费极低，此建议之原因与之相同。必须补充的是，俄方虽不要求抵押牌照，但其处理方式更加暴力：向所有未经许可便离港的船只开火。关于松花江抵押牌照一事，本署会向哈尔滨关税务司征询意见；但鉴于海关已充分控制中国轮船，因此不提倡要求其抵押牌照。

4. 关于俄国船只要求在大黑河和拉哈苏苏之间的华岸各地自由停靠或进行贸易一事，本署提议与俄阿穆尔水道局交涉，要求作为回报，中国轮船应在俄岸享有同等待遇。据本署所知，中国轮船迄今只敢在布拉戈维申斯克停靠，另有极少数情况下会在叶卡捷琳堡－尼科利斯克停靠；但是若能得到正式保证，不会有没收、征收以及其他危险，中国轮船希望有机会在俄国其他地点进行贸易。若俄方拒绝，则可对俄国轮船提出强制性要求，或办理松花江上施行的内港专照，或之后制定特殊章程要求其照章航行，或作为最后一步，仅允许其在拉哈苏苏分关、瑷珲口岸和大黑河口岸停靠，在华岸其他各地则只有停靠拿取木样之权利——不得装卸乘客或货物。

但此问题并非海关专属管辖之事，甚是微妙，关系到中国对远东共和国的总方针；因此本署谨提供建议，在未得贵署特别指示之前，不会采取任何行动，亦不会改变现行惯例。

此抄件发送至哈尔滨关税务司。

您忠诚的仆人

包安济（G. Boezi）

瑷珲关署理税务司

7. 为往返于黑龙江且在瑷珲关报关的俄罗斯船只船舶证件抵押办法事

[—29]

66   COMMRS.   INSPECTORATE GENERAL OF CUSTOMS,

gun   No. 90,380   PEKING,   21st July,   1922.

Sir,

With reference to I.G. telegram of

20th June, 1922 :

      enquiring what flag Russian vessels plying
on the Amur and reporting at Aigun fly
and what Customs treatment has been applied
by you or you propose to apply pending
official recognition of the Far Eastern
Republic by China;

to your telegram of 20th June, 1922, in reply :

      stating that such vessels have been flying
a red flag and also the flag of the Far
Eastern Republic and that you propose
to make no change in existing arrangements
except to demand deposit of ship's papers
and payment of fees like Non-Treaty Power
vessels;

and to despatch No. 58 :

      confirming your telegram of 20th June, 1922
and amplifying your statement concerning
existing arrangements;

                            I

The Commissioner of Customs,

    A I G U N.

I am directed by the Inspector General to say
that you should be careful neither to make nor
even to suggest to any local authorities any
change in existing procedure without definite
instructions.

     I am,

        Sir,

    Your obedient Servant,

        Audit Secretary
       for Chief Secretary.

致瑗珲关第 <u>66/90380</u> 号令　　　　海关总税务司署（北京）1922 年 7 月 21 日

尊敬的瑗珲关税务司：

　　根据 1922 年 6 月 20 日海关总税务司署电令：

　　　　"询问往返于黑龙江（俄称阿穆尔河）且在瑗珲关报关的俄罗斯船只悬挂何种旗帜，针对此类船只，瑗珲关现已采取何种措施或在等待中国政府对远东共和国进行官方承认期间建议采取何种措施。"

及贵署 1922 年 6 月 20 日电复：

　　　　"上述船只同时挂红色旗帜与远东共和国旗帜，瑗珲关建议对现有做法不做更改，但希望同非合约国船只一样，要求在放行前抵押船舶证件并缴纳相应费用。"

及第 58 号呈：

　　"重申 1922 年 6 月 20 日电呈内容，详细阐述现有做法。"

奉总税务司命令，现批复如下：兹通知，在未接到确切指示前，万勿改变或建议当地政府改变现有办法。

　　　　　　　　　　　　　　　　　　您忠诚的仆人

　　　　　　　　　　　　　　　　　　贝乐业（J. H. Berruyer）

　　　　　　　　　　　　　　会计科税务司受总务科税务司委托签发

8. 为在哈尔滨关结关驶向大黑河之轮船在松花江口将其所拖驳船转移给另一艘轮船之情况处理办法事

SE----- No. **33**

No. 27.   Service.

Aigun.   No. 811.

CUSTOM HOUSE,

Harbin___ , 15th November, 1922.

Sir,

    I have to acknowledge receipt of your Despatch No. 22 of the 2nd instant:

        Steamers cleared for Taheiho at Harbin, transferring their barges to another steamer at the mouth of the Sungari:

        information in re, soliciting;

and, in reply, to state that this practice is of old standing. Cargoes are, in such instances, passed and manifested for the barges concerned and not for the towing steamer. It has been generally recognised in this district that such barges are at liberty to change their towing steamer any where, merely informing the first Custom House en route in writing of the fact.

    The Amur Steamship and Trading Company invariably informed the Lahasusu Customs when such change of towing steamer had taken place or was about to take place, only in the latter case they were not always able to name the steamer which was going to take over the tow, hence the usual information as to transfer could not in such cases be entered on the manifest and thus conveyed to Taheiho Customs.

    The Amur Steamship and Trading Company have
                    been

To

    The Commissioner of Customs,

      AIGUN.

been working their tugs in this manner for
many years, a fact which old manifests on file
at Taheiho will probably bear forth.   I
therefore suggest that no breach of local Customs
Regulations has taken place in the instances
mentioned in your despatch under reply and that,
from a Revenue point of view, this transhipping,
as practiced, is in no way undesirable.

                    I am,

                         Sir,

          Your obedient Servant,

                                        Commissioner.

致瑷珲关第 27/811 号函　　　　　　　　哈尔滨关 1922 年 11 月 15 日

尊敬的瑷珲关税务司：

　　根据 11 月 2 日瑷珲关致哈尔滨关第 22 号函：

　　　"关于在哈尔滨关结关驶向大黑河之轮船在松花江口将其所拖驳船转移给另一
　　艘轮船一事，请提供相关信息。"

　　兹说明，此乃旧办法。在此种情况下，凡放行货物，均由驳船装载，而非牵引轮船。在
哈尔滨关区，驳船可在任何地方更换牵引轮船，只需要向沿途第一处海关办公楼提交书面
通知即可。

　　黑龙江轮船贸易公司在更换或计划更换牵引轮船时总是通知拉哈苏苏关。最近才发
生未能告知接替之牵引轮船船名之事，故而，在此情况下，无法将有关转移驳船之信息载
入舱单并传达给大黑河海关。黑龙江轮船贸易公司已经以此种方式经营牵引船多年，故
此，在大黑河存档的旧舱单或将更为实用。兹说明，贵署函文提及之情况并未违反当地
《海关章程》，此外，按照惯例，更换牵引船之办法可取。

　　　　　　　　　　　　　　　　　　　您忠诚的仆人

　　　　　　　　　　　　　　　　（签字）覃书（R. C. L. d' Anjou）

　　　　　　　　　　　　　　　　　　哈尔滨关税务司

9. 为提议拉哈苏苏分关、瑷珲口岸及大黑河口岸之间每周 交换一次口岸间往来的轮船清单事

SERVICE No. 35

No. 29, Service.

Aigun. No. 816.

CUSTOM HOUSE,

Harbin, 7th December, 1922.

Sir,

I have to acknowledge receipt of your

Despatch No. 24 of the 30th November:

Steamers Cleared for Taheiho at Harbin,
Transferring their Barges to Another
Steamer at the Mouth of the Sungari:
interchange between Lahasusu, Aigun and
Taheiho of weekly lists of steamers cleared
from one port for the other, in order to
control movement of steamers and barges,
suggesting:

and, in reply, to say that I am instructing the
Lahasusu Office to endeavour, as far as possible,
to enter a note of change of tow on the
Manifests of barges whenever such change takes
place at Lahasusu or is about to take place on
entering the Amur. I have, however, to repeat
that in the latter case the name of the steamer

which

To

The Commissioner of Customs,

AIGUN / TAHEIHO.

which is going to take over the tow is not
always ascertainable.   I am further instructing the
Lahasusu Office to supply your Office, commencing
with the 1923 Navigation Season, with a weekly
List of sailings from that port to Taheiho and/or
Aigun, such lists to distinguish between cargo
steamers, tugs and barges and to mention whether
the vessels carry cargo or not.

I am,

Sir,

Your obedient Servant,

Commissioner.

致瑷珲关第 <u>29/816</u> 号函   哈尔滨关 1922 年 12 月 7 日

尊敬的瑷珲关（瑷珲 / 大黑河）税务司：

根据 11 月 30 日瑷珲关致哈尔滨关第 24 号函：

"关于在哈尔滨关结关驶向大黑河之轮船在松花江口将其所拖驳船转移给另一艘轮船一事，提议拉哈苏苏分关、瑷珲口岸及大黑河口岸之间每周交换一次自一口岸结关驶往另一口岸的轮船清单，以便管控轮船及驳船之航行。"

兹说明，本署将指示拉哈苏苏分关在有船只于拉哈苏苏更换或在驶入黑龙江前计划更换牵引船时，尽快将有关更换牵引船之备注填写于驳船舱单内；然而，船只在驶入黑龙江前计划更换牵引船时，或将无法确定接替之牵引轮船船名。此外，本署将命拉哈苏苏分关提供 1923 年航运季开通以来，每周自拉哈苏苏分关驶往大黑河口岸和 / 或瑷珲口岸的轮船清单（载货轮船、牵引船及驳船各一份清单，且此等清单内均将列明相关船只载货与否之细目）。

您忠诚的仆人

（签字）覃书（R. C. L. d' Anjou）

哈尔滨关税务司

10. 为汇报大黑河轮船检查及港务课设立等事

98

I. G.

Aigun / Tahaiho 26th February, 1923.

Sir,

I have the honour to acknowledge the receipt of your Despatch No. 43/89,181 (in reply to Aigun despatch No. 42) :

Inspection of steamers on opening of Navigation: further report called for.

and to reply that I have carefully gone through your instructions and into the correspondence with the Harbin Office, that I have consulted with the Commissioner of Customs, Harbin, and that I have come to the following conclusions :

1. <u>Chinese Steamers</u>. These in most cases come from Harbin, where they have been inspected at the beginning of the navigation season; but in some cases they winter here (there were 12 in Harbour during the 1921 - 1922 winter season), or come from places along the Amur where they have been obliged to winter, having been caught by ice in the autumn. I would suggest that any steamer

wintering

The Inspector General of Customs,

P E K I N G.

wintering in Taheiho, or arriving without an
Inspection Certificate of the Harbin Office, be
subject to compulsory inspection before clearance.

2. Russian Steamers generally arrive in Taheiho
with a Certificate of Inspection issued by the
Amur Navigation Office, and are well manned and
officered. Very few of them winter in Taheiho,
but there is one such case this year, namely the
S. S. "Moskwa", flying the Russian Flag, but
ordinarily plying between Chinese Ports. The
Certificate of the Amur Navigation Office should,
in my opinion, be honoured, as I have reasons
to believe that the inspection on the Russian
side is thoroughly conducted. The inspection is
carried out regularly every year, and a more
comprehensive survey every 10 years in the case
of iron boats, and every 6 years in the case of
wooden boats. However if a Russian vessel carries
Chinese passengers the Customs may verify the
actual conditions of the steamer with a view to
their safety. Cases of steamers arriving in such
condition as to constitute a danger to the

Harbour

Harbour or shipping, would, of course, have to be specially dealt with. I propose that the Amur Navigation Office be informed that, unless Russian vessels are provided with a Certificate of Inspection issued by that Office, they must either submit to inspection by the C. M. Customs, or leave for Blagoveschensk in ballast to be inspected there, the same applying to Russian steamers wintering here which, at the opening of the navigation season, should either clear for Blagoveschensk in ballast, or submit to Chinese Inspection.

3.　　The inspection of boilers and machinery in Taheiho can be entrusted to Mr. V. I. Iankin, Aigun District Local Watcher and Mechanic, who is fully qualified and conversant with the excellent Russian Regulations (which are followed also in Harbin); we have no hydraulic pressure pump for water test of the boilers, but we may borrow one from the local Flour Mills. Inspection of the Hulls can be carried out by the Senior Outdoor Officer.

　　The fee may be the same as at Harbin (Hk. Tl. 0.400 per H. P.), the Horse Power being the
recognised

recognised standard measurement of vessels on this River; but, should you decide to apply the common scale of fee according to tons, there will be no difficulties to have vessels measured for Tonnage.

Two-tenths of the fee, as suggested by the Harbin Commissioner in his despatch No. 2343, may be paid to the Officer inspecting the boilers and machinery; and I believe that another two-tenths may be issued to the Officer inspecting the hull.

4.   The Taoyin-Superintendent is ready to support the Customs in their efforts to control shipping, and in this connection I have to report that he is anxious to have a Harbour Department opened at this Port, especially now that there is a Technical Adviser on Aids to Navigation paid out of River Dues Collection. The Senior Outdoor Officer fills already in practice the duties of Harbour Master; so that there would be little difficulty in establishing a formal Harbour Office. In deference to the wish of the Taoyin, Mr. Ignatieff could be appointed Harbour Master or Acting Harbour Master, in addition to his title as Technical Adviser,

without

without extra salary; but, as he will often be
absent on inspection duty, the Senior Outdoor Officer,
who gets now in this capacity an allowance of
Hk. Tls. 25 a month, may be granted the title and
allowance of Acting either full Tidesurveyor or
Assistant Tidesurveyor (and Harbour Master); the
present incumbent is, in my opinion, fully qualified
for the post.

The Harbour Regulations (submitted in my
despatch No. 40) should however be first approved
and promulgated, and I am asking the Taoyin-
Superintendent whether he may solicit the sanction
of the Regulations by the competent Boards.

It is very likely that a formal Harbour
Office, established under the auspices of the
Taoyin-Superintendent, would give us more effective
support than heretofore from that Official and
from the local Police, and greater consideration
from Shipping Companies and Merchants.

One copy of this despatch is being forwarded
to the Harbin Commissioner, and one to the

Coast

Coast Inspector, accompanied by a copy of Aigun despatch No. 42.

I have the honour to be,

Sir,

Your obedient Servant,

Acting Commissioner.

M E M O R A N D U M .

Custom House,

Harbin, 9th March, 1923.

To

The Commissioner of Customs,

A I G U N .

Harbin Commissioner's Comments on Aigun Despatch
No. 98 to I. G.; dated 26th February, 1923.

The question of Inspection of Steamers by the
Aigun Office was made the subject of S/O correspondence
between the Aigun Acting Commissioner and myself in
April and May, 1922.   A clear expose of the
question is given in two of my S/O letters to Mr
Boezi, copies of which are appended hereto for the
information of the Inspector General.

1.- Chinese Steamers.   Until the Aigun Office has
a staff competent to undertake the inspection of
vessels, as it is done here, it would be best for
that Office to confine inspection to Chinese vessels
trading on the Amur and to those wintering at
Taheiho clearing at the opening of the navigation
season for ports other than Harbin.   For the sake
of uniformity of practice and methods of inspection
a Memorandum will be prepared by Mr Abrahamsen and
sent to Aigun for the guidance of the Inspecting
Staff.

2.- Russian Steamers.   See S/O correspondence and
Harbour Master's remarks appended hereto.

3.   The inspection of boilers and machinery by
others than certificated Surveyors, Engineers, etc.,
should be avoided as much as possible to escape
criticism.   The fees for inspection of boilers
and machinery should be on the same scale as that

in

in force at Harbin, for the sake of uniformity.
At Harbin the Inspecting Staff receives no part of
the fees.   The measurement of vessels for tonnage
is not such an easy matter that it can be accurately
carried out by a layman.

4.   The appointment of the Technical Adviser on
Aids to Navigation as Harbour Master for the port
of Taheiho is not desirable.   I have exposed my
view on this subject in my Despatch No.2333.
Should it be necessary to establish a Harbour
Department at Taheiho, the present Senior Out-door
Officer, Mr Baukham, could very well fill the position
in addition to his present duties.

Commissioner.

APPENDIX.

APPENDIX No. 1.

Extract from the S/O to Mr Boezi, dated 24th April, 1922.

Dear Boezi,

. . . .

Inspection of boilers and Hulls.   Your proposal to inspect boilers of Chinese steam vessels has disturbed me so much that I did not hesitate to wire you asking for the postponement of these inspections until I had communicated with you.   We have worked so hard (against so many difficulties) these last three years to introduce a system of control over Chinese (and Russian) steam vessels that I fear any steps taken at your end without first coming to a perfect arrangement and understanding with this Office might destroy all the good work accomplished in the past. Frankly speaking I can not see any necessity for your office to inspect any vessels but those trading solely on the Amur.   All Chinese vessels now navigating the Sungari and Amur are owned by companies installed at Harbin - the centre of Chinese shipping - who may have agencies at Taheiho.   All these vessels are registered here, their owners have been educated to our requirements; it would be ill-advised to have the inspections of these steamers for safety to passengers performed anywhere else than at Harbin. Furthermore we have a trained staff to perform inspections and a very competent Mariner in our Harbour Master.   To start inspection of boilers and hulls at your end with a totally incompetent staff or with outsiders such as Mr Sperk who is an excellent man at his own job but unqualified for inspection of hulls

and

and ships' boilers would never do. I therefore propose that your Office does not undertake the inspection of vessels registered at Harbin for Sungari and Amur trade but that it limits itself to inspection of vessels navigating solely on the Amur. For the guidance of the Officer who will have charge of these inspections at your end Abrahamsen will prepare a Memorandum showing procedure adopted at Harbin which should be closely followed for the sake of uniformity at the two North Manchurian river port. I am not writing this in a spirit of criticism but on account of my experience at this port during the last three years and fear of a lack of uniformity in our methods of inspection which would bring outside criticism.

....

Yours sincerely.

(signed)   René   d'Anjou.

True   copy:

3rd   Assistant, A.

APPENDIX No. 2.

Copy of the S/O letter to Mr Boezi, dated 26th May, 1922.

Dear Boezi,

Your letter of 12th May; Inspection of Chinese and Russian vessels. I understand your point of view very well; but in the absence at your port of a competent Harbour Master and without first being acquainted with our modus faciendi I thought it advisable to ask you to postpone action at your port until you had heard my reasons. I will now explain our procedure vis-a-vis Chinese and Russian vessels. Chinese vessels. These vessels trade on the Sungari in accordance with the Sungari Provisional Regulations. Notwithstanding the fact that the Sungari is not considered as Inland Waters, these vessels take out I.W.S.N. Certificates renewable annually and follow the I.W.S.N. Regulations so far as the inspection of boilers, engines, hulls are concerned. We also inspect them for life-saving appliances, lights, internal structures, anchor and chains, etc., etc., The Inland Waters Steam Navigation Certificates only hold good on the Sungari. Properly these certificates should be surrendered at Lahasusu before clearance for Amur ports, but in practice these certificates are retained together with the ship's national papers issued by the Chiao Tung Pu which serve as Ship's papers when calling at Russian ports. Our inspection of life-saving apparatus, lights, interal structures, anchor, chain shackles, etc., is carried out by the Harbour Master in a very thorough manner, and in the last

two

two years things have improved to a great extent. We follow to a certain extent and especially as regards fire appliances and life-saving apparatus the Russian official navigation rules, a translation of which was made by this office last winter.

Until the enactment by China of Marine laws and under the veil of attending to the safety of passengers and to prevent obstruction of channels by vessels in charge of incompetent Masters, we exact by gentle pressure on the shipping companies that their Masters present themselves before the Harbour Master and be subjected to an informal examination as to their competency in navigation and in handling of ships. When found sufficiently competent to take charge of a vessel the Harbour Master stamps and signs any employment papers that may be presented. This is a tacit understanding with the Shipping Companies that the concerned is competent to handle a ship and may be employed. This is the thin edge of the wedge it is true but something had to be done to prevent the indiscriminating appointment of so-called Masters on Chinese ships with the attendant dangers to passengers, etc. A tremendous amount of discretion must be observed as you will readily understand, as we are skating on very thin ice. I have thought out another plan to arrive at the same result, which bids fair to come into operation next season, and that is to interest the Insurance Companies and obtain from them that they will not insure any cargo on any ship which has no Master approved of by a board of Examiners on which the Harbour Master will sit. I have all the foreign Insurance

Insurance Companies interested in this scheme, but
more anon.

Russian Steamers.   These vessels trade on the Sungari
in accordance with the Sungari Provisional Regulations.
In the past no inspection of vessels for safety of
passengers took place nor would the Russians have
permitted such inspection until quite lately. Generally
speaking Russian ships are kept in good repair, are
ably manned and follow the old Russian Navigation
Rules, which are very thorough.   As it was manifestly
unfair to make Chinese vessels take out I.W.S.N. papers
and pay fees for inspection of boilers, engines and
hulls we began this season to exact gentle pressure
on the Russian companies so that they should comply
with the same regulations as Chinese vessels.   These
vessels are now coming more and more under our control
and by interesting the Insurance companies as explained
above we hope to get all vessels under complete
control in good time.   In dealing with the inspection
of Russian vessels we have to use a great deal of
tact and discretion to make them respond to our
requirements.   They are very submissive because we are
considerate with them and assist them frequently in
their troubles with Chinese.

     At Taheiho you are in a somewhat different
position. You are on the Amur, a jointly-owned river
and Russian vessels only come within your cognizance
when entering at your port. If you take measures
that will irritate the Russians they will in their
return retaliate on Chinese vessels calling at Russian
ports and there will be a fine mess.   You have
                                   therefore

therefore to proceed carefully, remembering also that as a general rule Russian vessels are better manned and regulated by an old established code of laws. The question of river dues apart, you are interested in the safety of Chinese passengers only who may travel on Russian vessels, and that to a limited extent only. If Russian vessels calling at your port take no Chinese passengers you are not in the least concerned in the state of their boilers, machinery, hulls, or fire and life-saving apparatus. At the most you might interfere in case the vessel was unsafe or a danger to the Harbour (Chinese side). I would therefore strongly advise you not to tackle Russian vessels for the present but confine yourself to Chinese vessels, clearing from your port at the beginning of the season and to those entering without certificates of inspection from this office.

I hope this letter will clear the air and give you an idea of the situation.

Yours sincerely,

(signed) René d'Anjou,

True copy:

3rd Assistant, A.

Harbour Master's Office,   ^{To}   the Commissioner of Customs,

Harbin , 7th March , 1923.   H A R B I N .

Re - Inspection of Steamers and establishment of Harbour
Office at Taheiho .

     I have perused the Aigun/Taheiho despatch of Feb.
26th, 1923 and at your request for comments on same, the
following is submitted, numbered in rotation as per
despatch in question.

1.   Inspection is a necessity, and should be
compulsary, but if the vessel on her first trip is
bound for Harbin and has been inspected the previous
year the Senior Out-door officer could make a
throrough inspection of lights, fire appliances, life
belts etc., also, as far as conditions permit, have a
general look over the hull - the actual inspection
could then be deferred until the arrival of the
vessel at Harbin .

     It must be understood that our inspection is
based on safety to passengers principally, and the
above named factors really in this respect are the
most important, the state of the hull, unless
glaringly deteriorated is of less consequence on a
river where the vessel only navigates a few yards
from the river bank.

     If the boilers have been inspected the previous
year they should hardly become unsafe for another
trip to Harbin - on the other hand if the vessel

                    is

is bound elsewhere but Harbin, the usual
inspection should take place .

2.　　　　If the present authorities on the Amur
inspect vessels in the same manner as the
former government did then same can be considered
very satisfactory - and as there is no question
of extraterritorial privileges involved in regard
to Russian ships, there can be no exception
taken to verifying of document or even dispute
the Russian inspection while the vessel remains
in Chinese waters - discretion however should be
used to avoid the Russians retaliating on Chinese
ships berthing on the Russian side of the
River - reciprocating acknowledgment of inspection
would be best as a few differences of marine
technicalities would hardly effect the safety of
passengers .

　　　　　I concur that Russian vessels winter berthing
on the Chinese side should have the option of
going to Blagovestchensk in ballast for inspection
The berthing of 12 Chinese vessels at Taheiho,
winter 1921 - 1922 may be considered an exception.

3.　　　　There may not be the slightest doubt that
Mr. District Local Watcher Lankin is quite
capable of inspecting ships boilers and engines,
but, has he got a certificate to back such
authority in case of dispute ? If he has not,
then the protesting party will immediately raise
the question and the Customs would get no support
perhaps Mr. Lankin if he has no certificate

　　　　　　　　　　　　　　　　　　could

could easily obtain one at Blagovestchensk, this would at once alter his status.

Hydraulic pressure is extensively used for testing boilers, technical opinion however differ on this subject, some claim that hydraulic test is not conclusive, it is suggested as far as Harbin is concerned to obtain the Coast Inspector's decision on the matter.

It would be very practical if the same fees for inspection which are in force here and based on horse power could also obtain in Taheiho.

As to percentage of fees payable to the inspecting Officers, I understand that the Inspector General has since authorised another ruling.

4.   There seems to be a distinct misconception of the status of a Harbour Department compared with that of Aids to Navigation. They are two different institutions - i.e. the Harbour Office of a port controls Shipping and Navigation within the port limits, inspection of steamers, launches etc., - although Aids to Navigation co-operate with the Harbour Authorities their principle duties are to survey and mark the channels of the river beyond the Harbour limits.

I certainly agree that Mr. Baulham the present Senior Out-door Officer is capable of taking care of the duties of a Harbour Office at Taheiho and I fail to see why an employee

of

of Aids to Navigation as technical adviser to
same, should hold the concurrent appointment of
Harbour Master, even though he gets no renumeration
for such office, as while there are instances
where a Tidesurveyor & Harbour Master controls
Aids to Navigation beyond the Harbour limits I
do not know of one instance where a River
Inspector or Technical adviser holds the concurrent
rank of Harbour Master, special circumstances may
however justify an exception - even at the present
unsettled stage of authority on the Amur, and
should an Office be considered necessary it should
have the status of a River Inspector Office
rather than that of a Harbour Office as in some
of the ports on the Yangtze.

If however, last years agreement with the
Bolsheviks re - Aids to Navigation on the Amur
should be extended for another year, the establishment of any office except that of the Technical
Adviser would in my opinion be premature, even
for the time being superfluous.

It appears to me that if the status of
(even acting) Tidesurveyor & Harbour Master was given
to the Senior Out-door Officer at Taheiho it
would bring forth the solicited support both from
the Tao-yin Superintendent and the local Police -
greater considerations from shipping companies and
merchants would be a natural consequence.

(signed) H. Abrahamsen,

Harbour Master.

True Copy:

3rd Assistant A.

COAST INSPECTOR'S COMMENTS ON AIGUN/TAHEIHO No.98,

I. G., OF 26TH FEBRUARY, 1923.

In the circumstances the proposals made
would seem to be good provisionally. Mr. Boezi
knows the men to whom he refers and the local
conditions at Aigun and on the Amur, whereas
I only know the local conditions at Aigun, on
the Amur, Harbin, and on the Sungari.

                         (Signed) T. J. Eldridge,

                              Coast Inspector.

Coast Inspector's Office,

Shanghai, 8th March, 1923.

True Copy:

O.D. Sanders.

          Supervisor.

108

I. G.

Aigun/Taheiho   28th April, 1923.

Sir,

I have the honour to acknowledge the receipt of your Despatch No. 113/95,787 :

Inspection of Steamers and establishment of Harbour Office at Taheiho;

and, in reply, to state as follows:

Inspection of Steamers : The standard required in Russia for an Inspector of Boilers is a diploma of Mechanical Engineer, obtained from a Polytechnical School of the highest grade of the same standing as a University. A fully qualified Mechanical Engineer is now in charge of inspection of boilers in Blagovestchensk. Such qualification Mr. Lankin is far from possessing; nor could he get a diploma in Blagovestchensk - even if he had the knowledge, there is nothing approaching a Polytechnical Institute there. Mr. Lankin has completed a course in the Blagovest - chensk Industrial School, and holds a diploma as Assistant Fitter-Mechanic; in addition to this he

The Inspector General of Customs,
 PEKING.

followed

followed the course and passed the final examinations in the River School of the Ministry of Communications, which School forms mechanics and Captains for the Amur River exclusively. Mr. Lankin also acquired practical notions of Navigation by plying on the Amur, but, not having completed 18 months' practical apprenticeship afloat as prescribed by law, he does not hold a diploma. - Copy and Translation of the Papers concerning Mr. Lankin are enclosed.

If the Russian standard has to be adopted on the Chinese side, then Mr. Lankin, although quite capable of performing the inspection, and authorised to sign an Inspection Certificate for Machinery, could not sign one of inspection of Boilers nor could Mr. Ignatieff, who could very well inspect a steamer as far as machines, body, fittings, etc. go, because he does not possess the diploma as Mechanical Engineer.

In this case, we may fall back upon Mr. Sperk, originally recommended in Aigun Despatch No. 42, who possesses all the qualifications, and has been Chief Inspector of Factories for the whole

whole Amur Province for several years. Should
later, perchance, Mr. Sperk leave this Port, we
would have no difficulties in securing the
services of the Russian Inspector in Blagovestchensk. The services of an outside Inspector
spuld be remunerated, and I propose that the
remuneration be fixed at Roubles 15 to 25
according to conditions on the Russian side;
this sum, according to Mr. Ignatieff, was paid
to Railway Engineers when called to inspect
Steamers' Boilers in Habarovsk.

However, it is questionable, in my
opinion, whether the same rigid standard prevail-
ing abroad should be adhered in China, where
totally different conditions prevail, and Technical
Services generally are still in the embryo. P precedents of Exceptions to the rule of strict
qualification may be found in the Notarial and
Quasi-Consular functions of Commissioners, in the
functions of Harbour Master exercised in most
Ports by men without any proper Diploma or
Captain's Certificate, etc.; and I would like to
ascertain whether the Launch Inspector in Harbin

is

is a proper Mechanical Engineer, with diploma
from a Polytechnical High School.

It is to be pointed out, in this
connection, that the inspection here will
almost surely be confined to Chinese steamers
plying on the Amur, and to Russian steamers
plying on the Chinese side exclusively (a very
rare case) because the other Russian steamers
would certainly choose to clear in ballast for
Blagovestchensk at the opening of the River,
there to be inspected; and it is unlikely for
any Russian steamer to arrive from the Russian
side without a Certificate up to date.

As to your instructions to leave Chinese
steamers clearing from Aigun/Tahsiho at the opening of the River, for Sungari Ports, to be
inspected at Harbin, it is my opinion that an
informal, summary inspection should be held here,
before clearance, and the Steamer be given a
provisional Certificate (or Permit) valid only
for a trip to Harbin. This is in accordance
with Russian practice, for steamers clearing at
a Port to which no Inspector of Boilers is

attached.

attached, and makes things look more regular.

Furthermore if the Harbour Master at Aigun

(Taheiho) is in doubt as to safe conditions

of the vessel, or in case important repairs to

boilers have been effected during the winter in

Taheiho, or again if a steamer reaches Taheiho

having suffered damages, especially in the Boilers

a complete Inspection should be carried out here,

in order to avoid a possible disaster which

would reflect discredit on the general organisation

of Customs Inspection.

On the above points I have the honour

to solicit your instructions.

Harbour Regulations:

I regret that I unwillingly disregarded

the instructions of Circular No. 2060, in the

intention of pushing the Matter through the

Superintendent.

As to Special Notifications regulating

the junks and rafts traffic, I must explain

that my mention of them in Enclosure Nr. 3 to

Aigun Despatch No. 40, referred to eventual

separate Notifications to be issued in case

Rafts

Rafts and Junks should not be included in the
Harbour Regulations. In fact the original Draft
of Harbour Regulations submitted to you in Harbin
despatch No. 2110/74,773 stated (Article 1):

> „The term "vessel" in these Regu-
> „lations refers to vessels of Foreign
> „type. Regulations concerning Native-
> „type crafts are embodied herein only
> „so far as is necessary for their
> „due control when working in con-
> „nection with Foreign type vessels.
> „They are regulated in other respects
> „by special notifications.

It seemed to me more advisable to
have Junks and Rafts included in the Harbour
Regulations, thus avoiding the need of special
Notifications.

I may add that no Notifications what-
soever in the matter of shipping and the Harbour have ever been issued to the Public here
except those concerning the Tsheiho Harbour limits,
in confirmity with the instructions of your
Despatch No. 2110/74,773 to Harbin: control on
shipping has been gradually introduced and
strengthened, de facto, on the basis of verbal

decisions

decisions only, not by force of any written rules; but this Office has always been guided by the principles underlying the proposed Harbour Regulations.

As to the Regulations, I must again state that it would be preferable that the Russian translation be made either at the Inspectorate or at Harbin; if this is not possible, I shall be obliged for a copy of the Russian version of the Harbin Harbour Regulations, to be used as a guide in making our own translation.

Copies of this despatch are being sent to the Coast Inspector and the Harbin Commissioner.

I have the honour to be,

Sir,

Your obedient Servant,

Acting Commissioner.

Aigun Despatch No. 108 to I. G.

———

<u>Enclosure.</u>

Copies and Translations of Certificates concerning

Mr. V. Z. Lankin, Aigun District Local

Watcher and Mechanic.

———

А Т Е С Т А Т Ъ

БЛАГОВѢЩЕНСКАГО РЕМЕСЛЕННАГО УЧИЛИЩА,
имени графа Муравьева-Амурскаго
ЛАНКИНУ Василію Захарьевичу
на званіе подмастерья.

На основаніи ВЫСОЧАЙШЕ утвержденнаго 15 іюня 1908г
закона, ЛАНКИНЪ Василій, какъ успѣшно окончившій
курсъ Благовѣщенскаго Ремесленнаго Училища, имени гра
фа Муравьева-Амурскаго, опредѣленіемъ Педагогическа-
го Совѣта, 18 Октября 1914 г. удостоенъ званія
"Слесарнаго" подмастерья.

Выданъ 22 Ноября 1914 г. № 482.

Предсѣдатель Совѣта/подписалъ/ Орловъ.
Члены/подписали/Свящ. А.Покровскій.

Руководитель работъ А.Полячекъ.
К.Шемуновскій.
В.К. Ине.

Секретарь Совѣта В.К. Ине.

№ 187

СВИДѢТЕЛЬСТВО.

Выдано сіе свидѣтельство Гражданину Василію Захаровичу
Ланкину вѣроисповѣданія ------------- родившемуся
20 Августа 1896 г. въ томъ, что онъ въ 19... году
окончилъ теоретическій курсъ ученія въ Благовѣщенскомъ
Рѣчномъ Училищѣ I разряда по механическому отдѣленію
и на выпускныхъ испытаніяхъ оказалъ слѣдующіе успѣхи:
По Закону Божію..........................

"	Русскому языку	Четыре съ полов.	4,5
"	Ариѳметикѣ	Пять	5
"	Геометріи	Пять	5
"	Физикѣ	Четыре съ половиной	4,5
"	Пароходной механикѣ	Четыре	4.
"	Электротехникѣ	Три	3.
"	Черченію	Пять	5.

Въ бытность свою ученикомъ былъ отличного поведенія
и находился въ практическомъ плаваніи по рѣкамъ
Амурскаго бассейна

          г. Благовѣщенскъ 1920 года /марта/ "20" дня Апрѣля
Предсѣдатель Экзаменаціонной комиссіи
Начальникъ училища /подписалъ/ инж. А.Николаевъ
Члены экзаменаціонной комиссіи
/подписали/   П. Козловскій
               П. Мизгиревъ
               Пь Масюковъ
               И. Смирновъ
               инж. С. Нечаевъ
               Ап. Чрепановъ
               Н. Барановъ
               Н. Яковлевъ
Секретарь Педаг. Совѣта /подписалъ/ Яковлевъ
                              Примѣчаніе:

Примѣчаніе: Настоящее свидѣтельство должно быть
обмѣнено на аттестатъ по доставленіи Начальнику
Благовѣщенскаго Рѣчного Училища удостовѣреній,
законнымъ порядкомъ засвидѣтельствованныхъ, что онъ,
Ланкинъ, прослужилъ на паровыхъ судахъ въ плаваніи
по окончаніи курса училища срокъ, дополняющій
совершенное имъ во время прохожденія курса плаваніе,
до 18 мѣсяцевъ, при чемъ удостовѣренія эти
препровождаются и особымъ прошеніемъ Начальнику
Благовѣщенского Рѣчного училища не позже 15 марта.

/подписалъ/

Начальникъ Училища TRANSLATIONS.олаевъ

Diploma of the Blagovestchensk Industrial School
"Count Muraveff-Amursky" issued to Jankin, Vasilly
Zaharovich, as Assistant Master.

In accordance with the law sanctioned by the
Sovereign on 15th July, 1908, Vassilly Lankin, having
successfully completed the course in the Blagove-
sctchensk Industrial School "Count Muraveff-Amursky",
by a decision of the Pedagogical Council of 18th
October 1914, is found worthy of the grade of
Assistant Fitter Mechanic.

Issued 22nd November, 1914. No. 483.

The President of the Council (signed) Orloff

Members of the Council (signed) Priest
                                                A. Pokrovsky
                    The Director of Works: A. Poliatchek
                                                K. Shemunovsky
                                                V.K. shné.
                    The Secretary of the Council : V. K. Shne
                    ========

No. 187

Certificate

                                                        This

This Certificate is issued to Citizen Vasilly Maharovitch Iankin, religion . . . . ., born on 20th august, 1896, to the effect that in the 19.. year he completed the highest theoretical course of instructions in the Blagovestchensk River School, Mechanical Department and that in the final examinations he obtained the following results

In the Laws of God
in the Russian language	four and a half		4,5
" " Arithmetic	five		5
" Geometry	five		5
" Physics	four and a half		4,5
" Steam-Engine Mechanics	four		4
" Electrotechnics	Three		3
" Drawing	Five		5

While a student he was of excellent conduct and did practical navigation on the rivers of the Amur Basin.

Blagovestchensk, 20th march *april* , 1920.

The President of the Examining Board
Head of the School (signed) Ing. A. Nikolaieff

Members of the Board (signed)
P. Koslovsky   Ing. S. Hetchseff
P. Misgireff   I. Baranoff
P. Maslukoff   Ap. Cherepanoff
I. Smirnoff   B. Yakovleff

The Secretary of the Ped. Council (signed) Yakovleff .

Observation: The present Certificate must be exchanged for a Diploma on presentation to the Head of the Blagovestchensk River School of evidence, attested in the legal form, to the effect that he, Iankin, served on steam vessels in navigation, after ending the course of studies, a period, which will make up 18 months together with the navigation made while following the course; and this evidence must be submitted with a separate demand to the Head of the Blagovestchensk River School not later than 15th March. / The Headmaster (signed) Ing A.Nikolaieff.

True Copies and Translations:

Acting Commissioner.

16 MAY 1923

MEMORANDUM

Custom House,   The Commissioner of Customs,

Harbin, 9th May, 1923   A I G U N.

Harbin Commissioner's comments on Aigun Despatch
No. 108 to I. G. : dated 28th April, 1923.

When commenting on Aigun Despatch No. 98 to I. G.
It was far from my mind to bring about such a
controversy on the question of inspection of boilers
etc. nor was it ever suggested, or even thought of,
to apply the Russian standard of inspection to the
Chinese side, nor to ask for the same qualifications
from the Inspecting Staff as are demanded in Russia -
which we know from experience to be often more
theoretical than practical.- nor do I doubt Mr. Lankin's
qualifications to inspect Boilers and machinery. Anyway
as such inspections will be limited to very few
instances - rare in the case of Chinese Steamers plying
exclusively on the Amur and rarer still - if ever- in
the case of Russian steamers plying exclusively on the
Chinese side of the Amur, it seems to me that undue
importance is being given by Mr. Boezi to this question.
So long as the inspection is performed by a competent
officer - whether from the Customs Staff or otherwise -
it is quite immaterial who performs it.   In any
case the same fees for inspections as have been
authorised at Harbin should be charged for the sake
of uniformity of practice.   Copy of Harbour Master's
remark accompany these comments.

Appendix.

Commissioner

Appendix .

Harbin, 7th May, 1923.

Sir,

I have as per your instructions perused the Taheiho despatch to the I.G. No. 108 relating to the status of a Launch Inspector in connection with inspections of ships as understood by the Chinese Maritime Customs, and at your request my comments are stated bilow:

The qualifications necessary to hold a position as Inspector of steamers in Russian territory has never been intended to be used, even as a comparison, for our requirements.

Naval Architects (Marine Architect) with a university education as mentioned in the Taheiho despatch are men who plan and build engines and ship, and have the authority to pass a vessel for what is generally called, a Lloyds survey and whose qualitifications are accepted by a Court of Law to settle technical questions in case of disputes etc.

A Marine Engineer (in most other languages called a Machinist) has no university education, but is a graduate from a Marine Engineering school after having served 5 years as a blacksmith and fitter etc. The grade of the Certificates varies according to the Law in various countries, but are generally issued in three grades i.e. 1st, 2nd and 3rd Class. These men run and look after the engines of ships from the ocean going liner to those of the coal Tramp. They are known to be practical and capable men while their education includes considerable technical training.

In most countries the ruling exists that a 2nd and 3rd class deep-sea certificate entitles the holder to sail as Chief Engineer on vessel in Inland water trade.

The basis for the inspection of vessels by the Customs is that they should be safe for the travelling public but in no way comes into the category of Lloyds survey etc.

In most of the small ports in China an engineer from a steamer who happens to be in port, does the inspection for which he receives

the

the full fee charged by the Customs; the Harbour Master or his Deputy whether certificated or not inspects the Hull, fittings, steering gear lights and other equipment for which he receives no remuneration.

In Shanghai Marine Engineers from the Marine Staff (Marine Engineer who has served in the Cruisers) are appointed as Inspectors and draw a monthly salary according to their ranks.

From the above it will be seen that if a man is certified by law to run an Engine he is from the Chinese Customs points of view considered qualified to do the inspection.

The point in Mr. Lankins case is - has he got the right by law to go in complete charge of the engines of a River steamer? - if he has not, how can it be expected that in case of a dispute with a certificate Engineer that his ruling will be accepted?

Mr. Lankins knowledge and qualification has not been disputed and it is therefore unnecessary to raise that question. The contention is that an Inspector should substantiate his signature with a diploma qualifying him to take charge of the Engines he inspects.

I fail to see where the Harbin Launch Inspector qualifications in any way effects Mr. Lankins status but it may serve as an elucidation to the Taheiho Office to know that Mr. Launch Inspector Stoyanoff can produce official documents to prove that he has sailed as 2nd Engineer on large ocean going steamers (about 7000 gross tons) in trade between Vladivostock and the Black sea, he has also sailed as Chief Engineer on River steamers, this backed by 13 years in charge of our workshop should be considered sufficient qualifications for the duties he performs.

The question of Mr. Lgnatieff's qualifications is superfluous as the I.G.'s ruling in a previous despatch is that he is to attend to the duties of a Technical adviser in connection with Aids to navigation only.

(signed) H. Abrahamsen.

Harbour Master.

Commissioner of Customs,

    H A R B I N.

呈海关总税务司署 <u>98</u> 号文　　　　　　　瑗珲关 / 大黑河 1923 年 2 月 26 日

尊敬的海关总税务司（北京）：

根据海关总税务司署第 43/89181 号令（回复瑗珲关第 42 号呈）：

"关于在航运开通时查验轮船一事，请做出进一步汇报。"

兹汇报，根据海关总税务司署之指示以及与哈尔滨关之通信，现将轮船查验一事做出如下总结：

1. 中国轮船：中国轮船大多由哈尔滨关出发，待航运开通时，则于哈尔滨关接受查验；但亦有部分轮船于大黑河过冬（1921 年至 1922 年冬天，12 艘轮船泊于大黑河港口），或因秋末被浮冰所困留于黑龙江沿线过冬。因此兹建议，凡于大黑河过冬或抵港时无哈尔滨关查验证明书之轮船，出港前皆须接受查验。

2. 俄国轮船：俄国轮船抵港时通常持有俄阿穆尔水道局签发的查验证明书，且状况良好。俄国轮船少有于大黑河过冬之例，但今年悬挂俄国旗帜之 "莫斯科" 号轮船确于大黑河过冬，该船经常往返于中国各贸易市场。兹认为，俄方对于离港轮船之检查很是彻底，因此对于俄阿穆尔水道局签发的查验证明书应予以承认。俄方每年皆会例行查验船只，除此之外，铁船每 10 年全面查验一次，木船每 6 年全面查验一次。但若遇俄国船只搭载中国乘客之情况，海关为乘客安全着想或可查验轮船之实际情况，而若轮船状况不良，有危及港口或航运之险，海关必会特殊处之。兹提议，应告知俄阿穆尔水道局，若俄国船只未持有该局签发的查验证明书，则须接受中国海关查验，或者空载驶往布拉戈维申斯克（Blagovestchensk）接受查验；该办法同样适用于于大黑河过冬的俄国轮船，即待航运开通后，或空载离港驶往布拉戈维申斯克接受查验，或交于中国海关查验。

3. 大黑河口岸锅炉及机械的查验工作可由瑗珲关就地巡役兼匠董兰金（V.Z.Lankin）先生负责，其熟悉俄国轮船查验章程（哈尔滨关亦照此章之规定查验轮船），完全有资格接任此职；大黑河口岸尚无测试锅炉水压所需之液压泵，或可借于当地磨坊。至于船体之查验工作，可由超等外班关员负责。

查验收费标准可与哈尔滨关相同，即每马力 0.40 海关两；马力为黑龙江航道公认之船只计量标准，但若贵署认为，收费标准应以吨计量，则亦为可行之法，毕竟测量船只吨位亦非难事。

兹认为，可按照哈尔滨关第 2345 号呈中之建议，取查验费用之十分之二支付给负责锅炉及机械查验工作之关员；此外，建议另取十分之二支付给负责船体查验工作之关员。

4. 道尹兼海关监督已表示会竭力支持海关管理航运工作，认为既然现已有一名航务专门顾问，且其薪俸由江捐税收支付，则可于大黑河港口设立港务课。目前，超等外班关员实际上已承担理船厅之职责，因此成立正式港务课将不会有何难处。依道尹之意，易保罗（P. I. Ignatieff）先生除任航务专门顾问外，还可兼任理船厅或代理理船厅，无需额外薪俸；但因其需要外出巡查经常缺席，故可由超等外班关员（此职每月津贴 25 海关两）任头等总巡或二等总巡（兼理船厅），并发放相应津贴；兹认为，现任超等外班关员完全有资格接任此职。

然而，首要之事应为批准并发布《理船章程》（瑷珲关第 40 号呈），关于此事，本署已请道尹兼海关监督向税务处请示批准。

对于成立正式港务课一事，与警方相比，道尹兼海关监督之支持于海关而言或许更有效果，船运公司及商人亦会因此而更加尊重海关。

此抄件发送至哈尔滨关税务司及巡工司，兹附瑷珲关第 42 号呈抄件。

您忠诚的仆人

包安济（G. Boezi）

瑷珲关署理税务司

通函

由：	致：
哈尔滨关	瑷珲关税务司
1923 年 3 月 9 日	

1923 年 2 月 26 日瑷珲关致海关总税务司署第 98 号呈收悉：

关于轮船查验一事,瑷珲关署理税务司已于 1922 年 4 月至 5 月间与本署通过半官函进行商议。本署致包安济（G.Boezi）先生的两封半官函中皆明确提及此事,兹附函文抄件,以供参考。

1. 中国轮船: 在如哈尔滨关一样拥有查验轮船的合格人选之前,瑷珲关查验对象,应仅限于在黑龙江航道上进行贸易之轮船,以及在大黑河过冬并于航运开通时离港前往哈尔滨关以外港口之轮船。为统一轮船查验惯例及方法,阿布兰森（H.Abrahamsen）先生将编制一份轮船查验税贴,发送至瑷珲关以指导关员查验轮船。

2. 俄国轮船: 参阅半官函及随附理船厅之意见。

3. 关于负责查验轮船锅炉及机械之关员,最好为有资格的测量师和机师等,其余人等尽量不予考虑,以免遭人诟病。查验费用方面,为统一起见,应按照哈尔滨关现行收费标准予以收取,但哈尔滨关并未抽用该费用以支付负责查验之关员。此外,外行若要准确测量船只吨位,绝非易事。

4. 由航务专门顾问任大黑河口岸理船厅一职,绝非理想之策。本署已于哈尔滨关第 2333 号呈中说明对此事之观点。若必须于大黑河港口成立港务课,兹认为,现任超等外班关员博韩（G.E.Baukhan）先生,除其现有职责以外,亦非常适合兼任理船厅之职。

覃书（R. C. L. d'Anjou）

哈尔滨关税务司

附录1

1922年4月24日致包安济（G.Boezi）先生半官函之摘要

尊敬的包安济（G.Boezi）先生：

锅炉及船体查验：瑷珲关查验锅炉之提议着实令本署困扰,望商定之前暂缓查验事宜。过去三年里,为管理哈尔滨关范围内之中俄两国轮船,本署励精图治,排除万难,终于建立了颇为有效之制度,遂恐贵署会在与本署达成共识,制定周全安排之前采取行动,以致前期之成果毁于一旦。坦白相告,兹认为,瑷珲关只需查验在黑龙江航道上进行贸易之轮船,余者并无查验之必要。目前凡航行于松花江及黑龙江上的中国轮船均属于哈尔滨船运公司——哈尔滨关亦为中国轮船往来之中心——当然,这些公司亦有于大黑河设立代理处者,但所有轮船均登记于哈尔滨关,船主亦遵照哈尔滨关之要求行事,因此于哈尔滨关以外之地查验轮船（为确保乘客安全）,并非明智之举。且哈尔滨关由一名训练有素之关员负责轮船查验工作,理船厅亦配备一名非常合格之水手。若由瑷珲关一名不能胜任此职之关员或是如施佩克（Sperk）先生（其本职工作出色,但并非查验船体及锅炉的合格人选）一样的外行负责船体或锅炉的查验工作,恐难以完成。兹提议,瑷珲关仅查验在黑龙江航道上进行贸易之轮船,凡于哈尔滨关登记并于松花江及黑龙上进行贸易之轮船均不予查验。为指导瑷珲关负责查验工作之关员,阿布兰森（Abrahamsen）先生将编制一份轮船查验税贴,说明哈尔滨关现行查验程序,因此,为保证北满洲两个口岸的统一性,望瑷珲关严格按照此程序进行查验。然此函并无批评之意,仅为哈尔滨关过去这三年的经验之谈,亦恐因两口岸查验工作不统一而招致批评。

您真挚的

（签字）覃书（R. C. L. d'Anjou）

此抄件内容真实有效,特此证明

三等帮办前班

附录2

1922年5月26日致包安济（G.Boezi）先生半官函之摘要

尊敬的包安济（G.Boezi）先生：

贵署5月12日关于中俄两国轮船查验工作之函收悉。本署对于函中之观点表示理解；但因大黑河口岸尚无合格之理船厅，且不熟悉哈尔滨关轮船查验之惯例，遂请于本署阐明之前，暂缓行动。首先需明晰中俄两国轮船查验之程序；中国轮船：凡于松花江上进行贸易之轮船皆照《松花江临时章程》行事，尽管松花江并未被认定为内江，但此等轮船仍须办理内港专照，且每年皆需换新，还须依照《内港行轮章程》接受海关对其锅炉、发动机和船体进行查验。此外，哈尔滨关亦负责船只救生设备、灯、内部结构、船锚及锚链等查验事项。因内港专照仅适用于松花江航道，故按照规定，凡欲前往黑龙江各口岸之轮船，均须将内港专照呈交拉哈苏苏分关以办理结关手续，但实际上，轮船通常将该内港专照与交通部签发的船舶证件一起留存，待停靠俄国港口时，作船舶证件之用。哈尔滨关轮船救生设备、灯、内部结构、船锚及锚链等查验工作皆由理船厅负责，查验较为彻底，轮船各项状况于过去两年间已改进良多。关于轮船查验程序，尤其涉及消防及救生设备方面，哈尔滨关在一定程度上参照了俄国官方《航务条例》（去年冬天已完成译本）之规定。

鉴于中国尚未颁布《海商法》，哈尔滨关以保证乘客安全，防止因船主能力不足而致船只堵塞航道为由，向船运公司施压，令各船主至理船厅处接受非正式检查，包括检查船主航运和理船之能力。查船主有理船能力者，理船厅便于其所呈雇用文件上盖章签字，船运公司亦默认凡有理船厅盖章签字之船主，皆属有理船能力者，可予以雇用。当然此仅为试行之法，但海关需要采取措施以防止中国轮船委任船主之时不加以区分，最终危及乘客安全。然此行如履薄冰，务必慎重。为此，本署另有一策，或可于明年航运季实行，即若船主未获验货委员会（理船厅坐堂）之认可，则劝说保险公司不为其所属船只之货物提供保险服务。目前，外国保险公司均表示予以支持，不久还会有更多保险公司加入进来。

俄国轮船：凡于松花江上进行贸易之轮船皆照《松花江临时章程》行事。然此前哈尔滨关未曾以乘客安全为由对俄国轮船进行查验，且俄方亦未曾允许此等查验事项。虽然俄国轮船大多保养良好，船主操作得力，且照俄国旧《航务条例》航行，但相比之下，中国船只须办理内港专照，支付锅炉、发动机及船体查验之费用，实有不公之处，因此本署于本航运季开始便向俄国船运公司施加压力，令其船只同中国船只一样行事。目前，服从哈尔滨关管理之船只已日益增多，望得保险公司相助之后，俄国船只可完全受本关管制。然关于查验俄国船只之事，本关一向谨慎行事，尽量为其考虑周全，帮助其解决与中国船只频起之纠纷，正因如此，俄国船只方会服从于哈尔滨关之管理。

但大黑河口岸之处境有些不同，黑龙江乃两国共有之航道，俄国船只仅于进入大黑河港口之后，方入瑷珲关管辖范围之内。而且若瑷珲关有任何举措致俄方不满，中国船只停靠俄国港口时势必会遭其报复，后果不堪设想。因此瑷珲关对俄国船只进行查验之事务必谨慎，须依照惯例行事，但俄国船只一向遵守俄国旧《航务条例》，自身管理较为得当。实际上，于瑷珲关而言，除江捐征收事宜外，值得关注之事仅限于搭载中国乘客之俄国船只是否安全，而此类船只之数量亦十分有限。若俄国船只停靠于大黑河港口时，并未搭载中国乘客，其锅炉、机械、船体或消防及救生设备之状况则非海关顾及之事。然若俄国船只有危及大黑河港口之险，贵署当可加以阻挠。因此兹建议，瑷珲关目前勿对俄国船只行查验之事，而中国船只方面亦应限于在航运季开始从大黑河港口出港之轮船，或无哈尔滨关查验证明书之轮船。

望此函可使贵署明晰当前之形势。

您真挚的

（签字）贾韦（R. C. L. d'Anjou）

此抄件内容真实有效，特此证明。

三等帮办前班

通函

由：	致：
理船厅办公室	哈尔滨关税务司
1923 年 3 月 9 日	

关于大黑河港口船只查验及港务课设立之意见

应税务司之要求，本人已缮写关于 1923 年 2 月 26 日瑷珲关（大黑河）第 98 号呈之意见，并按照其呈文问题之顺序依次列下。

1. 兹认为，中国轮船之查验工作实有必要，应强制执行；但若轮船自航运开通后的首次航行即为驶往哈尔滨关，且已于前一年接受过查验，则超等外班关员只需彻底查验灯、消防设备及救生设备等，若条件允许，亦可全面查验船体；待轮船抵达哈尔滨关后再接受全面查验。

海关查验工作之主要目的为确保乘客安全，因此切实关系乘客安全之项最为重要，而船体若无明显受损之处，通常不会对航道造成严重之影响，毕竟轮船航行之处不会距江岸过远。

若轮船锅炉已于前一年查验过，则首航驶往哈尔滨关时，基本不会有何安全隐患——但若轮船驶往别处，海关则须对其进行常规查验。

2. 若俄阿穆尔水道局查验轮船之标准一如从前，则无可担忧之处；但因俄国轮船并不享有治外法权之特权，所以对于行驶于中国航道之俄国轮船，中国海关均可核查其文件，甚至可对俄国查验之结果提出异议；但于此需慎之又慎，以免中国轮船停靠俄方口岸时，遭其报复，因此最好承认俄方之查验结果，毕竟两国船舶技术之细节有很大差异，且几乎不会对乘客之安全造成影响。

关于允许于华岸过冬之俄国轮船空载驶往布拉戈维申斯克接受查验一事，本人表示赞同。但 1921 年至 1922 年于大黑河港口过冬的 12 艘中国轮船应属例外。

3. 毫无疑问，就地巡役兰金（V.Z.Lankin）先生完全有能力负责轮船锅炉及发动机的查验工作，但其是否有相关证书，以备发生争议之时使用，若没有，异议方提出质疑时，海关亦无从支持；兰金先生或可前往布拉戈维申斯克获此证书，而后其身份便会随之转变。

关于查验锅炉方面，水压测试自是使用最多之办法，但关于这一点，技术方面却有不同之意见，有些人认为水压测试并不完全准确，兹建议，涉及哈尔滨关时，由巡工司决定查验之办法。

大黑河港口若可使用哈尔滨关现行查验收费标准（以马力为计量单位），将会切实有效。

关于抽取所收费用之百分比支付查验关员一事，据悉，总税务司已下达另一指示。

4. 此项显然对港务课与航路标志之职能有所误解，毕竟二者体制完全不同，港务课之职能限于管理口岸界限以内之船运及航务工作、包括查验轮船、汽艇等；虽然航路标志工作与港口事务有交叉之处，但其主要职能仅涉及港口界限以外之航道勘测及标注工作。

兹认为，现任超等外班关员博韩（G.E.Baukhan）先生确有能力料理大黑河港务课各项事务，但对于水道委员会之职员航务专门顾问可兼任理船厅（虽未得此职薪酬）之事，不敢苟同。当然，确有头等总巡兼理船厅管理港口界限以外航路标志之事例，但并未听说巡江工司或航务专门顾问可兼任理船厅之事；虽然目前黑龙江航道各事尚未确定，特殊情况或可特殊对待，但即使有设立港务办事处之需，亦应如长江沿岸各口岸一样设立巡工事务局而非设立港务课。

若去年与布尔什维克签订的黑龙江航务相关协定可续约一年，那么兹认为，除航务专门顾问办事处之外，其他任何办事处之设立均为时过早，目前来看甚至有些多余。

兹认为，若由大黑河超等外班关员出任（即使为代理）头等总巡兼理船厅之职，必可得到道尹兼海关监督及当地警方之支持，海关当然亦会受到船运公司及商人更加严肃之对待。

（签字）阿布兰森（H.Abrahamsen）

理船厅

此抄件内容真实有效，特此证明

三等帮办前班

关于瑷珲关致海关总税务司署第98号呈的意见

1923 年 2 月 26 日瑷珲关致海关总税务司署第 98 号呈收悉：

兹认为，以目前之情况而言，呈中所列提议尚好。包安济（G. Boezi）先生对其所提之人员，以及瑷珲关和黑龙江航道之情况有充分之了解，毕竟本人仅知晓瑷珲关、黑龙江航道、哈尔滨关及松花江当地之情况。

（签字）额得志（T.J.Eldridge）

巡工司

1923 年 3 月 8 日，江海关巡工事务局

此抄件内容真实有效，特此证明

劳德迩（H. G. Lowder）监事员

呈海关总税务司署 108 号文　　　　　瑷珲关 / 大黑河 1923 年 4 月 28 日

尊敬的海关总税务司（北京）：

海关总税务司署致瑷珲关第 113/93787 号令收悉：

"请汇报大黑河口岸轮船检查和港务课设立等事。"

兹回复如下：

轮船检查：根据俄国标准，凡负责轮船锅炉检查工作者，均需拥有高级理工学院（大学同级别）的机械工程师文凭。目前布拉戈维申斯克的锅炉检查工作便是由一名有此等文凭的机械工程师负责。兰金（V.Z.Lankin）先生尚无此类文凭，但因布拉戈维申斯克地区无此级别的学校，所以即使其有能力，亦无法获得此类文凭；目前其已完成布拉戈维申斯克技工学校的课程，并获得了助理机械师文凭；除此之外，还在布拉戈维申斯克江河学校（River School）（由俄交通部设立——专门为阿穆尔河培养机械师与船长）研读相关课程，并顺利通过理论课程考试，但因尚未按照规定完成为期 18 个月的航行实践，故还未获得毕业文凭。兹附兰金先生的资质证明抄件及译本。

由此，如果要在黑龙江流域中国一侧采用俄国标准，那么兰金先生虽有能力担起检查之责，且已获准签署机械设备检查证明，但终会因无所需文凭，无法签署锅炉检查证明；同样，即使易保罗（P. I. Ignatieff）先生在检查轮船机械装置、船体、设备等方面有着丰富的经验，亦会因不具备机械工程师文凭而无法签署锅炉检查证明。

若如此，恐怕唯有施佩克（B. E. Sperk）先生符合要求，其既拥有所需要的一应文凭，又曾在阿穆尔省担任全省工厂总检查员数年（参阅瑷珲关致海关总税务司署第 42 号呈）。若之后，施佩克先生离开大黑河，海关亦可于布拉戈维申斯克寻得一名俄籍检查员来负责检查工作；薪酬方面，亦可按照俄国目前的薪酬标准，定在每月 15 到 25 卢布。易保罗先生称，此亦为哈巴罗夫斯克（Habarovsk）铁路工程师应邀检查轮船锅炉时的酬金数额。

然兹认为，中国与俄国情况不同，中国的技术服务仍在萌芽阶段，未必一定要严格按照国外标准行事；而且，关于严格要求资质证明一事，海关亦有很多例外，比如海关税务司并非均有要求的公证人与半领事资质，比如大多口岸的理船厅并无要求的船长资格证书等文凭。另外，不知哈尔滨关小轮工司是否持有高级理工学院授予的机械工程师文凭。

同时本署需要指出，大黑河口岸的检查对象几乎皆为往来于黑龙江上的中国轮船，而俄国轮船中，只有极少数仅于黑龙江华岸一侧往返，大多数均会选择在黑龙江开江后，空载离港驶往布拉戈维申斯克接受检查；迄今为止，凡自黑龙江俄岸而来的俄国轮船，几乎皆持检查证明文件。

鉴于贵署已下达指示，凡于航运开通后由瑷珲关/大黑河结关离港，驶往松花江沿岸各口岸的中国轮船，均须在哈尔滨关接受检查，兹认为，此等轮船在结关前应于大黑河口岸接受一次非正式初检，合格者可获得至哈尔滨关单次有效的临时证明（或许可证）。俄国对于在未设锅炉检查员的口岸办理结关的轮船便是照此办理，以使检查程序更加正规化。但若有轮船经瑷珲关（大黑河）理船厅检查后被判定存在安全隐患，或者轮船锅炉于冬季在大黑河进行过大修，又或者轮船抵达大黑河时已有所损坏，特别是轮船锅炉出现问题者，均应在大黑河口岸接受全面检查，以免发生重大事故，损害海关检查部门的信誉。

对于上述几点，敬请予以指示。

《理船章程》：

首先，本署就未能照海关总税务司署第 2060 号通令指示行事一事深表歉意，当时确系为得到海关监督批准，方有此举，望得贵署体谅。

另须说明，本署在瑷珲关致海关总税务司署第 40 号呈附件 3 中所提之规定民船及木筏航运事项的《专项公告》，是指在民船和木筏不应列入《理船章程》的情况下，将颁布单独的《专项公告》。

根据海关总税务司署致哈尔滨关第 2110/74773 号呈所附之最初草拟本《理船章程》第 1 条中所列：

"本章程中'船舶'一词系指洋式船舶而言。章程中有关华式船只之规定，仅以共与洋式船只有关之作业为限；其他方面有关华式船只之管理，见各专项公告。"

兹认为，将民船及木筏的管理办法纳入《理船章程》更为合理，亦无须再另行发布《专项公告》。

另外，依照海关总税务司署致哈尔滨关第 2110/74773 号令指示，本署所发布之船运及港务相关公告均仅与港口界限有关；加强船运管理一事虽已开始进行，但仅有口头约束，本署并未发布任何具有强制约束力的书面规定；瑷珲关一直照拟订的《理船章程》行事。

关于《理船章程》的俄文译本，呈请再次说明，最好由海关总税务司署或哈尔滨关完成；若此法不可行，望将哈尔滨关《理船章程》的俄文译本抄件发与本署，以供瑷珲关参考。若可如此，本署将不胜感激。

此抄件发送至巡工司及哈尔滨关税务司。

您忠诚的仆人

包安济（G. Boezi）

瑷珲关署理税务司

瑷珲关致海关总税务司署第 108 号呈附件

瑷珲关就地巡役兼匠董兰金（V.Z.Lankin）先生资质证明抄件及译本

助理机械师毕业文凭

由布拉戈维申斯克 阿穆尔斯基技工学校授予兰金（V. Z.Lankin）先生

鉴于兰金（V. Z. Lankin）先生已完成布拉戈维申斯克、阿穆尔斯基技工学校的规定课程，具备毕业资格，根据沙皇 1908 年 7 月 15 日颁布之法令，教育委员会于 1914 年 10 月 18 日决议授予其助理机械师文凭。

签发日期：1914 年 11 月 22 日 编号：483

教育委员会主席（签字）：奥罗夫（Orloff）

教育委员会委员（签字）：珀克洛斯基（A. Pokrovsky）

工会主席（签字）：普利塔吉克（A. Poliatchek）

赦穆诺斯基（K. Shemunovsky）

施尼（V. K. Shne）

教育委员会秘书（签字）：施尼（V. K. Shne）

编号：187

证明书

兹证明：兰金（V. Z. Lankin）先生,宗教信仰：　　　　,出生日期：1896 年 8 月 20 日,于 19　　年完成布拉戈维申斯克江河学校机械专业所规定的全部高级理论课程,结业考核成绩如下：

神学		
俄语	肆点伍	4.5
算术	伍	5
几何学	伍	5
物理学	肆点伍	4.5
蒸汽机机械学	肆	4
电工学	叁	3
绘图	伍	5

该生在校期间表现优秀,已在阿穆尔河流域河道上进行过航行实践。

1920 年 4 月 20 日

布拉戈维申斯克

审查委员会主席兼校长（签字）：
　　　　（工程师）尼克拉耶夫（A. Niklaieff）
审查委员会委员（签字）：克罗夫斯基（P. Kolovsky）
　　　　（工程师）赫挈夫（S. Hetchaeff）
　　　　　米基列夫（P. Misgireff）
　　　　　巴拉诺夫（I. Baranoff）
　　　　　马耶克夫（P. Masiukoff）
　　　　　切尔诺夫（Cherepanoff）

斯米诺夫（I. Smirnoff）

亚克列夫（N. Yakovleff）

教育委员会秘书（签字）：亚克列夫（N. Vakovleff）

说明：兰金（V. Z. Lankin）先生通过理论课程考试后，须完成为期18个月的航行实践（学习理论课程期间的航行实践时间亦包含在内），并于3月15日前将实践证明呈交至布拉戈维申斯克江河学校，同时向校长提交换取毕业文凭的申请，以将该证明书换为毕业文凭。

校长（签字）：

（工程师）尼克拉耶夫

该抄件及译本内容真实有效，特此证明：

确认人签字：包安济（G. Boezi）瑷珲关署理税务司

通函

由：	致：
哈尔滨关	瑷珲关税务司
1923 年 5 月 9 日	

1923 年 4 月 28 日瑷珲关致海关总税务司署第 108 号呈收悉：

本署在对瑷珲关致海关总税务司署第 98 号呈发表意见时，从未想过会引起锅炉检查问题的争议，亦从未建议过在中国实行俄国的检查标准，或是要求中国的检查人员具有与俄国检查人员一样的资质，毕竟根据经验，本署深知此等资质通常更侧重于理论而非实际。至于兰金（V. Z. Lankin）先生，本署从未质疑过其在锅炉及机械检查方面的能力。

实际上，需要接受此等检查的船只少之又少，毕竟仅仅往返于黑龙江上的中国轮船数量极少，而仅仅往返于黑龙江中国一侧的俄国轮船更在少数，因此兹认为，包安济（G. Boezi）先生高估了锅炉检查一事的重要性。

其实，只要负责检查工作的人员确有相应的能力，那么其具体是海关职员还是外聘人员，均不重要。然无论如何，瑷珲关检查收费标准应与哈尔滨关获准收取之费用标准保持一致。兹附理船厅意见抄件。

章书（R. C. L. d'Anjou）

哈尔滨关税务司

哈尔滨关税务司关于瑷珲关第 108 号呈的意见之附件

哈尔滨关 1923 年 5 月 7 日

尊敬的哈尔滨关税务司：

本人已照贵署指示详阅瑷珲关第 108 号呈，现就中国海关轮船检查工作中小轮工司之状况，给出如下意见：

在俄国境内，轮船检查人员均需持有必要的资格证书，但于中国海关轮船检查工作而言，并无此等要求，亦从未将此等证书作为任职资格的评判依据。

瑷珲关 / 大黑河呈文中所提到的造船工程师（持有大学文凭），通常负责船只发动机的设计和制造工作，且拥有对船只进行劳埃德测量（Lloyds survey）并放行的权力；若因遇到争议需要解决技术问题时，法院亦会承认其资质。

至于轮机工程师（其他语言中多称之为机械师），虽无大学文凭，但均毕业于海洋工程学院并具有至少 5 年的锻工及钳工经验，且在学习期间会接受技术培训，有较强的实践能力。证书等级因各国法律规定不同而略有差异，但通常分为一、二、三，三个等级。轮机工程师主要负责检查维修轮船发动机，包括远洋班轮和运煤货船。

根据大多数国家的现行法规，凡持有二级或三级深海资格证者，均可出任机师长，负责内陆水域的贸易运输。

海关轮船检查工作主要是为保证公众出行安全，无须进行劳埃德测量。

在中国大多数小口岸，检查工作可由当时在口岸的轮船工程师负责，海关收取的全部检查费用即为其酬金；理船厅及其副手，无论是否持有资格证书，均可对船身、配件、操舵装置及其他装备进行无偿检查。

在江海关，海上作业人员中的轮机工程师（曾于巡洋舰上工作）通常会被任命为小轮工司，根据等级按月领取薪俸。

由此可见，于中国海关而言，凡依法获得发动机检查资格者，均为轮船检查工作的合格人选。

兰金（V. Z. Lankin）先生的专业知识和能力无可争议，但关键在于作为轮船检查人员，其必须持有可以证明自己有资格签署发动机检查证明的文凭。若其尚未依法获得检查江轮发动机的资格，一旦与一名有资格证书的轮机工程师发生争议，其又如何能够让自己的决定得到认可呢？

此外，哈尔滨关小轮工司斯托亚诺夫（Stoyanoff）先生曾在大型远洋轮船（总重约 7000吨）上担任副手，往返于符拉迪沃斯托克与黑海之间，并连续 13 年担任江轮机师长，这些经验足以证明其确有资格担任小轮工司一职，且对于上述经历，其均可出示官方文件予以证实。因此，实不知斯托亚诺夫（Stoyanoff）先生的资格何以会成为兰金（V. Z. Lankin）先生拥有任职资格的依据。

至于易保罗（P. I. Ignatieff）先生的资格问题，实无讨论之必要，毕竟海关总税务司署已于此前令文中说明，其仅担任航务专门顾问一职。

（签字）阿布兰森（H. Abrahamsen）

哈尔滨关理船厅

11. 为瑷珲关对非商业用途的私人汽艇与摩托艇的管理事

III
. C.

Aigun/Taheiho 7th May, 1923.

Sir,

In accordance with the instructions of your
Circular No. 3404, II:

Motor Launches and Motor Boats, privately
owned and not engaged in trade :
report on Customs control of, called for;

I have the honour to inform you that there are
at this Port a few privately-owned Motor launches,
and **that**, in addition, the Port is constantly
visited by Motor Launches, the property of Government institutions or of private owners in Blagovestchensk.

Previous to 1922, these launches not engaged
in trade were allowed to go and come, practically
without control. At the beginning of the 1922
Navigation Season, however, a form of control was
introduced and on 27th June a Notification was
issued (copy enclosed) enjoining upon launches
proceeding to or coming from outside Harbour limits
to report to the Customs both before clearing and
on arrival; two points were allowed for launch
traffic

Inspector General of Customs
P E K I N G .

traffic, i. e. the Clearance Office, (Which was

formerly in the Winter Road Office and was lately

established on the Customs Pontoon moored opposite

the Custom House) and the Ferry Office, where an

Officer is invariably on duty. - Such simple

regulations were enforced without too much difficul-

ty : launches were searched on arrival and depar-

ture, and only a few exceptions were made for

launches conveying Officials. -

No registration has ever been enforced, and

it is my opinion that, given the scarce number of

such crafts on the Chinese side (10 in all,

including Customs launch), and the fact that no

registration is in force in Blagovestchensk, it is

unnecessary for the present to adopt this measure

in Tahsiho.

No launches have called at Aigun in recent

years, except the Customs launch on one occasion;

but, should any call at that Port, the same

practice may be followed as in Tahsiho.

Generally speaking, the control of launches

has been included in the proposed Harbour Regula-

tions, submitted in Aigun despatch No. 40 and

now

now about to be approved (see in particular
§ 1 and 4).

I must add that not infrequently launches
and Motor Boats ply between Taheiho and Blagovestchensk, carrying cargo: in such cases they
are treated like ordinary steamers: they must enter
and clear at the General Office, only they do
not hand proper manifests, the cargo being generally
of a uniform description (flour, wheat, etc.)

I have the honour to be,

Sir,

Your obedient Servant,

Acting Commissioner.

Aigun Despatch No. 111 to I. G.

———————

Enclosure.

Copy of Customs Notification No. 16.

The Public is hereby notified that, in accordance with Customs Regulations, all launches and boats proceeding to, or coming from, outside Harbour Limits, are to report to the Customs each time immediately before departure and after arrival. During Office hours, Motor and Steam launches and Boats can report either at the Ferry Office or the Clearance Office; after office hours, they must report at the Clearance Office. If they carry any merchandise, they must clear and enter through the General Office during Office hours.

愛琿關佈告 第十六號

為佈告事照得小火輪小汽船及一切小船等
行駛本口或由口外來者應照關章每次來
埠之後或離埠之先到關報驗不得延誤
如在辦公時間須在橫江輪船辦公處
或官渡路驗船處報明如在辦公時間
以外則在驗船處報明如係載運貨物
應於辦公時間到海關公事房聲明
特此佈告各宜照辦此佈

愛琿關署稅務司包安濟

中華民國十一年六月二十七日

CUSTOM HOUSE,
Aigun/Taheiho, 27th June, 1922.

(Signed) G. Bocsz
Acting Commissioner of Customs

True Copy:
Wongymesik
Probationary Clerk

呈海关总税务司署 <u>111</u> 号文　　　　　　　　瑷珲关 / 大黑河 1923 年 5 月 7 日

尊敬的海关总税务司（北京）：

　　根据海关总税务司署第 3404 号通令（第二辑）：

　　　　"请汇报各口海关对非商业用途的私人汽艇与摩托艇的管理情况。"

　　兹汇报，大黑河口岸除有私人汽艇和摩托艇往来外，另常有隶属于政府机关的汽艇以及布拉戈维申斯克（Blagovestchensk）地区的私人汽艇到港。

　　1922 年之前，凡属于非商业用途之汽艇，均可自由往来本口岸，几乎不受管理。1922 年航运季伊始，瑷珲关出台相关管理办法，并于 1922 年 6 月 27 日发布海关公告（抄件已随呈附上），要求汽艇及摩托艇等小船在进港或离港之时必须向海关报验；报验地点包括结关处（此前设于海关冬令过江检查处；现设于海关办公楼对面的浮码头处）和横江码头检查处，两处均有执勤关员常驻。该项规定易于执行：凡到港或离港之汽艇和摩托艇均会接受检查，唯政府机关的汽艇偶有例外。

　　迄今为止，此等汽艇尚未登记入册，因黑龙江华岸的汽艇数量十分有限（包括海关汽艇在内共计 10 艘），且布拉戈维申斯克方面亦未对此类船只进行登记管理，兹认为，大黑河暂无施行登记制度之必要。

　　近年间，瑷珲口岸除海关汽艇停靠过一次外，再未有其他汽艇停靠于此；日后若有汽艇停靠该口岸，或可照大黑河口岸的管理办法办理。

　　汽艇管理办法已列入瑷珲关《理船章程》（参阅瑷珲关致海关总税务司署第 40 号呈），静待贵署批示（参阅第 1 条与第 4 条）。

　　此外，汽艇与摩托艇还经常载货往返于大黑河与布拉戈维申斯克之间；此等汽艇与摩托艇的管理办法与轮船相同，即进出港口时须至征税汇办处报明，但因其所载货物通常仅为小麦、面粉之类，故未要求提供载货单。

您忠诚的仆人

包安济（G. Boezi）

瑷珲关署理税务司

瑷珲关致海关总税务司署第 111 号呈附件

海关公告第 16 号抄件

　　特此公告，凡汽艇、摩托艇及一切小船等行驶本口或由外口来者，每次到港之后或离港之前，均须照《海关章程》之规定到海关报验，不得延误；如在办公时间以内，须在横江码头检查处或结关处报明；如在办公时间以外，则在结关处报明；如有载运货物，则应于办公时间至征税汇办处报明。

　　　　　　　　　　　　　　　　　　　（签字）包安济（G.Boezi）

　　　　　　　　　　　　　　　　　　　瑷珲关署理税务司

　　　　　　　　　　　　　　　　　　　1922 年 6 月 27 日，瑷珲关／大黑河

该抄件内容真实有效，特此证明：

录事：王友燮　试用供事

12. 为瑷珲关实施海关关于中国和非条约国船只船长及船员的管理合同事

3052

Harbin   93,906   9th April, 1923.

Sir,

I have to acknowledge receipt of your

despatch No. 2823 :

Masters and Crews of Chinese and Non-
Treaty Power vessels: Customs control of,
proposals in re forwarding ;

and, in reply, to say that the conditions which you

describe are deplorable and that the proposals

which you make to remedy them meet with my approval.

But it is necessary that in this matter you should

have the support of the Superintendent, and of the

Commissioner for Foreign Affairs - with whom

'Consular functions' in the matter of entry and

clearance of Russian vessels rest (Circular No.

3100); and, further, that the authority of the

Chinese Government for the Customs to act in the

manner you suggest be obtained.

Bye-Law

The Commissioner of Customs,

       HARBIN.

Bye-Law No.3 of the Rules regarding
Notarial Acts (Circular No.220) lays down
that in the case of Chinese-owned vessels,
Masters, Mates and Engineers (foreigners) are to
be shipped and discharged and are to sign
Articles before the Commissioner of Customs;
while for the enforcement of "Ship's Articles"
by the Customs under penalty of withholding
Clearance, we have a precedent in the case
of certain sequestrated enemy vessels which were
taken over by the Chinese Government in 1917
in Shanghai. I append copy of correspondence
with the Shanghai Commissioner in this connection,
from which you will see that these vessels
were provided with "Papers" by the Shanghai
Commissioner, and that the Master in each
case was required to sign a document (corresponding
to what is generally termed "Ship's Articles")
under which the officers and crews were to be
shipped, discharged and receive their wages in

the

the presence of a Commissioner of Customs or a Harbour Master, clearance being issued only after these regulations had been complied with; and, further, that the Chinese Government issued instructions that the legality of such " Ship's Articles" was to be recognised pending the promulgation of a Shipping Law.

It will be best, therefore, for you, in your communications to the Superintendent and the Commissioner for Foreign Affairs asking for their support to call their attention to the above Bye-Law and to the precedent already established at Shanghai, and to request them to lay the matter before the Chinese Government, recommending that the Customs be authorised to act in the manner you suggest, quoting at the same time in support of their recommendations the Bye-Law and the Shanghai precedent referred to, and forwarding copies of the Articles which the Masters, etc., will be required to sign.

It

It is very necessary that the Superintendent and the Commissioner for Foreign Affairs, in their communications to the Chinese Government, should thus refer to the Shanghai precedent; for the Chinese themselves attach great importance to precedent, and your own position will be strengthened thereby - all the more so as the prospect of fees might incline the local officials to push the Customs aside and thus keep the matter in their own hands.

You are requested also to forward copies of the "Articles" to the Inspectorate, and at the same time to return the document "Agreement and Account of Crew" (which formed enclosure 2 in Shanghai despatch No.14549) now sent for your information.

Copies of this despatch are being sent to the Aigun Commissioner and

to

to the Coast Inspector.

I am,

Sir,

Your obedient Servant,

(Sign.) C. A. V. Bowra.

Officiating Inspector General, ad interim.

Appendix.

Appendix.

The Inspector General to the Shanghai Commissioner.

No.9834   Commrs.   Peking,27th September,1917.

Shanghai No.66,577.

Sir,

    With reference to your telegram of the 11th instant:

        advisable warn Government Customs should be officially informed to whom the sequestrated ships have been chartered. Question of National Papers signing on of officers and crew and general regulations concerning them should also be settled;

I enclose, for your information and guidance, copy of Shui-wu Ch'u despatch No. 1299, from which you will see that the ships have been chartered to the Ta-ta S. S. Co. (大連輪船公司   ).

    The other matters referred to in your telegram are to be settled by the Commissioner of Foreign Affairs and the Superintendent of Customs in consultation with you. In regard to National Papers assuming that the ships will have obtained a Certificate of Registration from the Chiao-t'ung Pu by the time that they are ready to sail, it would be best for you, if you are called upon to issue any Papers, to adopt the form originally devised

                    for

for the China Merchants Steam Navigation
Company's steamers, which presumably they still
hold.   Steamers of this Company have from time
to time visited foreign ports and have not so
far as I am aware, experienced any difficulty.
The steamers should I think be re-measured on
passing to the Chinese flag and their tonnage
according to Chinese practice and rules should
be recorded.   On this point and on the question
of load line you should consult the Coast
Inspector. It would possibly be simplest to
adhere to the load lines that the vessels already
carry as a provisional measure pending issue of
Chinese regulations on the subject.   If there
are objections to this course British practice
should be followed provisionally. In the matter
of signing on officers and crew Circular No.
9 of 1873 authorises you to give such assistance
as may be desired. Only properly certificated
officers should be signed on and in regard to
the formalities to be observed you should follow.
the practice and, as far as possible, the forms.
of British shipping offices, charging a similar
fee for the formality.

You are to report further on this
question when you have consulted the authorities
named.

I am, Sir,
Your obedient Servant,
(Signed) F. A. Aglen,
Inspector General.

The

The Shanghai Commissioner to the Inspector General.

No. 14,549.

.I. G.

Shanghai, 18th December, 1917.

Sir,

1.   I have the honour to acknowledge receipt of your despatch No.9834/66,577 :

> instructing me to report on the question of the "Papers" to be carried by the sequestrated enemy vessels chartered to the Ta Tah S. S. Corporation and subsequently to certain of the Allied Governments;

and, in reply, to say that I have arranged to issue the National Registers - on the forms hitherto in use - upon receipt of :-

(a) the usual fee (Hk.Tls.300) and a request for the issue of the register from the Commissioner for chartering sequestrated vessels;

(b) Lloyd's Certificate regarding fitness of Hull, Machinery and Boilers;

(c) Lloyd's Load Line Certificate (based on former load line);

(d) Harbour Master's Certificate as to fitness of equipment. (This form, copy enclosed has been in use for three years);

                    and

and after

the Deck Officers' Engineers' certificates have been viséd and registered, and the Officers, Engineers and crew have "signed on", before the Harbour Master.

The vessels having passenger accommodation will of course be provided by me with passenger certificates on the form in use for vessels over 50 tons.

2. I have the honour to enclose a copy of the document "Agreement and Account of Crew" commonly known as Ships Articles, which has been based on that used on British vessels. The only drawback to this document is that there is no Chinese law at the back of it: this, apparently cannot be helped at present.

3. I also enclose copy of the Charter Party between the Ta Tah Steam Ship Corporation, to whom the Chinese Government originally chartered the vessels, and the Sub-charterers.

4. As there has been a good deal of discussion as to who should operate as Chinese Government Surveyor, I on the 17th November (after consultation with the Coast Inspector and the Harbour Master) wrote to the Charter Commissioner (formerly Commissioner of Foreign Affairs) to the following effect:

"I have the honour to bring the following to your notice in connection with the sequestrated German and Austrian steamers.

" The Maritime Customs exercises certain

control

control over Chinese steamers. The control we
so exercise is in respect to condition of hull,
machinery and boilers, in respect to equipment,
and as far as it is possible in respect to
competence of officers (vide my despatch No.
890 of 13th September).

"Apart therefore from any arrangement which
in respect to the sequestrated vessels, may have
been specially made by the Government, we would
act as follows.

"As regards the vessels which are to be
reclassified at Lloyd's we would accept the
statement of Lloyd's Surveyor regarding fitness
of hull, machinery and boilers and issue
registers on that statement. As regards equipment
we would survey and determine what was needed
ourselves. As regards Load Line we would accept
the statement of Lloyd's Agent.

' It is understood that Lloyd's Surveyor
has been engaged by the Government to survey
also the steamers which are not to be classed.
In regard to these steamers we would consider
that we had a responsibility different from that
of classed vessels and while being glad to
avail ourselves of the statement of Lloyd's
Surveyor, regarding hull, machinery and boiler,
the vessels would also be inspected by the
Customs Surveyor, which survey would, it is
anticipated, be an acquiescing one.

"The

"The foregoing is, I repeat, what would happen in the absence of other arrangements ordered by the Government; and I have now the honour to ask whether such other arrangements have been made.

"If I am notified by you that it is the Government's intention that the whole of the surveys, i.e. of hull, machinery, boilers and equipment are to be undertaken on its governmental behalf - as apart from its position as owners - by Lloyd's Surveyor, we will of course abstain from functioning. In that case, however, I shall have to consider that Lloyd's Surveyor is acting as Government Surveyor of steamers and he should sign as such.

' In the absence of such a notification it appears to me that I have no choice but to act as indicated above ";

my object being to avoid friction between Lloyd's and Customs Surveyors, at the same time to obtain a guarantee for the seaworthiness of the vessels. In this connection I may observe that the certificates of Lloyd's Register are recognised by the authorities of the following countries as exempting vessels from undergoing certain inspections at the hands of the officials of the several Governments, viz. Canada, Denmark, France, Greece, Norway, Russia, Spain, Sweden, and United States of America.

I

I append copy of the reply I received
from the Charter Commissioner which is to the
following effect :-

The Surveyor Fletcher is employed by the
"Commissioner for control of Shipping" to survey
the seized German and Austrian vessels, to
supervise the work of repairs to the said
vessels for re-entry in Lloyd's register, and
also to cause such other unregistered vessels
to be duly entered in Lloyd's register. The
said Surveyor having been engaged by the
Shipping Commissioner is bound to accept
the responsibilities of his duty as implied
by the above various requirements. If, after
his survey duties are completed for each
vessel and the repairs have been made, the
Customs Surveyor should find it desirable in
the interest of safety to conduct a further
survey of his own, the Commissioner for Shipping
is quite agreeable that he should do so.

5. Of the vessels concerned, so far the
"Hwa Jah " (late "China" and " Hwa Ting"(late
Deike Rickmers") have received their National
Registers and are ready for sailing as soon as
sub-charterers desire. The " Hwa Jah" has
already made one trip to Chinwangtao while awaiting
transfer to the sub-charterers.

I have the honour to be,
Sir,
Your obedient Servant,
(Signed)

(Signed) R. H. R. Wade,
Commissioner.

The

The Inspector General to the Shanghai Commissioner.

_____

<u>No.10,698</u>   Comm's.

Shanghai No. 72,596.   Peking, 20th March, 1919.

     Sir,

          With reference to your despatch No.14833:
reporting that the Chinese Consul at New
York had declared that the Ship's Articles
issued to the S.S. "Hwa Jah" - one of
the sequestrated enemy vessels chartered
to Allied Government - were not binding
on the Chinese crew;

     I append, for your information and guidance, copy of
Shui-wu Ch'u despatch No. 377, from which you will
see that the Chinese Consuls abroad have now been
instructed to recognise the legality of such ship's
articles pending promulgation of a shipping law
by the Chinese Government.

         The Shanghai Harbour Master's Office copy
of the S.S. "Hwa Jah's" articles forwarded in your
despatch No.14833 is returned to you under separate
cover.

               I am,

                 Sir,

           Your obedient Servant,

True copies :

   (Signed) A. H. FORBES,   (Signed) F. A. Aglen,

Acting Assistant Secretary.   Inspector General.

Replied to in No. 130.

109

I.G.

Aigun/Taheiho   28th April, 1923.

Sir,

　　Having received copy of Harbin despatch
No. 2823 to I.G. and of your despatch No.
3052/93,906 to Harbin :

　　　　Vessels: Masters and Crew of Chinese and
　　　　Non-Treaty Powers' : proposed control of,

I have the honour to forward, enclosed, a Memorandum by the Senior Out-Door Officer, Mr.
G. E. Baukham, showing that the Chinese side of
the Amur the same deplorable conditions obtain as
on the Sungari.

　　A most typical case of disregard for
contracts and justice on the part of owners and
charterers of vessels, is quoted by the Senior
Officer. Three Russian Pilots were engaged by
the Wut'ung Co. for the navigation season 1922.
I have seen the contracts, in regular form, in
Russian and Chinese. - Suddenly, when every steamer
　　　　　　　　　　　　　　　　　　　　　　　　　　had

The Inspector General of Customs.

P E K I N G.

had engaged her Staff, for the season, a telegraphic order from the Harbin Head Office of the ut'ung Co. dismissed these men without compensation, on the plea that the steamers for which they have been engaged would be laid up for the season. - I approached both the Wut'ung Co. and the Superintendent, pointing our the shocking injustice perpetrated at the expense of the three Pilots; the Company said that they had to act according to directions of the Harbin Head Office: the Superintendent said he would talk the matter over with the Company; but the results were Nil.

I am therefore convinced that the control by the Customs of Masters and Crews would be greatly beneficial to the concerned. It world also add to our prestige, on conditions that our decisions be not challenged by the local Authorities, and, consequently, that our control be established on the most solid basis.

I consequently propose to move the Aigun Superintendent and Commissioner for Foreign Affairs in support of the Harbin Commissioner's proposal;

the

the demarche here will be more especially justified
by its coincidence with the creation of a Harbour
Department in Tahsiho. But, before taking action,
I should receive copy of the Ship's Articles as
proposed by the Harbin Office, uniformity in these
matters being essential.

      Copies of this despatch are being sent
                         and
to the Coast Inspector ∧ to the Harbin Commissioner.

                      I have the honour to be,

                      Sir,

                      Your obedient Servant,

                      Acting Commissioner.

Enclosure to Aigun despatch No. 109 to I. G.

Senior Out-Door Officer's Memorandum re proposed control
by the Customs of Officers and Crew of Chinese and
Non-Treaty Powers' vessels.

Senior Out-Door Officer's Office
Aigun/Taheiho, 20th April, 1923.

I have perused the contents of the Harbin
Commissioner's despatch No. 2623 to the Inspector General,
and the Memorandum prepared by Mr. H. Abrahamsen, Harbin
Harbour Master, calling attention to the disgraceful way
in which Masters, Engineers and Crews of Vessels are
treated by their Chinese and Russian employers, against
whom there is no redress to be obtained. The same state
of affairs exists at this Port, and the same procedure
concerning engagement etc. of masters, officers and crews
occurs with steamers plying on the Amur as on the
Sungari.

Chinese vessels. The largest Chinese concern at
Aigun is the Wutang Steamship Company and the largest
Russian concern is the Government Water Transport; there
are other small companies, both Russian and Chinese, with
very few vessels. Even in the case of the largest Chinese Company, contracts with the Officers and Crew are
of no value to the Officers and Crews, and I particu-
larly wish to call attention to the incident which
occurred at this Port last year. In may, just before
the opening of the river, three Russian Pilots came to
me and stated that they had been engaged by the
Wutung Company for the navigation season (contracts
signed by the parties concerned) and just before the
ships started to run they received Telegraphic Communication from the Head Office of the Company at Harbin
that their services were no longer required and were

paid

paid to date without any compensation for the remainder of the season. As the Pilots explained to me, they had stood by their ships and just as the river opened they were discharged. If they had known that they were going to be discharged, they would have been on the look out for other ships, but now it was too late; all vacancies were filled and they were left without employment for the remainder of the season for no reasonable cause, and furthermore left to face a hard winter with nothing to fall back upon for existance. All three of these Pilots stated that they had large families to support. The matter was reported to the Commissioner who referred the case to the Superintendent but there was no result; no steps were taken to compensate the discharged Officers - I then advised these men to go to Harbin and lay their case before the Harbour Master which, they agreed to do, stating that they were afraid to take action against the Company (being Chinese and part a Government Concern) in a Chinese Court.

Russian vessels chartered to Chinese. The same procedure is applied at this Port, as at Harbin; the stipulations are the same : the Charterer can put on board any crew that he thinks fit and in many cases incompetent men that have not been afloat before. There is no authority to check him, and this is of course a danger to navigation; the charterer will try to run his ship as cheap as possible; for instance he will not, if possible, employ a qualified Engineer, but a mechanic or even a greaser, providing that he can stop and start the engines and make minor repairs; the small companies take into very small consideration the safety of passengers and the danger to navigation by employing incompetent crews.

Where Russian ships chartered by Chinese are concerned,

concerned, if you were to ask the crew under what
conditions they are employed, they will show you a piece
of paper which in most cases is hardly readable. This
is supposed to be their underline contract and is a worthless
piece of paper not officially registered by any authority. The owner or charterer of the vessel can ignore
the contract at any moment and refuse to pay his employees especially when the crew is Russian, and they
will not attempt to take action through the Chinese
Court, being afraid that they will get no protection.

    Russian -owned -and -operated Steamers. With Russian-
owned steamers with Russian crews the system is much
better, the matter being regulated by the Russian
Shipping Board. Masters, Officers and Crew are given a
Book (English sailor fashion) in which are stated
conditions under which they are employed, owner having the
option of discharging at a month's or two weeks' notice,
as the case may be; the contract is generally for the
season, especially in the case of Masters and Officers.
Now if it happened that the owner refused to pay the
crews' salaries, the crew would notify the Government
Water Transport who would send what is called the
Ships' Inspector to the vessel and advise the owner to
pay according to contract; and if the owner still refused
to pay, action would be taken against him through the
Court, and if he declared bankrupcy, his ship or property
would be sold by auction, and the crew's wages would be
a privileged claim against the proceeds.

    I firmly believe that, if the Customs will control
the engagement, etc, of Ships' Officers and Crews, this will
give more authority and prestige to the Customs and put
things more ship shape (as Mr. H.Abrahamseen stated) which
is certainly required both on the Sungari and Amur.

G.E.Baukham
Examiner A.- Senior O.B. Officer.

No. 130   Commrs.

Aigun   No.94,546

INSPECTORATE GENERAL OF CUSTOMS,

PEKING, 31st May, 1923.

Sir,

With reference to your despatch No.109 :

reporting that the Harbin Commissioner's proposals for the Customs control of the masters and crews of Chinese and non-Treaty Power vessels would also be beneficial on the Amur;

I am directed by the Inspector General to say that you are authorised to act in the manner you propose. You should obtain a copy of the Ship's Articles as proposed by the Harbin Commissioner and consult with the latter before making definite proposals, so that the essential uniformity may be maintained.

A copy of this despatch is being sent to the Harbin Commissioner.

I am,

Sir,

Your obedient Servant,

Chief Secretary Officiating.

The Commissioner of Customs,

HARBIN.

Entered in Card-Index.

[4.—29]

No. 170.   COMMRS.

INSPECTORATE GENERAL OF CUSTOMS,

Aigun.   No. 98,543.

PEKING, 28th April 1924.

Entered in Card-Index.

Sir,

      With reference to your despatch No. 109 and to my despatch No. 130/94,546 in reply :

> Vessels, Masters and Crews of Chinese and Non-Treaty Powers: proposed control of by Customs ;

I append, for your information and guidance, copy of Shui-wu Ch'u despatch No. 474, from which you will see that the Articles for the Customs control of the masters and crews of Chinese and Non-Treaty Power vessels, as proposed by the Harbin Commissioner for adoption at his port, have received the approval of the Chinese Government for adoption at Aigun. You are requested, therefore, to see that these Articles are put into operation. The Harbin Commissioner is being instructed to introduce them

at

Commissioner of Customs,

   A I G U N.

at his port provided that the Harbin Superintendent raises no objection.

A copy of the Chinese version of the Articles, as amended here and as approved by the Shui-wu Ch'u, is also appended.

I am,

Sir,

Your obedient Servant,

Inspector General.

Appendix.

致哈尔滨关第 3052/93906 号令　　　　　海关总税务司署 1923 年 4 月 9 日

尊敬的哈尔滨关税务司：

第 2823 号呈收悉：

"呈送关于海关管控中国船只和无条约国船只船长及船员的提议。"

现批复如下：呈中所述的船只管理现状一塌糊涂，兹批准贵署的补救建议。但考虑到俄属船只进出港事宜需要海关监督和交涉员签发领事报单（第 3100 号通令），相关建议应获得他们的支持。而且，海关如要按照贵署建议的方式行动，还需获得中国政府的批准。

公证手续细则第 3 条附则（第 220 号通令）规定，凡华人自有船只，其船长与大副和机师（外籍）在海关税务司处签订《船长合同》之后方可上下船；如不签订，海关则不予发放结关单照。此项执法已有先例，1917 年曾在江海关扣押数只敌船，这些船后被中国政府接收。兹附与江海关税务司关于此问题讨论的往来通信。据此可知，江海关税务司为这些船只提供了"证明文件"，各船长需在海关税务司或理船厅在场的情况下签订一份文件（通常称为《船长合同》），然后船只驾驶员及船员方可依法上下船，领取工资。等到船只遵守这些规定后，始准发放结关单照。此外，中国政府曾给出指令，在等待《海运法》颁布之际，该《船长合同》的合法性应予以承认。

因此，贵署最好与海关监督和交涉员积极联络，获得他们对以上附则的关注和支持，并且要特别提醒，在江海关已有执法先例。然后请他们上呈中国政府，并在呈中建议海关按照贵署建议的方式行事应予以批准；同时引用前文提及的附则和江海关执法先例，为其建议提供佐证；并随呈附上需要船长等人签订的《船长合同》副本。

海关监督和交涉员需要在致中国政府的函中提及江海关先例，这一点非常重要，因为中国政府格外重视先例，贵署的立场也会因此得以更加明确，从而收费可能更倾向于交给地方官员，将海关撤开，将此事掌控在他们自己手中。

贵署也需要将《船长合同》副本上交至海关总税务司署。同时，附送"船员协议和账目"文件（江海关第 14549 号呈附表 2），供贵署参考。

同时，此令副本已抄送至瑷珲关税务司及巡工司。

您忠诚的仆人

包罗（C. A. V. Bowra）

总务科税务司

附件

海关总税务司署致江海关税务司令

致江海关第 <u>9834/66577</u> 号令　　　　海关总税务司署（北京）1917 年 9 月 27 日

尊敬的江海关税务司：

关于本月 11 日电呈：

"建议告诫中国政府，其应正式告知海关将扣押船只租给了哪家机构。船只驾驶员和船员国家证明文件的签署及关于此等人员的一般规定等问题均需解决。"

为了便于贵署顺利执行，兹附中方税务处第 1299 号令，以供参考。据该令所示，船只已租给大达轮船公司。

电呈中提及的其他事项需由贵署与交涉员和海关监督共同协商解决。关于可以表明船只在准备起航前已领有交通部轮船注册凭单的国家证明文件，贵署如需颁发证明文件，最好采用最初为中国商办招商局公司轮船设计制作的表格，目前该公司应该仍然持有类似表格。该公司的轮船有时会到达外国口岸，据我所知，其目前并未遇到任何困难。我认为，凡船只通过中国领海，应当重新丈量，并根据中国惯例和细则记录船只吨位。关于船只吨位及载货吃水线，应当咨询巡工司。在中国政府颁布此类章程之前，将船只载货吃水线作为临时标准不失为目前最简单的处理办法。倘若此种办法遇有异议，则暂时遵循英国惯例。关于船只驾驶员及船员的合同签署事宜，根据第 1873 号通令第 9 条，贵署可以予以援助。只有拥有合格证书的驾驶员方可签字。关于办理手续，贵署应当尽可能遵循惯例，按照英国海运监督事务所的方式办理，类似地征收一定手续费。

在咨询相关官员后，请另行汇报关于此问题的后续事宜。

您忠诚的仆人

（签字）安格联（F. A. Aglen）

海关总税务司

江海关税务司致海关总税务司署呈

呈海关总税务司署 14549 号文   江海关 1917 年 12 月 18 日

尊敬的海关总税务司：

1. 第 9834/66577 号令收悉：

"命令我汇报关于所扣押敌船在租给大达轮船公司后应携带的'文件'。"

现答复如下：兹告知本署安排，要领取（至今仍在使用的）"国家海关证明书"，必须先上交以下费用及文件：

（1）为租赁扣押船只办理国家海关证明书的手续费（300 海关两）及申请书；

（2）船体、机械和锅炉状况完好的劳埃德证书；

（3）劳埃德载货吃水线证书（基于原载货吃水线证书）；

（4）理船厅设备完好证书（此表格已使用三年，表格副本已附寄）。

并且

"船舶驾驶员机师证完成签注，驾驶员、机师和船员在理船厅处已经'签署'合同。"

凡设有乘客吃住安排的船只，需提供 50 吨以上船只使用的乘客证明书。

2. 兹附"船员协议和账目"文件，该文件通称《船长合同》，基于英国船只使用的版本制定。此文件的唯一缺点是尚无中国法律依据，显然在目前还不能发挥效用。

3. 另外，随附大达轮船公司（最初从中国政府租赁船只的总承租人）与分租人之间的租船合同副本。

4. 关于由谁担任中国政府测量师已有大量讨论，于是（在与巡工司和理船厅协商之后）在 11 月 7 日，本署向租船税务司（原交涉员）致函，大意如下：

"敬请注意以下关于扣押的德国和奥地利船只问题。

海关已对中国船只实施了一定的控制措施。我们目前实施的控制既与船体、机械和锅炉状况有关，又与设备有关，并且尽可能与驾驶员能力有关（参见 9 月 13 日第 890 号函）。

除由中国政府专门针对扣押船只做出的安排以外，我们将遵循以下办法执行：

关于欲在英国劳埃德船舶登记簿进行重新分类的船只，我们将会认可劳埃德测量师关于船体、机械和锅炉完好情况说明，并根据该说明发放海关证明书。关于设备，我们将会自己测量，并确定需要的内容。关于载货吃水线，我们将会认可劳埃德保险代理人的说明。

据悉,劳埃德测量师受雇于中国政府,负责调查还未归类的船只。关于上述船只,我们认为,我们对此所承担的职责与已归类船只不同,同时很高兴可以利用劳埃德测量师关于船体、机械和锅炉的情况说明,但也希望默许海关测量师对这些船只进行检验。

我需要强调,前述办法都是在找不到中国政府相关命令的前提下才会实施;现在我想询问是否已出台类似其他实施办法。

倘若贵署告知,中国政府意欲由劳埃德测量师代其执行全部调查(即船身、机械和锅炉以及设备),以撇开其作为船主的立场嫌疑,我们当然会停止这一方面的工作。但是在这种情况下,本署认为,劳埃德测量师作为中国政府的船只测量师,应同样签字确认。

如无上述通知,本署似乎除了遵照上述办法执行外,别无他法。"

本署的目的是避免劳埃德测量师和海关测量师之间出现矛盾,同时为船只适航性提供保证。此外,我观察到,加拿大、丹麦、法国、希腊、挪威、俄罗斯、西班牙、瑞典和美国政府均承认劳埃德船舶登记簿的证明书,可以免除某些船只检验。

兹附租船税务司给予本署的答复,大意如下:

"富乐嘉(Fletcher)测量师受雇于掌管海运的税务司测量扣押的德国和奥地利船只,监督上述船只修复工作,以使船只重新登记在万国船只登记簿中,同时负责让未入簿船只正式列入万国船只登记簿。按照前文所述各种要求,以上受雇于负责船政的税务司的测量师应承担其相应的责任。在其完成各船测量和修复工作之后,倘若为安全起见,海关测量师认为应当自行再做一次测量,负责船政的税务司则非常乐意其能这样做。"

5. 在船只中,目前"Hwa Jah"号(原"China"号)和"Hwa Ting"号(原"Deike Rickmers"号)已领取国家海关证明书,只要分租人愿意,即可扬帆起航。"Hwa Jah"号已开到秦皇岛,等待分租人认领。

您忠诚的仆人

(签字)威厚澜(R. H. R. Wade)

江海关税务司

海关总税务司署致江海关税务司令

致江海关第 <u>10698/72596</u> 号令　　　　海关总税务司署（北京）1919 年 3 月 20 日

尊敬的江海关税务司：

　　"根据第 14833 号呈：中国驻纽约领事已宣布，颁发给'Hwa Jah'号轮船（租用给盟国政府的扣押敌船之一）的'船员雇用合同'对中国船员不具有约束效力。"

　　为了便于贵署顺利执行，兹附税务处第 377 号令副本。据该令所示，在等待中国政府颁布《海运法》之际，已命令中国驻外领事承认上述《船长合同》的合法性。

　　第 14833 号呈送交的江海关理船厅关于"Hwa Jah"的船员雇佣合同副本另行回函，单独归还贵署。

您忠诚的仆人

（签字）安格联（F. A. Aglen）

海关总税务司

此副本内容真实有效，特此证明。

确认人签字：（签字）福贝士（A. H. Forbes）

代理总务科副税务司

呈海关总税务司署 <u>109</u> 号文　　　　　　　　瑷珲关 / 大黑河 1923 年 4 月 28 日

尊敬的海关总税务司（北京）：

哈尔滨关致海关总税务司署第 2823 号呈抄件及海关总税务司署致哈尔滨关第 3052/93906 号令抄件收悉：

"关于由海关管理中国及无约各国轮船船长及船员雇用事宜的建议。"

随呈附上超等外班关员博韩（G. E. Baukham）先生的报告，据报告所示，黑龙江华岸之现状与松花江一样堪忧。

博韩先生于报告中列举了一件船主与租船人忽视合同与公平之事。戊通航业公司于 1922 年航运季雇用了三名俄籍引水员，雇佣合同本署已见，乃常规俄汉双语合同。然就在所有轮船皆已雇用当年航运季的船员时，戊通航业公司哈尔滨总部突然发来指示，以相关轮船将在当年航运季中暂停使用为由，解雇了该三名引水员，且未给予任何补偿。本署与戊通航业公司和海关监督取得联系后，指出这一轻率解雇三名引水员且不给予补偿之行为着手令人震惊，且非常不公。戊通航业公司表示其必须听从哈尔滨总部的指示，而海关监督虽表示会与戊通航业公司商讨，但最终仍是不了了之。

因此，若能由海关管理船长和船员的雇用事宜，相信情况必将有所改善，亦会使海关更有威望。只要当地政府能够不加阻拦，海关便可建立起坚实的管理体制。

兹提议，说动瑷珲关海关监督兼交涉司支持哈尔滨关税务司之提议；与此同时，若可于大黑河口岸开设港务课，此次行动将更为合理。但在行动前，本署希望能收到哈尔滨关所提之《船长合同》（Ship's Articles）抄件，毕竟各方保持一致至关重要。

此抄件发送至巡工司及哈尔滨关税务司。

您忠诚的仆人

包安济（G. Boezi）

瑷珲关署理税务司

附件

关于由海关管理中国和无约各国轮船船长及船员雇用事宜的建议

超等外班关员办公室

瑷珲关 / 大黑河 1923 年 4 月 20 日

本人已仔细阅读了哈尔滨关税务司致海关总税务司署第 2823 号呈以及哈尔滨关理船厅阿布兰森（H. Abrahamsen）先生的报告，对于哈尔滨关区轮船船长、工程师以及船员受到其中国及俄国雇主不公对待，又得不到补偿之情况已然了解。事实上，大黑河口岸亦是如此，黑龙江上轮船船长、驾驶员以及船员的雇用情况与松花江上相同。

中国轮船：在瑷珲关，最大的中国船运机构是戊通航业公司，最大的俄国船运机构则是俄阿穆尔国家水运局；当然，也还有其他一些小公司，但所拥有的轮船数量与上述两大机构毫无可比性。然而，即使是最大的船运机构，其与驾驶员和船员所签订的合同亦毫无保障可言。

以去年发生在本口岸的一件事情为例：当时正值 5 月，航运开通之前，三名俄籍引水员找到本人，称戊通航业公司原本雇用他们于今年航运季期间为其工作（双方已签署合同），然而就在即将开船之时，戊通航业公司哈尔滨总部却发来电报，称不再需要他们继续工作，薪水仅发放至电报送达当日，对于航运季剩下的时间亦无任何赔偿。三名俄籍引水员表示，他们一直遵守合同等待开船，却在航运开通之时收到被解雇的消息，若早知会被解雇，还可以去其他轮船应征，但如今其他轮船均已满员，为时已晚，在航运季剩下的时间里都将难以找到任何工作，还要面对整个冬季都难以维持生计的困境，而戊通航业公司对于这一切却连一个合理的解释都没有；而且三名俄籍引水员皆声称自己还背负着养家糊口的重担。本人随后将此事呈报税务司，税务司又将此事告知海关监督，但最终也未得到任何解决；没有任何一方对这些惨遭解雇的船员予以任何帮助或补偿。本人建议他们前往哈尔滨，向理船厅投诉此事。他们接受了本人的建议，但同时也表示不敢在中国的法庭上与戊通航业公司正面对抗，因为该公司是中国公司，又在一定程度上隶属于政府。

中国人租赁的俄国轮船：在雇佣手续和规定方面，瑷珲关与哈尔滨关完全相同：租船人可以雇用任何其认为合适的船员，而受雇之人大多毫无航海经验，无法胜任船员工作；但又无权力机构对船员进行资格检查，如此势必会威胁到航运安全。租船人往往以压低运营成本为首要考虑；比如，只要情况允许，其绝不会雇用一名合格的工程师，而是会选择雇用一名机师，或是润滑工，只要他们会启动关闭发动机，会进行一些简单的修理即可。小公司很少考虑雇用不称职的船员会给乘客的人身安全以及航运安全带来怎样的危害。

如果向那些在中国人租赁的俄国轮船上工作的船员询问当初是如何被雇用的，他们往往会出示一张纸，上面的字迹多已模糊不清，难以辨认。这就是他们的合同，亦是一张毫无法律效力的废纸。船主或租船人可以随时忽视这份"合同"，拒绝向船员支付薪水；如果船员是俄国人，那么这种可能性会更大。而俄籍船员大多不会尝试通过中国法庭讨回公道，因为他们担心中国法庭并不会给予他们应有的保护。

俄国人所有并经营的轮船：对于俄国人所有并经营的轮船（船员亦为俄籍），船员雇用等事宜皆由俄国船运委员会（Russian Shipping Board）管理，制度颇为完善。凡受雇之船长、驾驶员以及船员，均会收到一本册子（样式与英国水手名册类似），上面载有雇佣详情。船主若想解雇员工，必须提前一个月（或两周）向该员工发出通知；合同有效期通常为一个航运季，特别是对于船长和驾驶员。船主若拒绝支付船员薪水，船员可向俄阿穆尔国家水运局投诉，水运局会委派一名"专员"到船上，告知船主按照合同支付薪水；船主若仍不照办，便会被告上法庭；船主若申请破产，其轮船及财产将被批准拍卖，拍卖所得收益优先用以偿付船员薪水。

兹坚信，若由海关管理轮船驾驶员及船员的雇用事宜，不仅可以提高海关在松花江和黑龙江上的威信，更有利于推进相关事宜的"规范化"（阿布兰森先生如是说）。

博韩（G. E. Baukham）

二等验货前班

超等外班关员

致瑷珲关第 <u>130/94546</u> 号令　　　　海关总税务司署（北京）1923 年 5 月 31 日

尊敬的哈尔滨关税务司：

　　根据第 109 号呈：

　　"哈尔滨关税务司关于海关管控中国和非条约国船只船长及船员的提议，同样对黑龙江的管理也十分有益。"

　　奉总税务司命令，兹告知：批准贵署按上述提议执行。贵署应当向哈尔滨关税务司索要一份《船长合同》（也称《船员雇佣合同》）副本，并与之协商之后，再拟定具体提议，以便在重要事项上保持一致性。

　　同时，此令副本已抄送给哈尔滨关税务司。

您忠诚的仆人

威厚澜（R. H. R. Wade）

代理总务科税务司

致瑷珲关第 <u>170/98543</u> 号令　　　　　海关总税务司署（北京）1924 年 4 月 28 日

尊敬的瑷珲关税务司：

　　根据第 109 号呈及海关总税务司署第 130/94546 号令批复：

　　　　"关于海关管控中国和非条约国船只船长及船员的提议。"

　　为了便于贵署顺利执行，兹附华方税务处第 474 号令，以供参考。据该令所示，为了增强海关对中国和非条约国船只船长及船员的管理，哈尔滨关税务司提议在其口岸实施《船长合同》（也称《船员雇佣合同》），中国政府已批准在瑷珲关实施该《合同》。因此，贵署需督促该《合同》的落实。若哈尔滨关监督对此没有异议，哈尔滨关税务司即可奉命在其口岸实施该《合同》。

　　随函附寄经修订且由税务处批准的《合同》中文版副本。

您忠诚的仆人

安格联（F. A. Aglen）

海关总税务司

13. 为免税放行东北航务局轮船自用薪材数量不超过 40000 俄丈事

[A.—29]

No. 254   COMMRS.

Aigun   No. 104,843

INSPECTORATE GENERAL OF CUSTOMS,

PEKING,   23rd September 1925.

INDEXED

Sir,

With reference to I. G. despatch No. 80/91,299 :

Wood fuel for use of steamers of the Wu T'ung Navigation Company（戊通航業公司）to be passed free of duty up to a maximum quantity of 40,000 sajen a year:

I append, for your information and guidance, copy of Shui-wu Ch'u despatch No. 1167, from which you will see that the Wu T'ung Navigation Company having been reconstructed into the North East Navigation Bureau（東北航務局）, under the auspices of the Government of the Three Eastern Provinces, the duty exemption originally accorded to the wood fuel for the use of the steamers

of

The Commissioner of Customs,

A I G U N.

of the former and afterwards revoked by the Kirin Provincial authorities owing to the privilege being abused, is to be renewed and wood fuel for the use of the steamers of the North East Navigation Bureau is to be exempted from duty up to a maximum of 40,000 sajen a year.

You are requested to act accordingly and to make arrangements with the Harbin office whereby the aggregate quantity of wood fuel passed free by both offices for the steamers of the North East Navigation Bureau is kept within the maximum laid down.

I am,

Sir,

Your obedient Servant,

Officiating Inspector General, ad interim.

Appendix.

Appendix.

I. G. despatch No. 254 to Aigun

稅務處令第一一六七號 中華民國十四年九月十九日

准據歲上將軍公署咨開兼東北稅務局常務董事王顧存經理王錫爭呈稱查該局輪船

二十二艘每年燃用木样不下數萬斤曩如照前捐或徵鉅前戊通公司會於民國十

一年間呈准交通部及成務處分別令行吉江兩省財政廳及嫩江開監督准

照我國江內各輪船自帶燃用柴斤一律免稅成例凡係戊通輪船自用木样每年以四萬

沙龍爲敕一律免前捐戈通有在吉林境內將瓦項免稅木样轉運人前事

政吉林省令將前案取前兩江省至今尚予難待原案茲藏局係由戊通收運爲東三省官

有事案每年歲局自用燃料自應援照成例請免稅前在職局改組伊始欵項支絀容免瓦

項戊款於局務不無裨益慶前每年均以四萬沙龍爲敕純係職局輪船自用决不得轉運

入懲分別每行就務處及吉江兩省一律准予難待原案容免稅前等商查該局輪船所燃

用木样既與我國內江各輪船自帶之燃料事同一律自應援照免稅成例與前戊通公司

之當案一列辦理以示難待容行轉筋照辦等因前來查本處前於民國十一年九月間會

准财政部来函以戊通航业公司本届官商合办年来药枭越钜其自用木柴拟可准予酌
免戎捐等因当以论船自享燃用菜厅间准免戎戊通就枭公司各论船所用木柴亦系供
作论烟嵩料之用既藻该公司藻海年来药枭越钜应通融准予免戎每年以四万沙柜为
限至木石局捐应由部博前一审酌免等语於迠月十三日令行滨江辉春爱煇等捐盗营
缝慝戎务司薄令各该辉戎务司运辨各在案此灭柬亡戎捐局请将该局论船自用木柴
爰案备免戎捐既蒸案辨该局系由戊通文祖为柬三百官有事柬且规该局论船自用
决不專每他人後與戊通就枭公司自用木柴免戎戎案同属用将应册通融准予免戎每
年为以西万沙柜为限至木石局捐应否一审备免应出财政部後辨余否復嵌並分令外阳
应令行代理熟戎扬司薄令滨江延旨爱煇等捐充务司查照辨理此令

宜连山司校
周铭明司校

致瑷珲关第 <u>254/104843</u> 号令　　　　海关总税务司署（北京）1925 年 9 月 23 日

尊敬的瑷珲关税务司：

根据海关总税务司署第 80/91299 号令：

"戊通航业公司轮船自用薪柴免税放行，每年以 40000 俄丈（沙绳）为限。"
为了便于贵署顺利执行，兹附税务处第 1167 号令，以供参考。据该令所示，戊通航业公司重组并入东北航务局，受东三省政府的庇护。据载，原戊通航业公司轮船自用薪材最初享有免税优惠政策，但之后由于滥用特权，吉林省省政府撤回政策，现将恢复免税政策，东北航务局轮船自用薪材予以免税，每年以 40000 俄丈为限。

请遵照此令执行，并与哈尔滨关协商安排，确保两关免税放行的东北航务局轮船自用薪材数量不超过 40000 俄丈。

您忠诚的仆人

泽礼（J. W. Stephenson）

暂代代理海关总税务司

14. 为建议在航海季雇用轮船工程师事

MOTOR BOAT ENGINEER: competent man to be engaged as, for navigation season only, recommending.

412

I. G.

Aigun   21st March, 1929.

Registered.

Sir,

I have the honour to submit for your favourable consideration a recommendation that a qualified chauffeur be taken on locally to be put in charge of the Aigun Customs motor-boat.

My experience here with Chinese Boatmen trained for the purpose has been anything but satisfactory. Last summer, for example, a defect in the pump of the engine was not noticed by the Boatman in charge until a cylinder had heated up and cracked entailing expensive repairs this winter.

As it happens, many experienced Chinese and Russian chauffeurs in Taheiho are out of employment during the summers when the roads are too soft for motor-buses to ply. A competent man from amongst these can be engaged each year for the navigation season from 1st May to 1st November (7 months) at $50 per month. He

would

THE INSPECTOR GENERAL OF CUSTOMS,
SHANGHAI.

would replace a Boatman who would ordinarily
be kept on at from \$25 to \$30 per month the
year round, with little to do in the winter,
so that the expense to the Service would be
practically the same. At the same time we
would have the services of a competent and
reliable man who would give the engine the
attention it requires while running, and navigate
the motor-boat safely.

If my recommendation meets with your
approval I would propose to engage a suitable
man from the 1st May for the 1929 navigation
season at a maximum of \$50 per month; the salary
paying rate for the current month is Harbin
\$212 = Hk.Tls.100. The Boatman in charge of
the motor-boat last year was discharged in December
and was not replaced.

I should add that the time of Mr.
V. Z. Lankin, engaged originally as Mechanic on
the authority of I. G. despatch No. 77/91,035
sanctioning the purchase of the motor-boat, is
now fully employed in carrying out the duties of
2nd Class Tidewaiter but that he completely
overhauls the hull and engine of the motor-boat
every winter and has kept the engine in repair
in the summer.

I have the honour to be,

Sir,

Your obedient Servant,

Acting Commissioner.

呈海关总税务司署 <u>412</u> 号文　　　　　　　　　璦珲关 1929 年 3 月 21 日

尊敬的海关总税务司（上海）:

　　兹建议在当地雇用可以负责管理瑷珲关轮船的合格驾驶员，望贵署酌情考虑。

　　本署在此与受过专门培训的华籍船员相处之后，不甚满意。如去年夏天，因负责的船员未能察觉发动机泵有问题，以致气缸升温炸裂，为此今冬需要支付高额的维修费用。

　　与此同时，大黑河夏天道路过软，公共汽车不宜通行，很多经验丰富的中俄汽车司机因此而失业。其中一定有人可以胜任船员之职，便可于每年航运季来工作，即 5 月 1 日至 11 月 1 日（共 7 个月），每月薪俸 50 银圆。全年工作的船员每月薪俸为 25 到 30 银圆，但冬日几乎无事可做，因此该项工作的实际支出并无改变。此外，也需要一位合格可靠之人负责该项工作，既能留心发动机的运行状况，又能安全驾驶轮船。

　　若此建议获得批准，本署提议 1929 年航运季从 5 月 1 日起择一合适人选，每月薪俸最低 50 银圆；哈尔滨当月薪俸支付汇率为 212 银圆 =100 海关两。去年负责管理轮船的船员于 12 月卸职，未有接替之人。

　　需要补充的是，海关总税务司署第 77/31035 号令批准购买摩托艇，并任命兰金（V. Z. Lankin）先生为匠董。现在兰金先生全职担任二等稽查员，每年冬天对摩托艇的船体和发动机彻底检修，夏天进行发动机的保养工作。

您忠诚的仆人

铎博赉（R. M. Talbot）

瑷珲关署理税务司

录事：黎彭寿　四等二级帮办

专题五

江捐税率

1. 为汇报俄方拟议的江捐征收税率事

Aigun / Taheiho 23rd April, 1922.

Sir,

1.   With reference to your telegrams of 17th and 18th April, and to mine of 13th and 21st April :

> concerning the russian proposal to take in hand the Aids-to-Navigation on the Amur and to levy River Dues on both sides of the River to meet the expenses thereof ;

I have the honour to report that for some time past I had known that something on this line was being prepared by the Russians. On a visit to the Directors of the Russian Navigation Office on the 6th instant I was asked by these gentlemen to give my support in securing the cooperation of the Chinese Government to their plans for improving the conditions of navigation on the Amur. I agreed with them

Inspector General of Customs,
      P E K I N G.

them that the matter was urgent, but of course could not pledge my support without having first ascertained your point of view, and the opinion of the Chinese Authorities. I only added that I expected the Chinese Government to claim a share in the supervision, in return for the contribution towards the expenses - and they said it was their intention to call a meeting of the interested in order to discuss the question.

2.　　　　I immediately went and saw the Taoyin-Superintendent, and reported these matters, which were new to him; I explained how matters stood in the opinion of the late Mr. Garden, River Inspector, who was here in 1918, carried out an inspection of the Aids-to-Navigation on the Chinese side as far as Moho, and was in 1919 appointed to Taheiho with a view to partecipating in negotiations for a joint control by Russia and China of Amur "Aids". The points in which the Taoyin made up his mind were 1) that China should have supervision of the works and expenditure; 2) that the collection on the Chinese side should be in Chinese hands, and 3)

that

that a single Administration would be better. He

wired to the Provincial Authorities for instructions

and asked me to study the question and to get

information.

3.　　On the 10th the Board of Directors of

the Russian Navigation Office called on me, and I

tried to get all the information I could. The gene-

ral lines of the Tariff they propose to apply I

wired you in my telegram of 13th; they are as

follows :

For certain categories of goods, chiefly grains

and Piece-Goods, 1 cent (1 kopek) per pood;

For other goods generally, 2 cents a pood;

For Firewood, 15 to 20 cents a square (not

cubic, as wired by mistake) sajen;

For Timber, a tax corresponding to the amount

that would be levied if the timber was sawn

up into firewood (which is generally the case);

For Horses and Cattle, 30 cents a Head;

For Sheep, Goats, Pigs, 15 cents a Head;

For Passengers, 5% on the cost of the tickets.

The Tax to be the same (except for passengers)

for any distance travelled over along the Amur;

The Tax to be received only once on the same

goods; i. e. re-exports duly covered by receipts to be

exempted, and goods conveyed f om one shore to the

other to pay only once — with the exception of

goods

goods carried by Ferry, which should not pay at all, owing to the short distance travelled.

The Tax to be uniformly levied on Steamers, Junks and Rafts.

The Arrangement to be provisional for 1922.

The Tariff is rather heavy, but the Amur is a very long River with not much traffic.

I took the opportunity, the same day, to ascertain whether the Russians would agree to the principles tentatively laid down by the Taoyin; I made my enquiries without giving these principles as either decided upon by the Chinese Authorities, nor as my own ideas, but simply as what the Chinese Government _may_ ask for. - The Directors found these principles quite natural, and said for their part they would certainly not object. They explained that all the materials, the launches, the staff, the organisation was ready to start working at the opening of the navigation; what lacks, is money to run the "Aids". Their intention is to work on the most economical plans; in fact they said that, comparatively, the cost would be one tenth of the cost of upkeep on the Sungari (which seems an exaggeration).

I

I pointed out that moneys collected and contributed by China should, in my opinion, be used for the frontier section of the Amur, in the same proportion as the Russian receipts for the same stretch of the River, and they agreed, only hinting at the possibility of including the Ussuri and Argun.

They said that a meeting would be held in Blagovestchensk on the 23rd, and asked me to be present. - The same day they also called on the Taoyin, and spoke of their proposals to him.

4.   I then saw the Taoyin, and he decided to call a meeting of the Chamber of Commerce and Shipping Companies for the 13th, at which I was present. The Chamber of Commerce showed a preference for Tonnage Dues, the Hut'ung S. S. Co for River Dues; they all agreed that to apply the same tax for any distance would not be fair, and decided to study the question between themselves and to arrive at an understanding as to their desiderata before the meeting with the Russians. - I made it clear to the Taoyin that I could do nothing without having consulted you, and it was agreed that he would also wire to the

Shui Wu Ch'u

Shui Wu Ch'u and the Wai Chiao Pu reporting the circumstances and asking for instructions.

5.   On receipt of your telegrams of 17th and 18th, suggesting that a better plan would be to leave the entire collection in russian hands according to a Tariff to be mutually agreed upon, and to credit, say, one half of the total collection as China's share of cost of Administration, I again called on the Taoyin and asked his opinion on this suggestion which presents obvious advantages; but he clearly said that he would not favour this course from the point of view of Chinese amour propre, and because he thought it would be unsafe and open to abuses to let the Russians collect on the Chinese side. He further shoed me a telegram received from the Wai Chiao Pu, generally approving the Taoyin's suggestions, and asking him to arrange for a provisional agreement for 1922 ; he also stated that the merchants would like to pay the Dues to the Shipping Companies, which should, in turn, be responsible to the Customs. - As to the meeting in Blagovestchensk, the Taoyin thought it would be better not to go,

because

because the crossing is now slow and dangerous, and it is not impossible to be blocked by drifting ice once over there; also because the _agenda_ of the meeting includes any amount of questions which have nothing to do with the "Aids", and concern the internal russian organisation of their shipping. The Taoyin believes it is better to meet after internal affairs have been settled on both sides, and proposes himself to call a meeting in a few days, after having ascertained the best time for it, and which russian authorities are to be asked.

6.　　In compliance with your instructions, I have calculated the probable collection, should the proposed Tariff be applied independently by the C. M. Customs at Aigun-Taheiho, and I communicated the results in my telegram of yesterday (21st april).

The calculation is very rough because 1) goods imported by water and re-exported also by water should be exempted - but in our Returns we do not distinguish re-exports originally imported by River from those originally imported overland, so that the amount of re-exports which should pay River Dues

cannot

cannot be ascertained; 2) it is hard to guess the amount of goods carried by ferry; 3) I have no details as to which goods besides grains and piece-goods should pay one cent per pood - and the difficulty of crossing over prevents me from getting more accurate information; 4) because the weight of many commodities can only be guessed from the number of pieces or value, which alone are given in our Returns.

Excluding re-exports and ferry traffic, in 1921 there have been, roughly, 750,000 poods of grains and piece goods carried by water; @ $ 0.01 per pood, they would have yielded $ 7,500-

400,000 poods of other goods, @ 2 cents $ 8,000-

177 cattle and horses, @ 30 cents $ 5-

30,000 sajens firewood, @ 20 cents $ 6,000-

timber carried by steamers and junks, the equivalent of sajens 25,000 @ 20 cents $ 5,000-

up-river passengers, 14,585 - approximate value of tickets $ 47,000 @ 5 % $ 2,350-

passengers for the Sungari, 17,826 - value of tickets @ 123,000 @ 5 % $ 6,150-

Total excluding rafts $ 35,05-

Rafts

Forward $ 35,055-

Rafts (excluding amount subsequently exported by steamers and already accounted for under timber) the equivalent of 25,000 sajens, @ 20 cents $ 5,000-
                                                      ——————
        Total including rafts $ 40,055-

        In the idea of the Russians, however, goods carried between points unprovided with a Custom House should pay as well, according to Steamers' Manifests; I have no basis for estimating the amount that could be collected under this heading; but it would certainly be very much less than dues on goods taxed at Aigun-Tsheihe.

7.   You will see from the foregoing that the whole question is still rather vague: no documents have been exchanged, no definite proposals have been made, other than a few principles, and a tentative tax submitted by the Russians, while it is proposed to settle all details in a meeting; of course, many points are at issue, and things cannot be settled in a moment, I am afraid; but on the other hand I would like to do everything possible for a speedy arrangement, and I shall wire again in case of further developments.

        That the taking in hand of the "Aids" is

                                                      urgent

urgent is proved by the numerous accidents to shipping
during the 1921 season, mostly due to lack of information on the conditions of the channels and shallows.
The Russian Navigation Office had 27 ships damaged,
including two destroyed; the Wutung Company, one entirely destroyed and several damaged; other companies in
proportion. Insurance changes were also very high, not
so much on account of Hunghutze, which were almost
absent from the Amur, as of unsafe navigation.

The present moment is also very opportune
for concluding an Agreement which, although provisional,
will create usuful precedents. So far, in the semi-
official conversations which have taken place, the
Russians have admitted the principle of equality with
China; they have not denied the right of Chinese
Steamers to navigate the Amur to the sea; they have
not mentioned yet the question of compensation by
China for the work and materials previously expended
by Russia on Aids-to-Navigations, which will now benefit the shipping of both countries. On the other
hand, the present Administration of the Russian
Navigation Office is based on technical, rather than
political, grounds, and is likely to last, even should
the

the Government change - while the Far Eastern Republic is in better shape than before and may very well turn into a stable Government, possibly under the aegis of Moscow.

8.   The political issue, however, is for the Taoyin to consider, and he has already received instructions to negotiate, on the following basis :1) the Agreement to be valid for 1922; 2) Tariff to be arranged locally; 3) the collection to be preferably undertaken by the respective Customs in China and Russia; 4) joint Administration - or control by China on work and expenditure; 5) the materials to be supplied by Russia. I would add a) that the money collected in China must be solely used, in equal proportion with the Russian collection, in the upkeep of the "Aids" in the frontier waters; b) that China should not be responsible for expenses in excess of the collection which the Russians declare should be enough.

9.   From a technical point of view, I concur in the opinion of the late Mr. Carden, that **one** Administration for the two sides is essential to the smooth and efficient operation of the "Aids". I would

possibly

possibly exclude the Argun for the present, because there is very little navigation there, according to reports - as to the Ussuri, I would like to have the Harbin Commissioner's opinion on the advisability of including it, and on how duties may be collected.

10. As to the mode of taxation, I would prefer Tonnage Dues; collection would be very simple and easy, and the charge would be evenly redistributed upon the cargo, under the shape of a slight increase in freight rates. The only difficulty is, that the Russians have more steamers and less cargo than the Chinese, and are afraid of being the losers in the bargain. - The amount of Tonnage Dues to be levied could only be calculated after the Russians have supplied a budget of the estimated expenditure, and after having ascertained the tonnage of all the vessels plying on the Amur. In order to levy the $ 35,000 - 40,000 (collectable by applying the Tariff independently at Aigun-Paheiho) the rate should be about $ 2.50 per ton for the season on steamers, unless the tax on passengers be made a separate charge, in which case it would not be over $ 2.00 (for the Chinese side only). Should Tonnage Dues be

adopted,

adopted, I venture to suggest that it be levied monthly instead of quarterly, because steamers are easily laid up, and cannot afford to pay a heavy tax for nothing, even for a short period.

11.   The levy of River Dues would meet with certain difficulties : 1) we could only collect at Aigu - Taheiho, and, possibly, at Lahasusu; on cargo between intermediate ports, we could only collect _a posteriori_ according to Manifests - thus trusting Shipping Companies too much; 2) it is nearly impossible to graduate the rates of duty according to distances on a long River like the Amur (and eventually the Ussuri and Argun), where there are so many Ports of call on both sides -; on the other hand, merchants object, with reason, to a single rate for all distances, as proposed by the Russians; 3) to ascertain the weight of many goods which are not classified by weight according to our Tariffs, we must rely again on the Shipping Orders, unless we throw the task on our Examiners' shoulders, already burdened enough.

12.   The proposal conveyed in your telegram of 17th instant would simplify matters, both as regards

                                        collection

collection and administration. But the Taoyin is not

in favour of it, and I must add that it would be

inconvenient even for us to have the Russians

collect River Dues in Tsheihe or Aigun Harbour, on

the many steamers which do not touch the Russian

shore: especially with the present Russian Administra-

tion, which does not give yet full guarantees of

fair play, this course would be open to abuses, and

it would besides inconvenience the merchants who

should subject their goods and documents to the

double inspection of the Customs and the Administra-

tion of the Aids-to-Navigation, losing much time in

landing and shipping cargo.

In case an Agreement is reached, I believe

that a River Inspector, possibly with a good

knowledge of the russian language, or else with a

Russian Assistant, would be the most suited repre-

sentative of China in the Administration of the

Aids-to-Navigation, and I hope you could see your

way to appointing one, should the Chinese Government

require his services as in a previous occasion.

Copy of this despatch is sent to the

Harbin

Harbin Commissioner.

            I have the honour to be,

               Sir,

           Your obedient Servant,

             Acting Commissioner.

Garden's Report

FURTHER REPORT ON THE AMUR RIVER.

    The Inspector General in his despatch No.10,457/71,173, Shanghai, dated the 2nd November, 1918, asks for my views on the following questions concerning the administration of the Amur River:-

(a) Whether there would be any technical difficulties in the way of China administering the Aids service on the Chinese bank of the river?

(b) If the nature of the work is such that it could only be conveniently handled by one administration?

(c) In the latter case, would it be practicable for a joint Russo-Chinese Commission to undertake the work?

(d) What expenditure would this involve for China - supposing such an arrangement were made - in initial outlay, in ships, staff, etc?

    Before answering the above questions it would be as well to first consider the system of marking the Amur River and the actual conditions of the channels thus marked at the different stages of the water in the river.

    As I stated in my recent report on the Amur River, the river is marked by a system of beacons and, during low water, buoys in addition. The beacons are either single or transit beacons as will be seen on the accompanying chart of the Amur River.

    The single beacons indicate that the channel is on that side of the river nearest the beacon or mark a point vessels are to make or leave when crossing over from one side of the river to the other.

    The transit beacons, which may be either double or treble beacons, indicate, in the case of double beacons, that when kept in line they lead vessels through the deepest water in the channel.

channel up to the point where the next set of double beacons
come into line. In the case of treble beacons, which are beacons
having one beacon in common - generally the one nearest to the
river bank - they indicate that the channel above and below them
is between shoals and that the beacons, if kept in line
alternately, steering in on one pair of beacons and out on the
other, will lead vessels through the deepest water in the channel.

To understand more fully this system of beacons a study of
the accompanying chart of the Amur River will explain their uses
more clearly.

Buoys are used in conjunction with beacons, at low water
only, to mark the sides of the channel when the channel is
narrow and/or tortuous and to assist vessels in keeping in the
deepest water.

The main channel of the Amur River does not appreciably
change but many of the channels over the shallows change and
alter their course frequently, as will be seen by Appendix No.III
of my original report. The principle changes take place as a
rule after high water but many smaller changes, such as banks
forming, extending, etc., take place at other stages of the
water in the river. At times channels over the shallows will
silt up and others form in a different direction, and places on
the river which were considered shallows will scour out and other
shallows form some distance above or below them. These constant
changes, sometimes happening very quickly, call for careful and
constant watching of the channels, especially during the
critical periods after high water. The new channels formed have
then to be marked, beacons and/or buoys moved, perhaps from one
side of the river to the other, discontinued or new aids
established.

It will be seen from the above that when the changes in the
channels occur the marking of them has to be effected
expeditiously. To do this it is essential that such work, and
also the work of keeping track of the changes in the channels,

should be under one administration.

If China decided to administer the Aids on Chinese territory and in Chinese waters of the Amur River it would lead to confusion and perhaps friction between the Chinese and Russian river authorities. Delays in marking the channels would no doubt happen or aids would be left in position which were no longer aids to navigation and would therefore constitute a serious danger to shipping. Not only would such a state exist but when cases of this nature did occur the present system of marking the Amur River - which I may state here is a most excellent one, if it is lavishly administered, for the conditions existing on that river - would be disorganized. Even if the two river authorities did work harmoniously it would mean that the Chinese and Russian authorities would each have to keep a staff at the different shallows and other men for attending to the lights and aids at other parts of the river.

The captains and pilots of vessels trading on the Amur River and tributaries are all of Russian nationality and were more or less under the control of the Amur River Administration in pre-war days. The powers vested with the Amur River Administration was paramount and therefore their special rules and regulations, issued for the safe navigation of the Amur River and tributaries, were strictly enforced and obeyed. If China took over the administration of the aids on Chinese territory and in Chinese waters there would, no doubt, be difficulties in the way to enforce such regulations which would have to be made by the river authorities, especially with those Russian steamers which trade on the Amur River between Harbarosk and Blagovestchensk and which do not call at a Chinese port.

As regards question (a): My opinion is that there would be many technical difficulties in the way of China administering the Aids service on the Chinese bank of the river.

I may state here, in case the question may crop up as to

whether

whether it would be possible to mark the Amur River by having
aids on one side of the river only, that I was informed that
the Russian Authorities did try to mark the river by having aids
only on Russian territory - all aids being discontinued on the
Chinese side of the river - but after a short trial found that
it was impracticable.

My answer to question (b) is that the aids marking the Amur
River can only be conveniently handled by one administration.

As regards question (c): It would be practicable but not
advisable for a joint Russo-Chinese Commission to undertake the
administration of the Amur River. I contend that the results
would not be so satisfactory as by having the administration
under one authority, and there would be disadvantages and perhaps
complications by having such a commission. In this connection
and also as regards question (d) I may be permitted to point out
the following:-

As stated above, the conditions on the Amur River are such
that the control of the administration can only be handled
efficiently by one administration. The Russian authorities have
organized, established and administered the system of marking
and governing the Amur River and have enjoyed that privilege for
many years. The employees of the Amur River administration have
been trained and brought up for the work and the technical men
may be considered experts in their particular line for work
connected with that river. Quarters for the executive staff
and offices have been built and established on Russian territory
in the most suitable positions for the administration of the
Amur River. Launches, dredgers, lighters, etc., of all
descriptions most suitable for the work on the river have been
built and engineering works and docks have been established for
their up-keep and repairs. I was given to understand that the
staff, or at least the majority of the staff, are entitled to a
pension after a certain number of years service or if they were

disabled in the execution of their duty and, besides this, they enjoy many other privileges.

It would appear from what I have written that it would be the best and most economical way for China to pay a certain amount down to the Russian authorities for what has already been done in the way of conservancy work and improvements on the Amur River for the initial outlay in ships, equipment, staff, etc., etc., and afterwards to pay a yearly sum towards the administration and upkeep in place of establishing a staff, ships, etc., for administering her part of the river in conjunction with the Russian Authorities at an enormous expense with no results to warrant such expenditure.

I feel sure that if the above arrangement was made that it would prove in the long run the most advantageous to all concerned and avoid the possibility of any complications. The administration of the river would then continue to be run on the same organized system which has proved to be the most satisfactory for the conditions existing on the Amur River.

If, however, in the opinion of the Chinese Authorities it was considered necessary to have someone to represent them on the Amur River then I would suggest that a technical man with tact and a knowledge of the Russian language, which is essential, or given an opportunity to learn it, be appointed. His headquarters should be at Taheiho so as to be in touch with the headquarters of the Amur River Administration at Blagovestchensk and at the same time he would be in the best position to attend to any part of the river requiring his services. He should have authority, which no doubt could be arranged between the two countries concerned, to have access to their premises, works, plans and charts of the river and the use of their vessels for inspection purposes when necessary. If the use of the vessels could not be arranged he should be provided with a suitable launch, having a small motor boat as tender and for work on the shallows, and a

man,

man, preferably of Russian nationality, with a thorough knowledge of the Amur River and its tributaries appointed as launch officer.

If it were necessary to carry out the above suggestions the estimated initial outlay in ships, staff, etc., in addition to the amount paid to the Russian Authorities for the improvements and work already done on the Amur River and for its yearly upkeep would be as follows for the first year:-

	Roubles.
One shallow draughted launch, preferably steam and wood consuming.	252,000.00.
One kerosene motor tender.	12,600.00.
One River Inspector @ Hk.Tls.500 per month.	75,600.00.
One Launch Officer @ Hk.Tls.100 per month.	15,120.00.
One Laodah @ Hk.Tls.14 per month.	2,116.00.
One No.2 Laodah and one Sailor-Carpenter @ Hk.Tls.12 per month each.	3,628.80.
Two Sailors @ Hk. Tls.10 per month each, for 6 months only.	1,512.00.
One No.1 Engineer @ Hk.Tls.50 per month.	7,560.00.
One No.2 Engineer @ Hk. Tls.25 per month.	3,780.00.
Two Firemen @ Hk. Tls.12 per month each, for 6 months only.	1,814.40.
Stores, oil, etc., for launch for 6 months.	15,120.00.
Total Roubles	390,852.00.

The rate of exchange is taken at the same rate as that given for the estimates in my original report, viz., Roubles 8.40 to one dollar or Roubles 12.60 to one Haikwan Tael.

The wages of two sailors and two firemen, also the cost of consumable stores, are only estimated for 6 months as the Amur River is only open to navigation for approximately six months in the year and therefore the services of these sailors and firemen would only be required when the launch was in commission.

In conclusion may I be permitted to point out that if China
  or pay towards the upkeep of,
decided to administer, the aids on Chinese territory and in Chinese waters marking the Amur River, which forms the boundary

between

between Chinese and Russian territory, the question may be brought up with regard to the administration of the Argun River, a branch of the upper part of Amur River and which also forms another part of the boundary between Chinese and Russian territory in the western part of Manchuria.   The Argun River is marked for a certain distance by a similar system as that by which the Amur River is marked and is under the same administration.   Up to the time of my recent inspection of the Amur River, however, no vessels under the Chinese flag had gone beyond Mo Ho T'ing and only two vessels under the Chinese flag had been to that place.

River Inspector.

呈海关总税务司署 44 号文　　　　　　　瑷珲关／大黑河 1922 年 4 月 23 日

尊敬的海关总税务司（北京）：

1. 根据海关总税务司署 4 月 17 日与 4 月 18 日电报，及瑷珲关 4 月 13 日与 4 月 21 日电报：

> "关于俄方提议由其管理黑龙江航路标志工作，并于黑龙江航道两岸征收江捐以支付相应支出之事。"

兹汇报，本署此前便已获悉俄方正在筹划此事。俄阿穆尔水道局各督办于 4 月 6 日与本署会面时便提出，希望本署可协助确保中国政府配合其计划，以改善黑龙江航务状况。本署认同此事十分紧急，但在未确认海关总税务司署及中国政府意见之前，不能贸然允诺，故仅表示期望中国政府承担相关费用后，可参与监督工作——俄方则表示希望双方可召开会议予以讨论。

2. 本署返回后便向道尹兼海关监督当面汇报此事，但道尹此前并不知晓此事。本署随后又向其说明已故巡江工司贾登（H. G. Garden）先生之意见。贾登先生于 1918 年巡查了黑龙江航道华岸（远至漠河一带）的航务情况，又于 1919 年接受任命来到大黑河口岸，以期参与中俄联合管理黑龙江航路标志的谈判工作。道尹认为：（1）中方应有权对航路标志工作及一应支出进行监督；（2）中方应于黑龙江航道华岸征税，及（3）该项事宜最好由单方管理。道尹已向省政府发送电报请求指示，同时命本署研究此事，获取信息。

3. 本署于 4 月 10 日与俄阿穆尔水道局各督办再次会面，并已尽量获取所有信息，随后于 4 月 13 日向海关总税务司署发送电报说明俄方提议使用的关税方针；如下：

特定种类货物，主要为谷物及按件货物，每普特 1 分（1 戈比）；

其他普通货物，每普特 2 分；

木桦，每平方（非立方，电报有误）俄丈 15 到 20 分；

木料，若木料锯成木桦（通常如此），按量征税；

马匹和牛，每头 30 分；

绵羊、山羊和猪，每头 15 分；

乘客，票面费用的 5%。

黑龙江航道沿线的货物运输（除乘客以外）无论里程长短，税率相同。

相同货物仅征一次税；即，复出口货物提供完税收据则免征税，从一岸运至另一岸的货物仅征一次税；但渡船所运货物除外，因运输里程较短，无须交税。

轮船、民船、木筏统一征税。

1922 年将做临时安排。

关税虽重，但黑龙江航道之航线虽长，运输却不是很多。

本署于 4 月 10 日亦借机确认俄方是否会暂时同意道尹所定之原则，但并未将此番原则说成是中国政府之决定，或本署之观点，仅将其称为中国政府或求之事。俄阿穆尔水道局各督办认为提出这些原则完全在情理之中，当然不会反对，并说明所有材料、汽艇、职员以及各项组织事宜，均已为航运季开始后的工作准备完毕；唯缺少"航路标志"资金，遂打算采用最为经济之办法；实际上俄方表示，黑龙江航道的维护费用可能仅为松花江航道维护费用的十分之一（似乎言过其实）。

本署指出，中方于黑龙江航道华岸所征税收及所供费用，应该用于黑龙江航道边界河段，且应与俄岸相同河段征收比例一致；俄方对此表示赞同，但暗示可能要将乌苏里江及额尔古纳河包括在内。

俄方提出会在 4 月 23 日于布拉戈维申斯克（Blagovestchensk）召开会议，邀请本署出席。此外，俄方同日亦拜访道尹，说明建议。

4. 本署遂面见道尹，道尹决定于 4 月 13 日召集商会及船运公司举行会议，本署亦列席。商会倾向征收船钞，而戊通公司倾向征收江捐；双方一致认为不分里程征税乃不公平之举，遂决定相互研究此事，以期与俄方开会之前，可按双方希求达成共识。同时，本署亦向道尹说明，在与海关总税务司署商定之前不会有任何行动，道尹亦会向税务处及外交部发送电报报告此情况，请求指示。

5. 收悉海关总税务司署 4 月 17 日及 18 日电报"建议最好经双方共同协定关税后，由俄方全权征税，征税总额的 50% 记入华方管理费用"后，本署便当面询问道尹对该建议（益处良多）有何看法；道尹明确表示出于民族自尊心，并不支持此做法，且若由俄方于华岸征税，恐会不安全，甚至招致谩骂。道尹遂将外交部电报示于本署，电报内容大致批准了道尹之建议，命其拟订 1922 年临时协议；道尹亦说明商人希望向船运公司交税，再由船运公司向海关负责。关于布拉戈维申斯克会议，道尹认为不宜赴会，目前横渡慢且危险，一旦过江，亦有受到浮冰阻挡之风险；再者会议议程包括与"航路标志"无关之事，涉及俄方内部船运组织事宜。道尹认为双方解决内部问题之后再行会面为较好之策，提出数日后待确定好最佳时机，将亲自召开会议，邀请俄国当局参会。

6. 按照海关总税务司指示，本署已计算出由中国海关按照拟议关税于瑷珲口岸和大黑河口岸征税的大概税收金额，并于 4 月 21 日电报中汇报了计算结果。

但计算结果非常不确切，因为:(1)经水运进口的货物再经水运复出口时免征税——但税收中并不区分复出口的货物原是经水运还是陆路进口而来，因此无法确定应支付江捐的复出口货物量;(2)难以预测渡船载货量;(3)不清楚除谷物及按件货物以外还有哪些货物应按每普特1分支付关税——目前因过江困难而无法获取更多精确信息;(4)很多货物只能通过件数或价值猜测重量，单独列于税收之中。

1921年除复出口及渡船运输之货物以外，经水运运输之货物税收情况估算如下：

谷物及按件货物大约为75万普特; 每普特0.01银圆，共计:	7500 银圆
其他货物400万普特; 每普特2分，共计:	8000 银圆
牛和马匹177头; 每头30分，共计:	53 银圆
木杆3万俄丈; 每俄丈20分，共计:	6000 银圆
轮船及民船运输之木料约25000俄丈; 每俄丈20分，共计:	5000 银圆
上游乘客14585人，票价约47000银圆; 按票面费用的5%征税，共计:	2350 银圆
总计（不包括木筏）:	35053 银圆
木筏运输之木料约25000俄丈 （由轮船接替出口及已计入木料项下者除外） 每俄丈20分，共计:	5000 银圆
总计（包括木筏）:	40053 银圆

但俄方认为，未设海关之地之间的货物运输亦应根据轮船舱口单交税；本署并无依据来估算此项征收税额，但定少于瑷珲口岸和大黑河口岸所征之税额。

7.由上述内容可知，整个问题依然不甚明朗:除道尹提出几项原则，俄方拟议暂行关税方针之外，中俄双方既未互换文件，亦无明确提议，不过已有提议欲在会议上解决所有细节问题;当然所有问题尚于讨论之中,恐怕非一时可解;但本署愿尽一切所能加快安排，若有进展定会电呈贵署。

1921年航运季期间船运事故频发，大多因为轮船不知河道及浅滩之状况，由此可证

"航路标志"管理工作的确迫在眉睫。俄阿穆尔水道局有 27 艘船只受损,其中两艘已毁;戊通公司有 1 艘船只彻底被毁,数艘受损;其他船运公司之船只亦相应受损。航运的保险费用非常之高,主要原因并非为土匪(红胡子),因其已几乎绝迹于黑龙江,主要因为航运不甚安全。

目前亦适于中俄双方缔结协议,虽为临时协议,但不失为有益之先例。迄今,中俄双方已进行数次半官方会谈,俄方已承认中俄平等原则,亦不否定中国轮船有权于黑龙江上航行,但并未提及中国对俄国此前航路标志工作及物料相关支出的补偿问题,毕竟两国船运如今均会受益于此。另外,俄阿穆尔水道局目前乃依靠技术进行管理,而非政治,因此即使俄国或将发生政变,以后亦极有可能依然以技术为管理基础。远东共和国的状况已有所改善,政府日趋稳定,或是受到莫斯科方面的庇护。

8. 然而,政治问题应为道尹所虑之事,其已接到指示,将按以下几点进行谈判:(1)协议于 1922 年有效;(2)由地方制定关税;(3)最好由中俄双方海关各自征税;(4)中俄双方联合管理或由中方管理航路标志工作及支出;(5)俄方提供物料。于此,本署欲补充:a. 中方所征税额必须专项用于边界河道航路标志维护工作,与俄方摊款比例相同;b. 若费用超出所征税额(俄方宣称此额足矣),中方不应予以承担。

9. 从技术角度出发,本署赞同已故巡江工司贾登(H.G.Garden)先生之意见,即只有中俄双方使用一个管理组织,方能顺利有效地开展"航路标志"工作。根据报告,额尔古纳河上的航务工作甚少,因此可能要暂时将其排除在外——关于乌苏里江,本署欲向哈尔滨关税务司征求意见,将乌苏里江包括在内是否可行,应如何征税。

10. 关于征税方式,本署倾向征收船钞;按船钞征税简单方便,费用可以重新平均分配于货物之上,只需略微提高运费即可。唯一的困难是,俄方轮船比中方多,但货物却相对较少,因此会担心在交易中失利。然而,关于征收船钞之数额,须待俄方提供支出预算,且所有往返于黑龙江航道的船只吨位得到确认后,方可予以计算。但若欲使征收税额达到 35000–40000 银圆(瑷珲口岸和大黑河口岸可单独征收之税额),则或将航运季轮船征收税率定为每吨 2.50 银圆,或将乘客征税单独计费,但税率不超过 2.00 银圆(仅限航道华岸)。若征收船钞,本署冒昧建议不要按季度征税,而是按月征税,因轮船容易闲置,若无所得难以承担重税,短期亦不可行。

11. 征收江捐将会面临之困难包括:(1)只能于瑷珲口岸和大黑河口岸征收江捐,或亦可于拉哈苏苏征收江捐,但对于中途转运港之间的货物运输,只能按照舱口单后验征收——如此便会过多依赖船运公司;(2)几乎无法于黑龙江(最终另有乌苏里江及额尔古纳河）如此长的航道之上按距离制定江捐税率,何况黑龙江航道两岸口岸众多,另一方面,商人有理由反对俄方不同里程费率相同之提议;(3)根据本署关税,很多货物并非按照重量归类,若要确定货物重量,则必须再次依靠装货单,要么则需将此任务交由已肩负重担的验货员。

12.海关总税务司署 4 月 17 日电报提议简化征税办法及管理事宜,但道尹并不赞同。于此,本署必须补充的是,于海关而言,若由俄方于大黑河口岸或瑷珲口岸征收江捐(很多轮船并不停靠俄罗斯口岸),将有诸多不便;尤其现在俄方的管理无法完全保证公平处事,这一做法亦会招致谩骂;商人需提交两次货物及海关凭证供海关及航务管理机构检查,除有不便外,亦会因装卸货物耗时过多。

若中俄双方可达成协议,兹认为适合于中俄航路标志管理组织中担任华方代表之人选应为一名巡江工司,但其应有良好的俄语能力或有一名俄国助理。若中国政府下达此类要求,望贵署可设法任命一名巡江工司。

此抄件发送至哈尔滨关税务司。

您忠诚的仆人

包安济（G. Boezi）

瑷珲关署理税务司

巡江工司贾登（H. G. Garden）先生

关于黑龙江航道之报告

总税务司（上海）于1918年11月2日海关总税务司署第10457/71713号令中，询问本人如何看待黑龙江航务管理事宜的如下问题：

1. 若由中国管理黑龙江航道华岸的航路标志工作，是否有技术难题？

2. 若由一个组织管理航路标志工作，是否更为妥当？

3. 若黑龙江航道的航路标志工作的确更适合由一个组织来进行管理，那么，若由中俄黑龙江水道委员会承担此工作，是否切实可行？

4. 若如此安排，中国需要承担多少费用，包括初期经费、船只、人员等？

在回答上述问题之前，首先要考虑到黑龙江航道的航路标志体系以及航道上不同水位的航路标志现状。

如本人近期于黑龙江航道相关报告中所述，黑龙江航道的航路标志使用的是标桩（立标），另于低水位配以浮标。标桩为单一标桩或直线（引导）标桩（参阅黑龙江航道航图）。

单一标桩标示航道在距离标桩最近的一侧，或是标注船只从航道一侧横渡至另一侧时的驶离地点。

直线（引导）标桩通常为两个标桩或三个标桩为一组。若为两个标桩连成一线，则标示此处为航道水位最深处，船只可直行至下一组双标桩连线之处；若为三个标桩（有一个为共享标桩，通常离河岸最近），则标示其上游及下游之航道介于浅滩之间，若标桩依次排列，船只则只要从前两个标桩处驶入、第三个标桩处驶出，便可自航道水位最深处驶过。

黑龙江航道航图中附标桩用途之详解，可供研究参考。

浮标会与标桩连用，但仅用于低水位处，标示航道狭窄及/或弯曲，指引船只保持在水位最深处航行。

黑龙江的主航道并无明显改变，但经由浅滩之航道却经常发生改变（参阅本人原报告的3号附录）。航道通常于高水位过后发生改变，而水位发生其他变化时，亦会导致航道发生很多较小之改变，如形成或延长河岸。有时跨越浅滩的航道会发生淤塞，随后于不同方向形成新的航道，而航道上原来的浅滩之处则会被冲开，另于其不远处或下游形成新的浅滩。这些变化不断发生，有时变化非常之快，因此需要时刻监察航道之变化，高水位过后尤为紧要。待新的航道形成后，需要重新竖立标桩、移动标桩及/或浮标，有时要将标桩从航道一侧移至另一侧，甚至拆除或重新建立航路标志。

由此可见，航道一旦发生变化，则需尽快重新标注。而若要如此，则须由一个管理组织来负责此类标注事宜及航道监察工作。

但若中国决定管理本国境内及黑龙江航道华岸的航路标志工作，中俄两国航路厅之间恐会有发生混乱甚至摩擦之险。航路标志工作定会因此而发生延迟之情况，或者在已不需要航路标志的地方依然立有标桩，船运安全将岌岌可危。不仅如此，黑龙江现行航路标志体系（可谓最优之体系），可能会因中俄双方的"过度"管理变得杂乱无章。即使中俄双方航路厅可以和谐共事，亦意味着中俄政府需各派一名职员驻守于各浅滩，还需派其他职员监察管理航道其他部分的标桩及其他航路标志等。

鉴于黑龙江航道及其支流上那些贸易船只的船主及引水员均为俄籍，且战前基本皆受阿穆尔水道局之管理，又因阿穆尔水道局极有权威，故所有船只能一致严格遵守阿穆尔水道局为黑龙江及其支流航务安全所颁发的特殊规章。然而，若中国接管本国境内及黑龙江航道华岸的航路标志工作，那么航路厅制定的此类章程定会难以施行，尤其对于那些在哈巴罗夫斯克（Harbarosk）与布拉戈维申斯克之间的黑龙江航道上进行贸易的俄国轮船，而这些俄国轮船亦不停靠于中国口岸。

关于问题（1）：兹认为，若由中国管理黑龙江航道华岸的航路标志工作，会有很多技术难题。

此外，关于是否可能仅于黑龙江航道华岸建立航路标志一事（贵署或有此疑问），特此说明，本人已获悉俄国政府的确曾尝试过仅于航道俄岸建立航路标志，而停止于华岸建立航路标志，但短时间的试验后，发现并不可行。

问题（2）：黑龙江航道的航路标志工作的确仅便于由一个组织来管理。

关于问题（3）：由中俄黑龙江水道委员会管理黑龙江航道的航路标志工作，可行但不明智。兹认为，虽然联合管理之结果不会如单方管理之结果那样令人满意，但成立中俄黑龙江水道委员会亦会有缺点，可能会过于复杂。关于此问题及问题（d），解释如下：

如上所述，基于黑龙江航道之状况，只有由一个组织管辖，航路标志工作方能有效开展。而多年来该工作一向由俄国政府负责，包括组织、建立及管理黑龙江航道的航路标志。俄阿穆尔水道局之职员均为此受过培训，技术人员可谓是航道工作方面的专业人士。此外，俄国政府已于最适合之地点搭建了职员宿舍及办公楼，以便于管理黑龙江航道；建造了最适合航道工作的各种汽艇、疏浚船及驳船等，亦为维修船只组织工程工作，搭建码头。据悉，俄阿穆尔水道局之职员或至少大多职员于工作一定年限后，或于执行任务时不幸致残,均有权得到养老储金,甚至额外享有很多其他特权。

如此可见,于中国而言,最佳、最经济之办法似乎应为:为已完成的黑龙江航道维护工作,向俄方支付一定数额的初期经费,包括船只、设备、职员等相关费用,之后每年支付一定的管理维护费用,而无须为中俄联合管理黑龙江航道的华方管理工作委派职员、船只等,毕竟若如此行事,不但费用巨大,而且结果亦无法保证。

兹认为,从长远来看,上述安排定会使所有相关方实现利益最大化,同时避免问题复杂化。航道管理工作亦可继续有序进行,毕竟事实已证实如此管理最适合于黑龙江航道之现状。

但若中国政府认为关于黑龙江航道之工作必须有中国代表出面,则建议,任命一位谨慎且知晓俄语(或有机会学习俄语)的专业人士。其任职地点应设于大黑河,一方面便于与布拉戈维申斯克的阿穆尔水道局联络,另一方面便于处理有关黑龙江航道的必要事务。其应有权(中俄双方定可安排)进入俄阿穆尔水道局,了解各项工事和计划,查阅航道航线图,如有必要亦可使用其船只进行巡查。若无船只可用,俄方应提供适当的汽艇,配有小型摩托艇,可做驳船,亦便于浅滩工作,还需委派一名小轮驾驶员,最好为俄籍,且需充分了解黑龙江航道及其支流。

若按上述建议执行,除向俄方支付已完成的黑龙江航道改善工作及每年的维护费用以外,第一年的船只、职员等初期经费预算如下:

事项	卢布
1 艘浅吃水船(最好为汽艇)燃烧木料	252000.00
1 艘摩托艇(可作驳船之用)燃烧煤油	12600.00
1 名巡江工司,每月 500 海关两	75600.00
1 名小轮驾驶员,每月 100 海关两	15120.00
1 名水手长,每月 14 海关两	2116.00
1 名副水手长及 1 名水手兼木匠,每人每月 12 海关两	3628.80
2 名水手,每人每月 10 海关两,仅 6 个月	1512.00
1 名管轮,每月 50 海关两	7560.00
1 名副管轮,每月 25 海关两	3780.00
2 名火夫,每人每月 12 海关两,仅 6 个月	1814.40
汽艇仓储、用油等,仅 6 个月	15120.00
卢布共计:	390852.00

此乃按照本人原报告中所述之兑换汇率计算，即8.40卢布兑换1银圆，或12.60卢布兑换1海关两。

鉴于黑龙江航道的航运季仅开放约6月之久，而只有使用汽艇之时方可用到水手及伙夫，故两名水手及两名火夫之薪俸，以及仓储费用仅为6个月之预算。

然而，黑龙江乃为中俄两国之界河，若中国决定管理本国境内及航道华岸的航路标志工作，或摊付航路标志的维护费用，亦可能需要涉及额尔古纳河之管理问题，毕竟额尔古纳河乃黑龙江上游之支流，亦为中俄两国于满洲西部之界河。额尔古纳河虽仅有一段航道上建立了航路标志，但与黑龙江所使用的航路标志体系相似，管理办法亦相同。本人近期巡查黑龙江之时，并未发现挂中国旗的轮船驶出漠河廷，且只有两艘挂中国旗的轮船行至漠河廷。

贾登（H. G. Garden）

巡江工司

2. 为指示黑龙江航务江捐征收入账办法事

59   COMMRS.

No. 90,055

INSPECTORATE GENERAL OF CUSTOMS,

PEKING,   28th June 1922.

Sir,

    With reference to your despatches Nos.
44, 47 and 54 and to I. G. despatch No.58/90,054:

    Aids to navigation on the Amur:

and especially to I. G. telegram of 31st May 1922:

(a) informing you that the Shui-wu Ch'u had
reported that the Taoyin had signed an
Agreement with the local Russian Authorities
for the collection of certain taxes for
Aids to Navigation, the collection to begin
on the 1st June; that the actual terms of
the Agreement had not been communicated, but
that as the duration of the Agreement was
limited to the present year and the matter
was urgent, the Ch'u had approved and had
instructed the Superintendent to act
accordingly: and

(b) authorising you to undertake the collection
of such taxes as had been fixed by the
Agreement, but to retain 10% of the amount
collected by the Customs for cost of
                  collection.

The Commissioner of Customs,

    A I G U N.

collection, accounts instructions to follow
by despatch:

I am now directed by the Inspector General to
instruct you as follows:

1. The daily collection of the taxes is to be
   shown in a separate column in your B-6
   Report, but the collection is not to be
   passed through your Revenue Account.   It
   is, however, to appear in your Quarterly
   Trade Returns under the Tonnage Dues heading
   - as at Harbin - with the following
   explanatory footnote:-

   * "River Dues applied locally to Aids to
      Navigation".

2. The collection and disposal of the River
   Dues are to be accounted for in "Local
   Moneys Account" - A/c. D - a detailed
   statement of which should accompany your
   Quarterly Service Accounts.

3. As regards the 10% for cost of collection
   you are to write the amount off your

                                    Local

Local Moneys Account and to enter it in your Account D. under K. Unclassed.

I am,

Sir,

Your obedient Servant,

Chief Secretary.

致瑷珲关第 <u>59/90055</u> 号令　　　　海关总税务司署（北京）1922 年 6 月 28 日

尊敬的瑷珲关税务司：

根据第 44 号呈、第 47 号呈、第 54 号呈以及海关总税务司署第 58/90054 号令：

"黑龙江航务"

特别是根据海关总税务司署 1922 年 5 月 31 日电令：

"（1）通知贵署，税务处称黑河道尹已与俄当地政府签署某些税种的征收协议，以供修建维护航路标志之用，起征日期为 6 月 1 日；协议具体条款尚未沟通，但协议有效期仅今年有效，且情况紧急，税务处已批准该协议，并指示海关监督依此执行；以及

（2）授权贵署负责征收协议中确定的税款，但保留海关所征税款的 10% 作为征税开销，入账指示见后续令文。"

奉总税务司命令，特做出如下指示：

1. 每日征收税款应在贵署 B-6 报告一个单独列中填写，税款不经过贵署税收账户。但此款项应在贵署季度报表中船钞项下有所体现（与哈尔滨关一样），并做以下脚注：

＊江捐适用于地方航务。

2. 江捐税款的征收与使用都应记在 D 账户"地方公款清账"中，明细表应随附在贵署海关账户季报表后。

3. 至于征税所花销的 10% 经费，请从贵署地方公款清账中销账，然后登记到 D 账户第 K 项未分类栏目下。

您忠诚的仆人

包罗（C. A. Bowra）

总务科税务司

3. 为提议暂于一年之内向经水运往来于黑龙江航道华岸各地和瑷珲关之间的货物征收半税事

66

I.G.

Aigun / Taheiho 1st August, 1922.

Sir,

In my despatch No. 37 I had the honour to suggest that, as a counterpart to the concessions made by the Customs to the merchants in the matter of the taxation of the overland traffic, duty on cargo moved along the Chinese side of the Amur be levied in accordance with the Aigun Regulations and with practice on the Sungari and at Lahasusu.

My mind is not changed as to the right and opportunity of introducing this taxation which should have been started years ago, with the abolition of the duty free zone; even the merchants, during the discussions on the Liangchiat'un question, have repeatedly protested that they would not object to legal taxation. - But I realise the difficulties of

The Inspector General of Customs,

PEKING.

of imposing a new taxation on the local trade which is passing through a severe crisis just now ; I have therefore the honour to recommend and adopt the suggestion put forward by Mr. Yeh, the Chinese Assistant serving at this Port, that provisionally - for one year or until trade conditions improve - only half Tariff duty be levied on goods moved along the Chinese side of the Amur.

I add that collection may be started only from the beginning of the 1925 nagivation season - but the principle should be asserted and made to be accepted now, in connection with the adoption of the new procedure for taxation of overland cargo, just submitted in my despatch No. 64. We would thus give the merchants breathing time, and avoid the reproach of hampering trade in the present commercial depression ; we would have matters of principle settled at the good moment ; we could with leisure prepare the new procedure, issue the Revised General Regulations for Trade on the Amur, and make further enquiries with a view to the possible opening of Stations up and down river.

I

I would also like to remark that an extended control – fiscal and technical – by the C. M. Customs over the Amur frontier, made possible by the taxation of Amur Traffic and the probable consequent opening of new Customs Stations, will in my opinion greatly contribute to the strengthening of China's position vis-à-vis the Russians ; and I would again point out that opportunities such as China has now, should possibly be taken advantage of without delay, lest they may not present themselves again.

I have the honour to be,

Sir,

Your obedient Servant,

Acting Commissioner.

呈海关总税务司署 <u>66</u> 号文　　　　　　　　　瑷珲关 / 大黑河 1922 年 8 月 1 日

尊敬的海关总税务司（北京）：

　　本署曾于瑷珲关第 37 号呈中建议，鉴于海关在陆路运输征税问题上已向商人让步，因此对于向黑龙江航道华岸各地货物征税事宜，应按照瑷珲关章程及松花江和拉哈苏苏分关的惯例执行。

　　关于征税之权利与时机，本署依然认为，应于几年前废止免税区时，便开始征税；而在梁家屯问题的讨论中，商人亦反复申明不会反对合法税收。但本署意识到，当地贸易刚刚经历了严重的危机，若欲向商人征税，势必会困难重重；兹建议，采用本口岸华班帮办叶元章先生之提议，即暂时一年或直至贸易状况有所改善之前，向黑龙江航道华岸各地之货物按半价税率征税。

　　需要补充的是，或可于 1923 年航运季开始起征，但关于本署于瑷珲关第 64 号呈中所提的采用新征税制度向陆路货物征税一事，现在应坚持原则，予以施行。如此亦可予以商人喘息之时间，避免海关会因在目前经济萧条之情况下阻碍贸易而受到谴责；海关则应于此时立下原则，制定新的征税制度，修订并发布黑龙江贸易相关的总章程，查究黑龙江航道上游或下游是否有设立分关之可能。

　　此外，若能实现对黑龙江航道的货物运输征税，随后设立新的海关分关，则有望实现中国海关扩大黑龙江边境的管理范围（财政及技术方面），兹认为，由此亦可大大加强中国相对俄国之地位；而且中国现有的这些机会，可遇而不可求，应立即抓住。

　　　　　　　　　　　　　　　　　　　　　　　　您忠诚的仆人

　　　　　　　　　　　　　　　　　　　　　　　　包安济（G. Boezi）

　　　　　　　　　　　　　　　　　　　　　　　　瑷珲关署理税务司

4. 为江捐收入账管理及支出意见事

77.

I. G.　　　　　　　　　　　　Aigun/Taheiho 1st November, 1922.

Sir,

1.　　　　I have the honour to acknowledge the receipt of your despatch No. 74/90,942 :

　　　　　Aids to Navigation on the Amur: additional regulations generally approved; Mr. Ignatieff, appointed as Technical Adviser on Aids to Navigation; various information requested:

and, in reply, to state that I have refrained from recommending any scheme for the Administration of the Aids to Navigation; whenever asked of our intention for the future, I have invariably replied that your decision has not been made yet, and that much will depend on the collection and the estimated expenditure.

2.　　　　Mr. Ignatieff is therefore busy in making out estimates of the expenses for 1923, both in

　　　　　　　　　　　　　　　　　the

The Inspector General of Customs,

　　PEKING.

the event of the Russians continuing to work on
the whole of the frontier waters, and in case we
may be able to take in hand the upkeep of the Aids
on one section of the Amur, from Taheiho up- or
down-river. A decision on the future policy cannot
certainly be reached here, and I understand both
Russians and Chinese would prefer to *leave* the matter
for settlement by the respective Central Governments,
a local Arrangement presenting many inconveniences.

3.   Mr. Baukham, Senior Out-door Officer, completed
his tour of inspection of the lower river, while I
personally proceeded to inspect the works and installations of the Navigation Office on the Upper Amur.
The results of our investigations are now very useful in checking the accounts and estimates presented
by the Russians; generally speaking, the work has been
done to satisfaction, although on a very economical
scale - the Aids are in order, although it is hard
to verify,
the correctness of the position of the beacons with
very high waters, as ~~have been prevalent~~ *we had* this year.

4.   The collection has been somewhat over $
28,000, not including Lahasusu for the last month; considering that we only started collection in June, and
that

that this has been a very bad year for trade, the average collection for *a* whole season may be confidently put to nearly $ 40,000. The Russian returns of River Dues collected are still being scrutinized, and their estimated expenses still revised, after long and wearisome parleys, by the Technical Adviser. All should be definitely sanctioned in a few days, when I will forward exact figures and facts.

5.   As for the refusal of the Chinese to accept the proposed article whereby China's right to navigate the Amur to the mouth of the river were being implicitly recognised, the explanations given are very vague. The Taoyin was favourable to the clause, but he submitted the Articles to the sanction of the Provincial Authorities (an action on the correctness of which I have doubts) who vetoed the article in question. The Taoyin, who was considerably surprised, never communicated in writing the Provincial Governor's reply, and the only reason that he could understand was, apparently, that a Conference being on the point of meeting to decide on the Navigation on the Amur, this question should not be prejudiced.

6. Concerning

6.   Concerning Mr. Ignatieff's pay, and other expenses in connection with supervision of the Aids to Navigation, I am to ask for definite instructions as to Accounts treatment. - While in your despatch No. 58/90,054 you instructed to charge to A/c A the small initial expenses incurred, the Audit Secretary, in his semi-official letter of 6th october, in answer to my query, directed that Mr. Ignatieff's pay be issued from "River Dues Account" (Local Moneys Account) - i. e. from River Dues Collection -; and to the same Account are to be charged Mr. Ignatieff's travelling expenses incurred on first appointment, according to your despatch No. 85/91,680, just received.

        But I am afraid that, according to the Local Agreement under which we collect River Dues, any expenditure from the collection is to be sanctioned by the Joint Commission; and the Taoyin views things from this angle. And I am equally afraid that there may be claims by the Taoyin in the disposal of whatever balance there is left of the Collection, after meeting all the expenses for 1922, as he is the Chinese President of the Commission. - Such question, I believe, could not be raised locally

without

without friction, and would probably give no result. If, therefore, the Customs have full right to the disposal of the River Dues Collection, and of the expenditure of these funds, I would suggest that the Taoyin-Superintendent be instructed to this effect by the Wai Chiao Pu and the Shui Wu Ch'u. In the doubt, I have at once presented a demand for the inclusion of Mr. Ignatieff's salary to the end of December in the general estimate of expenses to be met by common funds, subject to your final instruction; both the Taoyin and the Director of the Russian Navigation Office have verbally agreed. — However, if the Taoyin is right in his contention that the Commission is to sanction any expenditure, I must also ask him to sanction pay to Mr. Ignatieff from balance of collection, after 31st December (to which date we are paying the Russian Staff). — Pending your instructions, all expenses are charged to Suspense Account.

> I have the honour to be, Sir,
>
> Your obedient Servant,
>
> Acting Commissioner.

[1-274]

93   Commrs.

Inspectorate General of Customs,

No. 92,051   *PEKING,* 21st November,   19^{22}.

SIR,

I am directed by the Inspector General to acknowledge receipt of your Despatch No. 77 :

requesting definite instructions concerning the accounts treatment of the pay issuable to Mr. Ignatieff, Technical Adviser to the Administration of the Amur Aids to Navigation and of other expenses in connection with the supervision of the Aids to Navigation;

and, in reply, to say that since Mr. Ignatieff has been appointed Technical Adviser to the local administration of the Amur Aids to Navigation, his salary, house rent, etc., are therefore to be a charge on the River Dues collection booked in Account D, Local Moneys Account, so long as he functions as such, i.e. so long as the provisional Local Agreement is operative.

With

the Commissioner of Customs,

AIGUN.

With regard to the question of control of the expenditure from the River Dues funds and its consequent bearing on the accounts treatment of Mr. Ignatieff's pay, I am to say that it is not the Customs but the Joint Commission of which the Commissioner is a member which controls the Aids expenditure and that consequently Mr. Ignatieff's appointment and the expenditure concerned therewith, as well as any other disbursements in connection with the Aids to Navigation, should be notified to the Commission and sanctioned by them.

It would seem, however, that these matters should be settled by the Commissioner locally in accordance with the Agreement and that they do not require further reference to the Wai-chiao Pu or Shui-wu Ch'u.

I am,

Sir,

Your obedient Servant,

Cecil A. V. Bowra

Chief Secretary.

呈海关总税务司署 <u>77</u> 号文　　　　　　　　瑷珲关／大黑河 1922 年 11 月 1 日

尊敬的海关总税务司（北京）：

　　1. 根据海关总税务司署第 74/90942 号令：

　　　　"黑龙江航务：基本批准补充细则；易保罗（Ignatieff）先生任航务专门顾问一职；请汇报具体信息。"

　　兹回复，关于为航务管理提供方案一事，本署已尽量避之；凡被问及海关将来之打算时，本署皆以海关总税务司署尚未做出决议，仍待查看征税结果及支出预算回复之。

　　2. 易保罗（P. I. Ignatieff）先生已开始编制 1923 年支出预算，该预算基于以下两种情况：一为俄方将继续管理黑龙江所有航道的航路标志维护工作，一为华方将管理黑龙江一段航道（大黑河上游或下游）的航路标志维护工作。然而，此事实难于地方做出决策，中俄双方更希望由各自中央政府出面予以解决，毕竟地方安排确有诸多不便。

　　3. 超等外班关员博韩（G. E. Baukham）先生已完成黑龙江航道下游的巡查工作，而本署亦已亲自前往黑龙江上游航道检查俄阿穆尔水道局各项工事完成之情况，以助于核查俄方所交账簿及预算；总体来说，俄方虽然非常节约用度，但今年工事之完成情况还比较令人满意——航路标志排列有序，唯于水位较高时，难以矫正标桩之位置。

　　4. 目前，海关已征税款 28000 余银圆，但拉哈苏苏分关上月所征税款尚未纳入此金额之中；今年自 6 月起方开始征税，又值贸易萧条之年，基于目前征税之情况，预计整个航运季的平均税收可达 40000 银圆。俄方江捐收益仍在仔细核查之中，而关于支出预算，双方已协商良久，但仍需航务专门顾问予以修订。待过些时日一切事宜确定之后，本署将呈送确切金额及各项明细。

　　5. 关于中国政府拒绝接受拟议条款（此条款含蓄承认中国有权航行至黑龙江航道口）一事，尚未有明确解释。道尹虽对该条款表示赞成，但却将之呈送至省政府请求批准（本署质疑此举之正确性），而省政府则对上述条款予以否决。道尹虽颇为诧异，但却从未向省长呈文沟通此事，其认为极有可能因黑龙江航务决策会议并未讨论该问题。

　　6. 关于易保罗（Ignatieff）先生之薪俸以及有关黑龙江航务监理方面的其他费用，请予以明确指示。海关总税务司署第 58/90054 号令指示将小额初期经费计入账户 A，而会计科税务司 10 月 6 日机要信函指示，由"江捐账户"（地方公款清账），即江捐税收，支付易保罗先生之薪俸；根据刚收悉之海关总税务司署第 85/91680 号令，易保罗先生任职之旅费将计入同一账户。

但依照《中俄黑龙江航行地方临时协议》之规定,凡江捐税收之支出均须由中俄黑龙江水道委员会批准。道尹既为中俄黑龙江水道委员会的中方委员长,亦会从该角度考虑问题,因此对于如何处理支付 1922 年所有费用后的税款余额定会有所要求。兹认为,若由地方提出此问题,必会引起冲突,亦不会有何结果。若要海关可以全权处理所征捐款,以及税款支出事项,建议由外交部和税务处向道尹兼海关监督下达指示。本署已向中俄黑龙江水道委员会提出,将易保罗先生至 12 月末之薪俸总额纳入支出预算之中,由共同资金支付,道尹和俄阿穆尔水道局督办均已口头表示赞成,但仍待贵署最终指示。然而,若确如道尹之主张,所有费用均须由中俄黑龙江水道委员会批准,则本署仍须请其批准 12 月 31 日（此为本署支付俄方职员薪俸之日）之后由江捐税收余额支付易保罗先生之薪俸。在等待贵署指示期间,所有费用将计入暂付款账。

您忠诚的仆人

包安济（G. Boezi）

瑷珲关署理税务司

致瑷珲关第 93/92051 号令　　　　海关总税务司署（北京）1922 年 11 月 21 日

尊敬的瑷珲关税务司：

第 77 号呈收悉：

"请示黑龙江航务管理部门专门顾问易保罗（P. I. Ignatieff）先生应发薪俸以及有关黑龙江航务监理方面的其他费用的入账办法。"

奉总税务司命令，现批复如下：兹告知，因为易保罗（P. I. Ignatieff）先生担任黑龙江航务专门顾问，所以只要他行使相应职责（即只要地方临时协议仍在生效中），其薪资、房屋租赁费等应由贵署 D 账户地方公款清账中的"江捐征收"项下支出。

兹通知关于江捐资金支出管理以及后续的易保罗先生薪俸入账办法问题，航务支出不是由海关而是由联合委员会掌管的，瑷珲关税务司只是其成员之一，因此易保罗先生的任命和相关费用，以及有关航路标志的其他开支，都应呈请联合委员会批准。

然而，这些问题都应由瑷珲关税务司根据协议在地方即可解决，无须呈交至外交部或税务处裁定。

您忠诚的仆人

包罗（C. A. Bowra）

总务科税务司

5. 为公布黑龙江江捐税则事

<u>Customs Notification No. 86.</u>

With reference to Customs Notification No. 16:
Provisional Regulations for collection of
Amur River Dues for 1922, notifying:

and to Customs Notification No. 59:

instructing that the River Dues Tariff be
doubled, with certain exceptions:

the Public is hereby notified that arrangements have been
made with the Heiho Taoyin and the Chamber of Commerce
whereby the River Dues is to be further increased, from
the opening of the 1927 navigation season, as follows:

Category I	Pood	$0.015
Category II	,,	0.03
Timber	Sq.ft.	0.00035
Passenger tickets		7½%
Gold	Catty	2.00

Flour is hereafter to be classified in first
category.

The Tariff on other cargo will remain the same as
before.

Goods carried by Junk or Raft will subject the
above Tariff at reduced half rate.

Deer horns and musk are charged River Dues at the
rate of 20% of the Customs duty, whereas ginseng at the
rate of 10% of the duty.

Acting Commissioner of Customs.

CUSTOM HOUSE,
Aigun/Taheiho, 9th May, 1927.

Таможенное Объявленіе № 86.

Ссылаясь на таможенное объявленіе за № 16, касающееся временнаго правила для взысканія попудноплеснаго сбора для 1922 года, и таможенное объявленіе за № 59, касающееся сбора которые будутъ взыскиваться въ двойнѣ;

Симъ доводится до всеобщаго свѣдѣнія,, что согласно соглашенія съ Даоиномъ и Коммерческимъ Обществомъ тарифъ попудноплеснаго сбора въ семъ году увеличивается согласно нижеслѣдующаго а именно:

Грузъ I-ой категоріи 0.015 за пудъ

    " II-ой категоріи 0.03 за пудъ

Лѣсъ   0.00035 за квадратн. футъ

Пассажирскій билетъ $7\frac{1}{2}$% со стоимости билета

Золото   2 дол. съ кетти

Оленій рога и струя 20% съ пошлины
/панты/

Жиншень   10% съ пошлины

А также доводится до всеобщаго свѣдѣнія публики, что мука въ будущемъ оплачивается какъ грузъ I-ой категоріи.

Тарифъ другихъ грузовъ остается по прежнему.

Грузъ возимый на джонкахъ и на шаландахъ плотятъ половину установленнаго сбора.

Управленіе
Китайской Таможни въ г. Сахалянѣ,
9-го Мая 1927 года

И.Д. Таможеннаго Комиссара.

95   Service.

Harbin.   No. 168.   Aigun   11th May, 1927.

          Sir,

                    I beg to confirm my telegram of the

          7th May, as follows:

                              Please instruct Lahasusu telegraphi-
                         cally to make following increases
                         and alterations in River Dues at
                         once for coming season: Category
                         one and two to pay one and one
                         half and three cents per pood
                         respectively; flour to be classified
                         in first category hereafter; River
                         Dues on all passenger tickets
                         increased to seven and half per
                         cent. Instructions follow by
                         despatch.

          and to my telegram of today's date which will be

          sent if the lines are in repair:

                              My telegram of 7th May: Please
                         notify Lahasusu telegraphically that
                         cargo originating on the Sungari
                         and destined for Amur or Ussuri
                                                       ports

The Commissioner of Customs.

          Harbin.

ports will be exempt from increase in River Dues until 20th May and any increase collected before that date may be refunded on production of River Dues Receipt.

I am appending in detail the alterations and increases that have been made in the present River Dues Tariff (the essential points of which were included in my telegram of the 7th May quoted above).

Enclosed you will also find a copy of Aigun Notification No. 86 in triplicate for posting at Lahasusu and Harbin.

With reference to the new tariff on timber the rate is per superficial square feet based on a thickness of 1 inch. Planks from 1 inch to 2 inches thick pay double and planks 2 inches to 3 inches thick pay triple, and so on, the tariff rate.

I should be glad if a copy of this

despatch

despatch could be sent to the Lahasusu Office.

I am,

Sir,

Your obedient Servant,

Acting Commissioner.

APPENDIX.

APPENDIX.

AMUR RIVER DUES TARIFF.

Name.	Classifier.	Steamer or Barge.	Junk or Raft.
Category I: Building Materials, Iron, Cast Iron, Steel & Lead Ware, Cereals, Flour, Hay & Fodder, Vegetables, Salt, Coal & Charcoal, Agricultural Machines other than wooden:	Pood	$0.015	$0.0075
Category II: Other goods:	Pood	0.03	0.015
Timber:			
1" thick or under	Sup.Sq.ft.	0.00035	0.000175
Over 1" thick not exceeding 2"	,,	0.0007	0.00035
Over 2" thick not exceeding 3"	,,	0.00105	0.000525
Over 3" thick not exceeding 4"	,,	0.0014	0.0007
Over 4" thick not exceeding 5"	,,	0.00175	0.000875
Gold:	Catty	2.00	1.00
Deer horns & Musk:		20% of the duty.	10% of duty.
Ginseng:		10% " " "	5% " "
Firewood:			
3/4 arshine long:	Sq.sajen	0.15	0.075
up to 1 arshine long:	" "	0.20	0.10
Live Stock:			
Large (horses & cattle)	Head	0.30	0.15
Small (pigs, sheep, goats)	"	0.15	0.075
Fowls:	Piece.	0.01	0.005
Passenger tickets:		$7\frac{1}{2}\%$	$7\frac{1}{2}\%$

海关公告第 86 号 ①

瑷珲关 / 大黑河 1927 年 5 月 9 日

根据海关公告第 16 号：

"公布 1922 年黑龙江江捐暂行章程。"

及海关公告第 59 号：

"指示除某项特例外，所有江捐税率赠加一倍。"

兹通知：本署与黑河道尹公署及商会协定，自 1927 年航运季开通起，实行复增江捐规定，具体如下：

第一种货类	每普特	0.015 银圆
第二种货类	每普特	0.03 银圆
木料	每平方英尺	0.00035 银圆
乘客船票	———	7.5%
金	每斤	2.00 银圆

面粉此后列在第一种货类之内。

其他货物江捐税率照常核算。

凡货物由民船或木筏运送者，一律照上述江捐税率之半数征收江捐。

鹿茸及麝香之江捐照正税征收二成，人参征收一成。

（签字）铎博赉（R. M. Talbot）

瑷珲关署理税务司

———————

① 注：原档为英俄文对照。

致哈尔滨关第 95/168 号函　　　　　　　　　　瑷珲关 1927 年 5 月 11 日

尊敬的哈尔滨关税务司：

根据瑷珲关 5 月 7 日电报：

"请通过电报指示拉哈苏苏分关，于航运季来临之际，务必立即增收江捐，将其修改为：第一种货类每普特征收大洋一分五厘，第二种货类每普特征收大洋三分；面粉此后列在第一种货类之内；客票值百抽捐七点五。"

及瑷珲关 5 月 11 日电报（内容或需更改）：

"根据瑷珲关 5 月 7 日电报，请电令告知拉哈苏苏分关，5 月 20 日之前，凡货物自松花江运往黑龙江或乌苏里江各口岸者，一律照之前税率征收江捐；该日期前对此等货物增收之江捐税款，或可凭江捐完税收据退还。"

兹附现行江捐税率所做变更及增加明细（要点请参阅上述瑷珲关 5 月 7 日电报）。

随附瑷珲关海关通告第 86 号之抄件（一式三份），请拉哈苏苏分关及哈尔滨关予以颁布。

新税则规定，木料每平方英尺所征税额，依照其厚度而定，1 英寸为基数；凡厚度超出 1 英寸但不足 2 英寸者，一律按双倍税率缴纳江捐；凡厚度超出 2 英寸但不足 3 英寸者，一律按三倍税率缴纳江捐等。

望将此函抄件发送至拉哈苏苏分关。

　　　　　　　　　　　　　　　　您忠诚的仆人

　　　　　　　　　　　　　　（签字）铎博赉（R. M. Talbot）

　　　　　　　　　　　　　　瑷珲关署理税务司

附录

黑龙江江捐税则

名称	单位	轮船／驳船	民船／木筏
		银圆	银圆
第一种货类： 建筑材料,铁、铸铁、钢铁及铅制品、谷物、面粉、干草和草料、蔬菜、盐类、煤和木炭、农具（非木质）：	普特	0.015	0.0075
第二种货类： 其他货物：	普特	0.03	0.015
木料：（厚度）			
1 英寸以下（含 1 英寸）	1 平方英尺	0.00035	0.00075
1 ～ 2 英寸（含 2 英寸）	1 平方英尺	0.00070	0.00035
2 ～ 3 英寸（含 3 英寸）	1 平方英尺	0.00105	0.000525
3 ～ 4 英寸（含 4 英寸）	1 平方英尺	0.0014	0.0007
4 ～ 5 英寸（含 5 英寸）	1 平方英尺	0.00175	0.000875
金：	斤	2.00	1.00
鹿茸／麝香：		20% 正税	10% 正税
人参：		10% 正税	5% 正税
木桴：（长度）			
3/4 俄尺：	平方俄尺	0.15	0.075
大于 1 俄尺：	平方俄尺	0.20	0.10
家畜：			
大型（马／骆驼）	头	0.30	0.15
小型（猪、绵羊、山羊）	头	0.15	0.075
家禽：	只	0.01	0.005
客票：	从价	7.5%	7.5%

6. 为 1927 年 5 月起上调江捐税率事

I.G.   Aigun   27th July, 1927.

Sir,

1.   With reference to Aigun despatch No. 311:

                        reporting, *inter alia*, the
                        receipt of instructions from the
                        Provincial Authorities, transmitted
                        through the Taoyin, that the
                        River Dues Tariff should be
                        increased:

to I.G. despatch No. 350:

                        directing that the proposed
                        increase be not put into effect
                        until the Taoyin received the
                        authority of the Shui-wu Ch'u:

to my telegram of the 2nd June, 1927:

                        stating that the increase had
                        already been put into effect
                        without reference to the Ch'u
                        following a precedent created
                        in June, 1925:

and to your telegram of the 3rd June in reply:

                        that the former increase was
                        not a parallel case; but that
                                                  the

The Officiating Inspector General of Customs,

        Peking.

the increase having been put
into effect was to be continued,
and that the Superintendent should
report to the Ch'u that River
Dues had been raised on
instructions of the Provincial
Authorities:

I now have the honour to report more fully on
the whole question and to inform you that the
Taoyin has transmitted to the Provincial Authorities
my request that the Ch'u be notified of the
increase.

2.   In my despatch No. 511, referred to
above, I related the circumstances leading up to
the proposal on the part of the Taoyin to
increase the River Dues and reported the receipt
of a letter from him (copy of which was enclosed
at the time) to the effect that he had been
instructed by the Provincial Authorities to raise
the Tariff in order to wipe out the yearly
deficit; laying down certain stipulations as to
the amount and manner of the increase and
requesting that the Chamber of Commerce be consulted

in

in the matter. The principal changes were to be
that goods in Categories I and II were, thereafter,
to pay 1½ and 3 cents per pood, respectively,
instead of 1 and 2 cents.

3.   A draft of the proposed new Tariff was
eventually drawn up and submitted to the Chamber
of Commerce. In addition to the general increase
in the rates applying to Categories I and II, I
proposed to raise the rates on timber (log in
rafts), to classify such articles as ginseng, musk
etc., as luxuries to which higher rates were
applicable and to levy a tax of $3 per catty on
the export of gold (which is mined near here).
The negotiations with the Chamber of Commerce
which followed were without special incident the
President having already agreed to the increases
in principle at the time it was decided to raise
the River Dues Tariff rather than levy a special
local surtax to cover the cost of digging the
channel in the harbour (Aigun despatch No. 311).
All suggested increases were eventually agreed to

                                                    with

with the exception of the tax on gold which the Chamber wished to fix at \$1 instead of \$3 per catty. They also recommended that wheat flour should be changed from Category II to I where, as a necessity of life, it would pay smaller dues. The opinion was also expressed privately that, in consideration of the immense profit the Tung Pei S/S Company made last year, the dues on passenger tickets should be raised from 5% to 7½%. A copy of the Chamber's letter of 2nd May in the above connection is appended.

Appendix No.1.
(filed in writer's office)

4.   On the 5th May I addressed the Taoyin, copy of letter appended, reporting the result of the negotiations with the Chamber. At the same time I proposed that gold pay \$2 instead of \$1 per catty and that, contrary to the Taoyin's own idea, the dues on passenger tickets be increased to 7½%.

Appendix No.1a.
(filed in writer's office)

5.   On the 9th May the Taoyin replied, copy appended, approving the Tariff agreed on with

Appendix No.2.

the

the Chamber together with my recommendations, stating
that the increases should be put into effect at
once and adding that besides notifying the local
interests concerned he was informing the Provincial
Authorities of the action that was being taken.
The raising of the Tariff took effect from the
9th May, when the Harbin office was requested to
notify Lahasusu of the new rates.

6.　　　　　　On the 10th May I received a letter
from the Taoyin, copy of which is appended,
requesting that the new rates be not applied to
traffic originating on the Sungari for a period of
ten days owing to the lack of notice that had
been given to the Harbin merchants of the increase

Appendix No.3.
(Filed in Writers Office)

7.　　　　　　I received your despatch No. 350,
referred to above, on the 26th May directing me
to make no arrangements to put the proposed
increases into effect until the Shui-wu Ch'u's
authority had been obtained and that the Taoyin
was to be requested to act accordingly. The
advisability of such action being taken had been

considered

considered by myself before the new rates were put into effect but finding that there was already a precedent for increasing the River Dues Tariff without reference to the Shui-wu Ch'u I had decided to begin the levying of the new rates at once - navigation was just opening when the heaviest collections of the year were to be made.

8.　　At the risk of making this despatch too long but in order to place more clearly on record the history of the application of the River Dues Tariff, and to explain my reasons for assuming that a precedent had already been created for increasing the Tariff on the instructions of the Provincial Authorities only, I will now refer to the correspondance and orders on record regarding the subject.

9.　　Aigun despatch No. 54 of 10th June, 1922, submitted the original River Dues Tariff as approved by the Shui-wu Ch'u. Paragraph 4 is liable to convey the wrong impression that it was subsequently altered to meet the wishes of the

local

local Chamber of Commerce. Reference to the Chinese enclosure shows, however, that the recommendation of the Chamber, that the Amur be divided into upper and lower sections and that half the tariff be levied on goods travelling on each, was included in the tariff regulations before they were submitted to the Ch'u.

on to the English Translation (vide desp. 67, Appendix, Remarks, &c)

10.   Aigun despatch No. 230, §6, reporting the raising of the Tariff to "full rates" is also ambiguous. It is stated in the opening sentence of that paragraph: "In my despatch No. 218 I submitted "that as the collection of River Dues at a half "tariff rate no longer provided sufficient funds to "meet current expenditure the proper course was to "collect at the full rate." On referring to Aigun despatch No. 218, which is alluded to, §5 discloses the following use of the terms "full rate" and "half rate": "My first proposal was to collect River Dues at a full tariff rate. At present, for "the purpose of assessing River Dues, the Amur is "divided into two sections, an upper section from

                                                    "Taheiho

349

"Taheiho to Pokrovka and a lower section from
"Taheiho to Kasakevich, and for each section one
"half of the tariff only is paid. The Russians,
"on the other hand, collect a full rate
"irrespective of distance travelled". It will thus
be seen that where a "full rate" was spoken of
in reality a doubling of the existing rates, as
originally approved by the Ch'u, was meant.

11.   Aigun despatch No. 230, referred to in
the preceding paragraph, reports that the collection
of the "full tariff rates" commenced on the 9th
June, 1925. The increase was put into effect on
the instructions of the Provincial Authorities only
and met with considerable opposition on the part
of the merchants.

12.   Commissioner's order to the General
Office notifying the change in River Dues Tariff
sums up the matter very clearly:

PRACTICE ORDER NO.95.

Custom House,
Aigun/Taheiho.9th June, 1925.

AMUR RIVER DUES:

With reference to Practice Order No.
14:

14:

Provisional Regulations for collection of Amur River Dues for 1922, notifying:

it has now been decided that Amur River Dues on cargo will be collected from this date and until further orders at double the rates laid down in the above order, as a result of arrangements made with the Heiho Taoyin and the Chamber of Commerce. Dues on passenger tickets will be levied at 5% as hitherto.

(Signed) R. F. C. Hedgeland
Commissioner.

In view of the above considerations I considered that it was not necessary, from a Customs stand-point, to refer the present increase, which was not so great as the former one, to the Ch'n for approval.

13.   This decision of mine was arrived at independently of the attitude assumed by the Taoyin, during the preliminary negotiations, that the fixing of the amount to be collected for River Dues was an intra-Provincial matter only.

14.   After the receipt of your despatch No. 350, referred to above, I called on the Taoyin acquainted him with your instructions to myself and asked

asked him, in view of the fact that the increase

had already been put into effect, to wire the

Ch'u for that Board's approval. He maintained the

position he had assumed all along that as the

Ch'u had sanctioned the collection of River Dues

by the Customs that Board was no longer concerned

or interested in how much or how little was

assessed and that such matters lay entirely within

the discretion of the Provincial Authorities. I

did not wish to argue about the relative amount

of authority the Inspector General (Shui-wu Ch'u)

and the Heilungchiang Authorities have over the

River Dues Collection but I pointed out that as

a matter of courtesy (and mere formality) the

Inspector General should be informed of the

increase through the Ch'u and that the present

position of the Taoyin was tantamount to that of

giving me orders over the head of yourself. The

interview was conducted in a friendly manner but

the Taoyin at one time went so far as to say

that, if the Aigun Customs was not prepared to

follow

follow the instructions of the Provincial Authorities in this instance, he might have to consider some other system of collecting River Dues. The interview wound up by the Taoyin requesting me to wire you stating his position and to request that the matter of increase be left entirely in the hands of the Provincial Authorities.

15.   I accordingly sent off the telegram of the 2nd June and duly received your reply of the 3rd June, both of which telegrams are referred to above. After consulting further with the Taoyin as to notifying the Ch'u it was arranged that I should address him asking to have the matter referred but that he should be written to as Taoyin and not as Superintendent. I did this on the 13th July and append copy of my letter.

Appendix No.4.
(Filed in Statis office)

16.   On the 19th July the Taoyin replied (copy of letter appended) that he had referred

Appendix No.5.
(Filed in Statis office)

the matter to the Provincial Authorities with whom he left the decision as to whether the increase should be reported to the Ch'u. On my part I

have

have reasons to believe that they will take the necessary steps.

17.   The Taoyin takes full responsibility for the increase in the River Dues Tariff as will be seen from what precedes. No protests against the nature of the increase have as yet been made either by the shipping companies or the merchants and I do not anticipate that there will be any. As a result of the increase the collection to date has been nearly double what it was last year.

18.   I am appending a statement showing the rates of the new Tariff as compared with that of June, 1925.

Appendix No.6.

I have the honour to be,

Sir,

Your obedient Servant,

Acting Commissioner.

Appendix.

Appendix No. 6.

A statement comparing the Amur River Dues Tariff

of June, 1925, to the present Tariff increased May, 1927.

Name.	Classifier.	June,1925.	May,1927.
Category I: Building materials, Iron, Cast iron, Steel & Lead ware, Cereals, Hay & Fodder, Vegetables, Salt, Coal and Charcoal, Agricultural machines other than wooden, and Flour.	Pood.	.01	.015
Category II:			
Other goods:	Pood.	.02	.03
Timber:		.005 per 1 piece of 3 saj. x 1 ver., and so on proportionately.	.00035 per 1 Sup.Sq.ft.of 1" thick or under, and so on proportionately.
Gold:	Catty	...	2.00
Ginseng:		II Category	10% of duty.
De Horns & Musk:		II Category	20% of duty.
Firewood:	Sq.sajen.		
3/4 arshine long		.15	.15
up to 1 arshine long		.20	.20
Live stock:	Head		
Large (horses & cattles)		.30	.30
Small (pigs, sheep, goats)		.15	.15
Fowls:	Piece	.01	.01
Passenger tickets:		5%	7½%

Note: Cargo carried by junks or rafts pay River Dues at half the
above rate.

呈海关总税务司署 325 号文　　　　　　　　瑷珲关 1927 年 7 月 27 日

尊敬的海关总税务司（北京）：

1. 根据瑷珲关第 311 号呈：

"报告已收到由道尹转达的省政府指令——上调江捐税率。"

及海关总税务司署第 350 号令：

"指示瑷珲关，在道尹得到税务处的授权后，方可执行对江捐税率的上调。"

又瑷珲关 1927 年 6 月 2 日电呈：

"虽尚未得到税务处的授权，但上调江捐税率一事已按 1925 年 6 月的先例付诸实施。"

及海关总税务司署 6 月 3 日电令回复：

"1925 年 6 月的先例与目前事例并不相符，但上调江捐税率一事既已付诸实施，则应继续进行；海关监督应将已按省政府指令上调江捐税率一事及时汇报至税务处。"

兹报告，道尹已向省政府传达了本署的请求，即及时向税务处汇报上调江捐税率一事。

2. 道尹来函（兹附道尹信函抄件）说明："为抵消年度赤字，已在省政府的指示下，上调了江捐税率，并对上调数额及方式作出了相应规定；且相关事项俱已通知商会，并要求商会尽快做出商榷。"税率的变化主要体现于类别 I 和类别 II 中的货物上，即每件货物的税率分别由原来的 1 分和 2 分增长至 1.5 分和 3 分。

3. 最终拟定的新税率已通知商会。除了对类别 I 与类别 II 中货物的税率予以上调外，本署建议对木料（用于木筏的原木）的税率也予以上调；人参、麝香等奢侈品，亦应收取更高的江捐；至于出口的黄金（开采于本地者），则宜按每斤 3 银圆的标准征税。与商会之间的后续商榷并无意外，商会主席已同意上调税率，并认为通过上调税率的方式来抵偿疏浚港口河道的费用，远远好过征收特殊的地方附加税的做法（参阅瑷珲关第 311 号呈）。除了黄金一项，其余所有上调税率的提案都已获得批准；至于黄金一项，商会表示希望按每斤 1 银圆的标准征税，而非每斤 3 银圆。商会还提议将作为生活必需品的小麦和面粉由类别 II 移入至类别 I 中，这样可以使生活必需品的税费降低，另外，商会私下表示，考虑到东北航路局去年所获利润丰厚，应将船票的税率由原来的 5% 增加至 7.5%。随函附上 5 月 2 日商会信函的抄件。

4. 5 月 4 日，本署致函道尹，告知与商会之间的商榷结果（兹附该信函抄件）。本署向道尹建议，黄金应按每斤 2 银圆征税，而非商会所提议的每斤 1 银圆，船票则应按 7.5% 的税率征税（这与道尹先前的意见有所不同）。

5.5月9日，道尹回复同意本署与商会之间的商榷结果，并同意本署于5月4日信函中所提的建议，上调税率一事可即刻付诸施行；同时道尹还补充说，除了已向地方的相关利益人发出通知外，其业已向省政府汇报了上调江捐税率一事（兹附该信函抄件）。调整之后的新税率将于5月9日起正式施行，哈尔滨关应及时将新税率通知拉哈苏苏。

6.5月10日，道尹致函本署（兹附道尹信函抄件），指出因哈尔滨关的商人尚未收到税率上调的通知，所以十天之内，不可于松花江上实施新税率。

7.5月26日海关总税务司署第350号令指示，瑷珲关应在得到税务处的授权后，再开始上调税率；届时，道尹也会按指示采取相应的行动。不过在新税率实施之前，本署已仔细考虑过上调税率之可行性，而且发现之前也曾有过在向税务处汇报之前先行上调税率之先例，因此，鉴于航运季伊始正是一年当中税收最多之时，本署遂决定立即按照上调后的税率征收江捐。

8.兹附与此相关之信函及令文摘要，以便更加清楚地了解历年江捐税率之情况，以及本署参照之先例（在仅有省政府指令的情况下上调税率）。

9.1922年6月10日瑷珲关第54号呈所提交的江捐税率为经税务处批准的原江捐税率。该呈第4段之表达容易让人误解为，之后是为了满足地方商会之要求而调整了税率。但根据中文附件，可知商会之提议为将黑龙江分为上游与下游两个部分，各部分分别按"半价税率"向货物征收江捐，且该提议已在呈交给税务处之前被纳入关税章程。

10.瑷珲关第230号呈（第6章）所报告之欲按"全价税率"征收江捐表意不清。兹引用瑷珲关第230号呈开篇之内容"本署已于瑷珲关第218号呈中指出，鉴于按半价税率征得的江捐已无法为目前的支出提供充足的资金，故应当在适当的航路上按全价税率征收江捐"。瑷珲关第218号呈（第5章）亦使用了"全价税率"和"半价税率"之表达："兹建议按全价税率征收江捐；目前为便于核定江捐税收，将黑龙江分为上游与下游两个部分，自大黑河至波克罗夫卡一段为上游部分，而自大黑河至嘎杂克维池一段为下游部分，每一部分仅按半价税率征收江捐；俄罗斯方面则不论航行里程，一律按全价税率征收江捐。"由此可知，所谓的"全价税率"实为税务处批准的原江捐税率之两倍。

11.瑷珲关第230号呈报告，自1925年6月9日起开始按"全价税率"征收江捐。此次税率上调仅有省政府之指令，遭到了商人们的普遍反对。

12.海关通过税务司谕令向致征税汇办处通知调整江捐税率事宜，因此参考此类税务司谕令，便可了解江捐税率调整的相关事宜。

第 95 号税务司谕令　　　　　　　　　　瑷珲关 / 大黑河 1925 年 6 月 9 日

黑龙江江捐：

根据第 14 号税务司谕令：

"根据 1922 年江捐征收临时章程，黑河道尹及商会协商后决定，即日起至收到
下一步指令之前，按照之前令文所定税率之两倍向黑龙江航道上的货物征收江捐。
同时仍按 5% 的税率向乘客船票征税。"

（签字）贺智兰（R.F.C.Hedgeland）

瑷珲关税务司

基于上述考量，兹认为，鉴于此次税率上调之幅度比先例中上调幅度小，因此从海关
的立场出发，实无向税务处呈报之必要。

13. 虽然道尹亦认为，在最初的商榷阶段，决定江捐征收数额仅为省政府内部之事，但
本署未将上调税率事宜呈报税务处之决定与道尹之态度并无干系。

14. 在收到海关总税务司署第 350 号令后，本署即刻面见道尹，告知其海关总税务司署
对本署之指示，并指出鉴于已开始按照上调之税率征收江捐，应尽快向税务处汇报此事，
以获批准。但道尹仍保持自己的一贯立场，认为税务处既已批准由海关来征收江捐，便不
会在意征收税率之额度，因此上调江捐税率之事完全可由省政府单方面决定。虽然（税
务处）总税务司与黑龙江省政府在征收江捐一事上权利相当，但本署并未就此事与道尹争
辩，只是指出，就算出于礼貌（或是例行公事），亦应通过税务处向总税务司呈报税率上调
事宜，且道尹如今之做法无异于越过海关总税务司直接向本署下达指令。此次会面气氛
融洽，不过道尹也表示，若瑷珲关不愿执行省政府所下达的上调税率之指示，那么其或许
会考虑由其他部门来征收江捐。会面结束时，道尹要求本署电呈海关总税务司署说明其
立场，并表示关于上调税率一事须由省政府全权决定。

15. 本署应道尹之要求于 6 月 2 日电呈海关总税务司署，并于 6 月 3 日收到贵署之批
复。随后，本署与道尹就向税务处呈报上调税率一事进行了进一步协商，最后商定由本署
向道尹正式致函请其呈报此事，但须于呈文中称其为道尹，而非海关监督。本署已于 7 月
13 日向道尹致函（兹附该信函抄件）。

16. 道尹于 7 月 19 日致函本署（兹附该信函抄件），告知已向省政府呈报此事，将由省

政府决定是否将上调税率一事汇报至税务处。本署相信省政府会采取必要的措施。

17. 从先前的情况可以看出，道尹需要为江捐税率的上调一事负全责。如本署所料，各航业公司及商人对税率的上调均无异议。税率上调后，迄今税收金额已达去年同期税收金额之两倍。

18. 兹附新税率与 1925 年 6 月税率的对比报表。

您忠诚的仆人

铎博赉（R. M. Talbot）

瑷珲关署理税务司

附表 6

黑龙江新旧江捐税率对比明细

（1925 年 6 月旧税率与 1927 年 5 月新税率）

物品	单位	日期	
		1925 年 6 月	1927 年 5 月
类别 I： 建筑材料，铁，生铁，钢，铅制品，谷物，干草与饲料，蔬菜，盐，煤炭，非木制农业用具，面粉	普特	0.01	0.015
类别 II： 其他物品	普特	0.02	0.03
木料		0.005 每件 （3 俄丈 × 1 俄寸）	0.00035 每件 （1 平方英尺 厚度小于 1 俄寸）
黄金	斤	…	0.20
人参		按类别 II	0.10
鹿角，麝香		按类别 II	0.20
木桩： 3-4 俄丈长 不超过 1 俄丈长	平方俄丈	0.15 0.20	0.15 0.20
家畜： 大只（马、牛） 小只（猪、绵羊、山羊）	只	0.30 0.15	0.30 0.15
家禽	只	0.01	0.01
乘客船票		0.05	0.075

注：由民船及木筏运载的货物只需支付上述税率的一半即可。

此抄件发送至哈尔滨关税务司

录事：屠守鑫　四等帮办后班

7. 为拉哈苏苏分关代瑷珲关征收乌黑两江江捐相关事

監督來函第一二七號

逕啟者案准

貴稅務司第一二一號復函備悉查愛琿關徵收此項旅票捐本署於濱江道

署來文奉省令請撥本關江捐計金四千三百元案內得知大概此事已於本

月十八日轉請

查核辦理在案惟拉分關並非屬於愛琿關何以比照該關徵收旅票捐鄙意

度之或係代收性質如確係拉分關代理該關徵收旅票捐及其他江捐自開

辦截至上年止共徵收若干本年開江起至六月底止共徵收若干徵起之欵如

何撥付以上各節相應再行函請

貴稅務司查明見復以憑核辦為荷此致 中華民國十六年八月二十三日

Enclosure No.3 to Harbin Desp.No.83/Aigun.

復監督函第一二六號

逕復者關於請撥修濬烏蘇里江經費暨徵收旅票江捐各節迭准丙

字第二九〇第三〇〇號

公函均已備悉查拉哈蘇蘇分關所收烏蘇里江船隻及貿易江捐

完全係代愛琿關徵收所收各款向均由該分關直接交由愛琿關查收

尊意所度恰係事實貴關於此事現擬函詢愛琿稅務司並請其將

尊函所詢各節詳晰函復惟距該關路途甚遙往返需時倚稍寬

時日定能得一詳明答復也相應函復

貴監督查照為荷此致　民國十六年八月二十四日

Harbin No.87/Aigun.

Enclosure.

濱江關監督來函內字第三五九號

逕啟者案准吉林財政廳咨開為咨行事本年九月十九日本
省奉到令內開案查前因吉江兩省與俄方會修烏黑兩江本省應擔會
修烏江半數經費擬貴縣江省微收貨捐減案辦理督經電飭係蘭道尹
將海關年收捐款數目詳查查報在案茲據呈復以遵查烏江貨客
各捐上年八月即已開微該稅務司事前未經呈准擅自微收支配同江稅關對
於調查捐額又復不允開單並送未免駭視主權等情令應令查明各關捐
稅向來辦法核議具復因奉此查此案會修烏黑兩江本省應擔半
數經費等議加微貨捐及各關向來微收捐稅辦法徹應均無案可稽究
竟是何詳情除呈復外相應抄同原令咨請貴署查照希將此案前後
辦理情形及向來微收捐稅辦法鈔送過廳以憑核議實紉公誼等因准此查
拉哈蘇分關代理珲關微收江捐一事前准第一二六號函詢愛
關稅務司在案茲准前因有應行研究明晰以憑答復者(一)本關前定本江
捐捐率拉分關是否典辦微抑代愛關收捐後即不重微本關江捐(二)拉分關於
上年八月起即代收此項捐款該分關屬本關管轄代微伊時是否係總稅
務司令飭馬前稅務司轉行遵辦抑懂係愛關稅務司委託辦理並曾否
報明本關有案以各節及拉分關所收此項江捐捐率自問微起每月
微收數目相應玉請
貴稅務司分別查明見復以憑核轉為荷此致
中華民國十六年十月十八日

復濱江關監督函第一五六號

逕啟者昨准兩字第三五九號

公函當即電詢璦琿關稅務司去訖茲准電復稱茲本關對於濱江關監督

第二九〇第三〇〇號之復函業已寄發想不日即達

貴關等同准此查關於

貴監督內字第三五九號函內所詢各節似尚須函詢璦琿關方能悉

其詳細茲就本稅務司所知者先為告知拉哈蘇蘇分關於代理璦琿關

徵收烏黑兩江捐外並為本關徵收松花江捐此種權宜辦法係由璦琿

關與本關兩方面稅務司參酌辦理因關員和衷共濟具有合作之精

神故亦毫無困難至吉林省政府此次所擬調查各項本稅務司甚願

勉盡棉薄調查奉告惟吉林財政廳對於此事終以直接向璦琿關

監督調查為宜准至前因相應函復

貴監督查照轉復為荷此致中華民國十六年十月二十五日

Enclosure No.2 to Aigun No.100/Harbin.

M E M O R A N D U M.

Technical Adviser's Office,	To
Custom House,	Commissioner of Customs,
Aigun/Taheiho, 24th October,1927.	A I G U N.

After the Sino-Russian Agreement of the 27th June, 1922, for the joint upkeep of Aids on the Amur (from Pokrovka to Harbarovsk) had been signed the Customs began the collection of River Dues at Taheiho, Aigun and Lahasusu. At Lahasusu the collection for 1922 amounted to $5,754.31. But that office did not show separate figures for traffic proceeding up the Amur as distinct from that destined for points below the Sungari and for the Ussuri. It may be estimated that traffic under the latter category paid some $2,500 for 1922. Steamers were stopped from plying to Harbarovsk after 1922 and proceeded thereafter to the Ussuri via the Kasakevich Waterway, and a new Agreement was drawn up in 1923 accordingly.

The figures for the River Dues Collection since 1922 at Lahasusu on steamers plying the Amur below the Sungari (to SuiYuan) and on those trading on the Ussuri have been as follows:

1922 approx.	1923	1924	1925	1926	1927 approx.	Total
$2,500	$1,371	$1,598	$3,496	$10,272	$15,800	$35,000

The figures for the collection for October and November of this year will not be known until later but an estimate of $2,000 for those two months is included in the above figure for the year 1927. Owing to the heavy floods on the Ussuri this year there was a large falling off

in

in traffic and consequent collection on that river. The collection of Dues on passanger tickets at Lahasusu for points to and from the Lahasusu - Sui-yuan stretch of the Amur and on tickets to or from points on the Ussuri began in 1926.

Aids on the Amur in Heilungchiang Province extend from Pokrovka to Lahasusu a distance of 1513 versts. In Kirin Province Aids have been placed as follows: Lahasusu to Sui-yuan 190 versts and Kasakevich Waterway to Hulin 336 versts, a total for Kirin of 526 versts. The expenditure on the joint upkeep, including overhead and maintenance, of Aids on the stretch from Lahasusu to Harbarovsk in 1922, from Lahasusu to Sui-yuan for 1923/4/5/6 and from Lahasusu to Sui-yuan and Kasakevich Waterway to Hulin for 1927 was as follows:

1922	1923	1924	1925	1926	1927	Total approx.
$2,895	$2,470	$3,344	$4,060	$4,902	$14,400	$32,000

It will be seen from the above that for several years Aids in Kirin Province were in arrears and only now is the collection at Lahasusu proving sufficient. As yet Aids are not maintained on the Kasakevich Waterway.

(Signed) P. I. Ignatieff
Technical Adviser.

Translation:

4th Assistant B.

通函

由：	致：
航务专门顾问办事处	瑷珲关税务司
瑷珲关（瑷珲／大黑河）1927 年 10 月 24 日	

中俄双方于 1922 年 6 月 27 日为共同维护黑龙江边界河道自波克罗夫卡至哈巴罗夫斯克（Harbarovsk）河段的航路标志签订协议后，大黑河口岸、瑷珲口岸及拉哈苏苏口岸的海关便开始征收江捐。拉哈苏苏分关 1922 年江捐税收总计 5754.31 银圆，但其中并未将前往黑龙江上游之货物与前往松花江下游各处及乌苏里江之货物（此类货物税收估计约有 2500 银圆）加以区分。然 1922 年后，中国轮船不再获准经哈巴罗夫斯克前往乌苏里江，只能改经嘎杂克维池水道；1923 年协议因此做出调整。

自 1922 年以来，拉哈苏苏分关对往来松花江下游至绥远（黑龙江上）河段及往来乌苏里江贸易之轮船所征江捐数额如下：

年份	1922	1923	1924	1925	1926	1927	总计
银圆	2500	1371	1598	3496	10272	15800	35000

1927 年 10 月和 11 月江捐征收数额尚难确定，估计约有 2000 银圆，已将之计入上述 1927 年江捐数额。1927 年乌苏里江遭遇大洪水，货物运输量骤减，江捐税收由此大幅减少。拉哈苏苏分关自 1926 年开始对往来黑龙江自拉哈苏苏至绥远河段各处及往来乌苏里江各处之乘客船票征收江捐。

黑龙江省内已安设航路标志的河道全长 1513 俄里，即黑龙江自波克罗夫卡至哈巴罗夫斯克河段。吉林省内已安设航路标志的河道共计 526 俄里，包括黑龙江自拉哈苏苏至绥远河段（长 190 俄里）及自嘎杂克维池水道至虎林河段（长 336 俄里）。

吉林省内的航政联合维护工程，1922 年仅涉及黑龙江自拉哈苏苏至哈巴罗夫斯克河段，1923 年至 1926 年涉及黑龙江自拉哈苏苏至绥远河段，1927 年新增自嘎杂克维池水道至虎林河段；具体费用细目（包括管理费和维护费）如下：

年份	1922	1923	1924	1925	1926	1927	总计
银圆	2895	2470	3344	4060	4902	14400	32000

由上表可知，1922 年至 1925 年吉林省内的江捐税收一直不足以支付航路标志维护工作所需费用，直到近两年拉哈苏苏分关所征税款方较为充足，然嘎杂克维池水道的航路标志维护工作尚未开展。

（签名）易保罗（P. I. Ignatieff）

黑龙江航务专门顾问

翻译：屠守鑫 四等帮办后班

8. 为巡查黑龙江的旅费由黑龙江江捐账户支付事

AMUR RIVER DUES ACCOUNT: refund from, of advances made from
Harbin Suspense Account to cover cost of Mr. Garden's
inspection trips on Amur in 1918/1919; copies of
correspondence with Taoyin in re, forwarding, and further
359. instructions, soliciting.

359
I.G.

I.G.   Aigun   23rd February, 1928.

Sir,

1.   I have the honour to submit copies of

correspondence that has passed between myself

and the Heiho Taoyin regarding the eventual

repayment by the Amur Aids Commission of a sum

of Hk.Tls.8,907.39, advanced originally by the

Harbin Customs to defray the late River

Inspector Garden's expenses on his trips of

inspection of Amur Aids during the summers of

1918 and 1919, and to request your further

instructions in the matter.

2.   The question was raised by the receipt

of your despatch No. 323/110,666:

                                    informing this office that the
                                    Harbin Customs had been
                                    instructed to transfer the sum
                                    of Hk.Tls.8,907.39, representing
                                                                the

The Inspector General of Customs,

    Peking.

the amount outstanding under the
heading "Amur Inspection Trip
Account" in Suspense A/c., to
"Aigun Customs Amur River Dues
A/c.", and that the Aigun
Customs was to note that the
amount in question was to be
repaid from Amur Aids funds
when the financial position of
the latter permitted.

3.　　　　Anticipating at the time that objections
might be raised by the Taoyin to the transferrance
of such an obligation to the Amur Aids I
mentioned the matter in my S/O No. 70 of 12th
January, 1927, to you and was instructed in your
S/O of the 17th February, 1927, in reply that I
was to make myself familiar with the circumstances
under which the advance was made before
approaching the Taoyin on the subject.

4.　　　　As there was very little on record in
this office regarding the circumstances of, and
authority for, the advances to Mr. Garden, Aigun
having been a sub-office of Harbin at the time,

I

I wrote the Harbin Commissioner requesting as much information as possible. The details supplied in return were not complete, in the light of further copies of correspondence between the Inspector General and the Harbin Commissioner recently supplied to me by Mr. Acting Commissioner Barentzen, and left me still considerably in the dark. By piecing the information I had received together with what was on record here it seemed to me that our expectations of repayment could not be strong. The fact that the Amur Aids Commission is such only in name and derived from the beginning a large share of its income from the taxation of Ussuri traffic, with the ultimate object of rehabilitating the Aids on that river, involves the Kirin authorities who are not concerned with Mr. Garden's inspection trips on the Amur. Further, from correspondence on file in this office and quoted below, part of Mr. Garden's time in Taheiho appears to have been taken up with Harbour matters. I

also

also gathered from a feeler put out that the Taoyin
considered the Heilungchiang Tuchun's original interest
in the Amur, which led to Mr. Garden's inspection
trips, as purely political and as antedating, and
disassociated from, the Amur Aids Commission's
technical activities.

5.   In March, 1927, the Annual Statement of
Accounts of the Amur Aids Commission was sent as
usual to the Taoyin as President of that Commission,
a copy being sent in Aigun despatch No. 313 to
I. G. At the time of making out this Annual
Statement an additional one was drawn up for your
information showing the advances made to that date
by the Harbin Customs and including the cost of
Mr. Garden's inspection trips which had already been
debited to Amur Aids Account by Harbin. A
translation of this latter statement was also sent
to the Taoyin. Therein he noted the item of
Hk.Tls.8,907.39 debited to the Amur River Dues Account
by the Harbin Customs and wrote me on the 7th May.

1927.

Appendix No.1.   1927, copy of letter appended, that as all Aids

expenditure must first have the approval of the

Provincial Authorities he had submitted the matter

to them.

6.   I replied fully to his letter on the 9th

Appendix No.2.   May, 1927, copy appended, giving the circumstances

of the advances, explaining that he was wrong in

assuming that the advance had already been included

in local Aids Account without his sanction, stating

that the debiting of the account by the Harbin

Customs was more in the nature of a book

transaction by the latter Office, that the repayment

of the advance would only be expected when the

Amur Aids Commission was well able to do so and

asking him to forward my letter to the Higher

Authorities to supplement his.

7.   My letter was duly forwarded by the Taoyin

but the reply from the Governor, transmitted by the

Taoyin on the 7th June, 1927, of which copy is

Appendix No.3.   appended, was to the effect that Mr. Garden had

been

been brought to Taheiho for the purpose of investigating the advisability of establishing a Harbourmaster's Office and his expenses should not be paid out of Amur Aids funds but by the "appointing department concerned".

8. On receipt of this letter I called on the Taoyin to point out the erroneous assumptions of the Governor and said that while the question of establishing a Harbour Office at Taheiho may have been in the air at the time (Vide I. G. despatch No. 10,766/73,071 to Shanghai) it was incidental to Mr. Garden's trip to the Amur. The survey from Lahasusu to Mo Ho T'ing, the expense of the motor boat brought from Harbin for the purpose, his salary and other expenses made up the advances to Mr. Garden now reclaimed and could only have concerned the question of Aids.

9. The Taoyin took the position that the expenditure was made long before the Commission was formed (as already stated above) and that it was a matter between the Harbin Commission and the

Heilungchiang

Heilungchiang Authorities or between the latter and
the I. G. through the Shui-wu Ch'u. He confessed
that his records of, and his own ideas on, the
subject were rather vague; but he was sympathetic
in this and subsequent interviews and said that,
while he could not reopen the question himself
with the Provincial Authorities, if I would address
him again he would forward my letter. About this
time he contemplated a trip to Tsitsihar and I
relied on him to make matters plain to those
concerned.

10.   The Taoyin's visit was eventually postponed,
however, and on the 25th October, 1927, I sent a
Appendix No.4.   second letter, copy appended (together with a
correction), as suggested by him, reviewing what I
had said in my first communication and what I had
told him as just related above. A reply has now
been received to this letter dated 20th January,
1928, copy appended, and from this it can be seen
Appendix No.5.   that the question of establishing a Harbour Office
at

at Taheiho is again made largely responsible for the advances, that the question of Mr. Garden's detachment for the inspection of Aids is practically ignored and stating that as the income from River Dues must be used for present demands, and for the repayment of the loan from the Sungari Aids funds, the whole matter should be referred to the Shui-wu Ch'u and the advance recovered from that Bureau.

11.   Although I was in Harbin at the time of Mr. Garden's death and was subsequently appointed to the charge of Aigun my recollections of his activities are rather vague. It would appear from the statement of his advances, appended, that he made two trips to this region, one in 1918 and the second in 1919. The first was made from Harbin to Mo Ho T'ing in the Harbin Customs M/L "Heilung" while in 1919 he proceeded from Harbin to Taheiho by steamer with his wife and remained at this place

Appendix No.6.

12.   The question seems to have been raised originally early in 1918 by the Heilungchiang Authorities requesting the assistance of the Harbin

Commissioner

Commissioner in making an inspection of the

existing Amur Aids with a view to the commencement

of Chinese shipping operations on that river.

Harbin despatch No. 1706 to I. G. of 12th March,

1918, reports Mr. Grevedon's attitude in the matter

and encloses copies of his correspondence with his

Superintendent. The opening paragraph of I. G.

despatch No. 1879/70,042 of the 30th July, 1918,

to Harbin states that "the Heilungchiang Tuchun

"has requested that an inspection of the river

"from the mouth of the Sungari to Mo Ho T'ing

"(漠 河 廷) should be undertaken by the

"Maritime Customs with a view more especially to

"obtaining and recording particulars of the Aids

"to Navigation established by the Russian

"Government." This despatch goes on to say that

Mr. Garden has been selected for the work, and §4

states that "the advances made to him will

"ultimately be recovered from Revenue Account".

I. G. despatch No. 2111/74,778 to Harbin informs

the

the latter port of the progress of negotiations toward a provisional agreement between the Sino-Soviet Authorities which would enable Chinese steamers to operate on the Amur to the same extent as Soviet steamers operated on the Sungari. A very interesting and informative resumé in English of all the correspondence between the Shui-wu Ch'u and the Inspector General on the Amur River question to the date of the despatch - 29th August 1919 - was enclosed. (A copy of this despatch was only recently supplied to me by the Harbin Commissioner, as remarked in §4).

13.   In looking back over the S/O correspondence between Mr. Grevedon and Mr. Mansfield, the latter being Assistant-in-Charge of the port at the time, very little light is thrown on the subject of Mr. Garden's activities on the Amur. There is nothing at all on record about the inspection trip of 1918 the first allusion to Mr. Garden's local activities being Mr. Mansfield's S/O of the 27th May, 1919.

to

to Harbin in which he says: "Garden turned up on
"the 20th. He is living with me and will do so
"until he goes. I took him to call on the Taoyin
"who tells me he had no official communication
"regarding Garden's arrival or duties here. The
"Taoyin seems keen on the appointment of a
"Harbourmaster here presumably as supervisor of Aids,
"etc. Garden told him that he had already handed
"in his report, further copies of which had been
"asked for by the Chiao T'ung Pu, before he left
"Shanghai. The Taoyin appears to be of the opinion
"that Garden will be asked once more to assist in
"connection with the Chinese share in Amur Aids.
"Whilst Garden is here it would be a good
"opportunity to try and arrive at some sort of
"understanding regarding Harbour Limits and extent of
"Chinese jurisdiction, points which have never been
"settled".

14.   On the receipt of this S/O Mr. Grevedon
appears to have written privately to the Inspector

General

General enclosing a copy. The Inspector General
replied by wire a copy of which was forwarded to
Aigun in Harbin S/O of 9th June, 1919: "Copy of
"I. G.'s telegram of 7th June:- Your letter of 3rd
"June: by all means let Garden occupy himself fully
"in consultation with Mansfield and Taoyin regarding
"all matters pertaining Harbour control. Let him
"suggest Harbour Limits and Harbour Regulations adapted
"local conditions based on treaty port traditions and
"practice. N.B. question of Aids must wait until
"Chinese Government has settled question with some .X..
"Russian Authorities. *mutilated - might be "recognized".

15.   On the 5th June, 1919, Mr. Mansfield stated
in an S/O to Harbin: "Garden's Appointment: the
"Taoyin's interpreter has been here and informs me
"that the Taoyin has received a telegram from the
"Ministry of Communications notifying him of Garden's
"appointment. The Board says that it is proposed to
"establish a Harbourmaster's Office at Aigun and that
"the Inspector General has been approached on the
"subject. I presume instructions will come in due
                                        "course".

"course". It is not clear to what position Mr.
Garden was "appointed" whether in connection with
Aids or Harbour matters.

16.   Mr. Mansfield's S/O of the 17th July,
1919 to Harbin states: "Harbour and Navigation:
"Garden sent you the other day copy of a letter
"received from Mr. Shen, the Taoyin's Secretary,
"and its enclosure. From this you will see that
"General Howarth was instructed by the Russian
"Minister to go into the question of Aids with
"the Wu T'ung Kung Ssu!!!!"...... "Yesterday the
"Taoyin sent to say that he was coming to see
"us on business connected with the Harbour, etc.
"To save time Garden and I went to see him.
"He showed us a despatch received by him from
"the Wai Chiao Fu which is somewhat at varience
"with the Chiao T'ung Fu's telegram which formed
"the enclosure to Mr. Shen's letter"..............
"From the Wai Chiao Fu's despatch to the Taoyin
"you will see that on the recommendation of

                                        "Minister

"Minister Liu at Vladivostook it is proposed to

"draw up, in collaboration with the Russian

"Government (the Koltchak Government I presume),

"provisional regulations for the navigation of

"Chinese shipping on the Amur. You and the Heiho

"Taoyin are designated, as being well acquainted

"with the subject, to cooperate in discussing the

"matter with the Russian authorities. The Wai

"Chiao Pu goes on to say that the Shui-wu Ch'u

"has already been requested to instruct you

"accordingly so I suppose there will shortly be a

"despatch containing instructions from the I. G. on

"the subject. As far as I can see the matter

"referred to by the Wai Chiao Pu - i.e. navigation

"on the Amur by Chinese vessels covers the "Aids"

"question and can have nothing to do - or at any

"rate only indirectly concerns - Taheiho Harbour

"regulations which are a matter entirely for the

"Chinese Government ...."

A copy of I. G. despatch No. 2089/74.295 to Harbin

is

is on file at this office. It authorizes the
expenditure of a certain sum for the survey of
Taheiho Harbour, presumably to be undertaken by
Mr. Garden. As he was stricken by his fatal
illness about this time nothing was done about
the projected survey.

17.   From the foregoing it may be concluded
that Mr. Garden's trip to this region in 1918
was entirely taken up with a survey of Amur Aids
as they then existed, while there seems to be
much confusion regarding the reason for his
presence here in 1919 and what little he did was
limited, owing to his untimely death, to drawing
up Harbour Regulations and making certain
recommendations in connection therewith. In the
resumé, already referred to, of correspondence
between the Inspector General and the Shui-wu Ch'u
on Amur questions: D. No. 82 to Ch'u, 22nd April,
1919, last sentence, reads: "The Inspector General
"does not see that, at this stage, the placing
                                        "of

"of a Harbourmaster at Aigun (Taheiho) would be
"of much assistance in the solving of any of the
"above questions, but he will send Mr. Garden to
"Aigun for a few months as it may be of
"assistance to have a technical man to refer to".
The summaries from the same source of D. No. 884
from, of 5th June, 1919, and D. No. 134 to Ch'u,
of 14th June, 1919, rather imply that for the
time being Mr. Garden's energies are to be
expended on Harbour Office rather than Aids
questions.

18.   Since the exchange of correspondence with
the Taoyin touched on above, I have received copy
of a further despatch to Harbin (I. G. despatch
No. 3938/115,668) instructing that Office to debit
"Aigun Customs Amur River Dues Account" with the
advance of Hk.Tls.1,024.43 hitherto outstanding at
Shanghai in connection with the preparations of
plans, etc., on Amur Aids by Mr. Garden. I
consider that this transfer should also be
reported to the Taoyin but before doing so I

shall

shall await your further instructions as to the

attitude you wish me to adopt toward the question

in general.

I have the honour to be,

Sir,

Your obedient Servant,

Acting Commissioner.

Appendix.

Appendix No.6 to Aigun despatch No.359 to I.G.

AMUR INSPECTION TRIP ACCOUNT.

Authority: I.G. Despatches Nos.1861/69,669, 1879/70,042, 1493/
60,873 to Harbin and 73,071 to Shanghai.
(April 22 - May 9, 1919)

Date	To whom paid	Particulars	Roubles	Hk.Tls.
31 7. 18	H.G.Garden,R.Insp	Salary for July, 1918	5,840.00	
"	"	Transfer Allowance	1,062.50	
5. 8. 18	"	Advance for Amur inspection	10,000.00	
16. 8. 18	Standard Oil Co.	Kerosene for Launch	13,457.01	
7. 9. 18	"	Kerosene Oil for M/L "Heilung"	30,839.68	
19.10. 18	Churin & Co.	Stores for inspection trip	5,734.90	
"	H.G.Garden,R.Insp	Sundries " " "	1,130.25	
"	"	Washing mess linen	30.90	
"	"	Expenditure on trip	8,010.55	
"	"	Refund of advance	*10,000.00	
"	"	Proceeds of sales of empty tins	*-3,557.00	
28.10. 18	"	Salary for October, 1918	5,884.00	
"	"	Mileage allowance to Shanghai	460.80	
"	"	Hotel room expenses	556.00	
"	Wagon Lits	Passage for Mr. Garden to Shanghai	490.35	
18.11. 18	Dr. Chun	Medical attendance	28.39	
4.12. 18	Sh'ai Works Dept.	2 sets of square drawing pen	79.31	
12.5. 19	H. G. Garden	Transfer allowance	3,250.00	
31.5. 19	"	Salary for May @ 400	16,041.60	
28.6. 19	"	" " June "	15,818.80	
30.7. 19	"	" " July	21,789.84	
		Forward:	140,504.88	

Date	To whom paid	Particulars	Roubles	Hk.Tls.
		Forward:	140,504.88	
30. 8.19	H.G. Garden	Salary for August	26,513.20	
19. 8.19	Ch.Post Office	Expenses on transporting surveying instrument	279.95	
15. 7.19	H.G. Garden	Refund of travelling expenses	1,885.00	
29. 9.19	"	Part of September pay	15,328.40	
"	"	Post-mortem pay	57,482.40	
30. 9.19	Mrs. Garden	Passage from Taheiho to Harbin	651.00	
	"	Rent allowance	9,180.00	
"	Wagon Lits	Passages for Mrs. Garden to Shanghai	3,104.30	
12.11.19	J. Steinscher	Cartage on Mr. Garden's luggage	30.00	
15.11.19	A/c. A.	Cartage on surveying instruments	14.36	
2.12.19	Chi.Tel.Adtion.	Telegram sent during September to November	129.60	
24.12.19	"	Telegrams sent	3,161.00	
			258,264.09	
		Less refund of advance*	-13,557.00	
		Total advance in Roubles @ various rates =	244,707.09	8,102.07
30. 8.18	H.G.Garden, R. Inspector	Salary for August Sh.Tls. 445.60		400.00
30. 9.18	"	Salary for September Sh.Tls.445.60		400.00
17.12.20	Mr.Talbot,Asst.	Repairs to surveying inst.		5.32
				8,907.39

*The

*The total Rouble advances - Roubles 244,707.09 - were brought forward to Hk.Tls. advances on 12th June, 1921 at various rates and which Roubles advances had been made.

True copy:

4th Assistant B.

Note: The dates given in the heading of this Appendix are as supplied by the Harbin Office.

呈海关总税务司署 <u>359</u> 号文　　　　　　　　　　　瑷珲关 1928 年 2 月 23 日

尊敬的海关总税务司（北京）：

　　1. 兹呈送本署与黑河道尹就黑龙江水道委员会结付哈尔滨关账户中未结账款 8907.39 海关两一事的往来信件抄件。该笔欠款为哈尔滨关为贾登（H.G.Garden）先生 1918 年和 1919 年巡查黑龙江航路标志预支的旅费，请求海关总税务司署予以进一步指示。

　　2. 海关总税务司署第 323/110666 号令曾指示：

　　　　"通知瑷珲关，哈尔滨关已收到指令，将暂付款账中黑龙江巡查账户条目下的未结账款 8907.39 海关两转至瑷珲关黑龙江江捐账户下，待瑷珲关黑龙江江捐账户资金充足之时，以黑龙江航路标志资金结付该笔未结账款。"

　　3. 本署曾于 1927 年 1 月 12 日瑷珲关致海关总税务司署第 70 号机要文件中指出，黑河道尹或许会反对将该笔欠款转移至黑龙江航路标志账户项下。海关总税务司署 1927 年 2 月 17 日机要文件批复，指示本署在与道尹接洽此事之前，应了解该笔欠款的详细情况。

　　4. 然而，鉴于该笔欠款发生之时，瑷珲关仍为哈尔滨关之分关，因此关于批复给贾登先生预支款一事，并未有太多的记录。本署遂致信哈尔滨关税务司，希望获取更多信息。然而，本署参考了哈尔滨关署理税务司巴闰森（Barentzen）先生提供的海关总税务司与哈尔滨关税务司之间往来信件的抄件之后，发现信息仍不完整，故依然无法摸清此事的来龙去脉。不过，结合已收到之信息和相关记录，本署认为，对于由黑龙江航路标志资金支付该笔欠款一事不可有过高之期待。原因在于，黑龙江水道委员会只是一个名义上的组织，而且从一开始，其主要收入便来自于对乌苏里江航运所征之税款；且其目的在于将来可重新于乌苏里江航道上建立航路标志，此事亦涉及吉林省政府，但贾登先生在黑龙江上进行巡查一事并非吉林省政府关心之事。况且，从瑷珲关存档的通信中可以看出，贾登先生在大黑河期间，有一部分时间是投身于港务事务的；而本署亦探知，道尹认为当初乃是因为黑龙江督军欲了解黑龙江，方指派贾登先生前往巡查，故此次巡查实属政治性质，而且哈尔滨关预支贾登先生巡查黑龙江之旅费时，黑龙江水道委员会尚未成立，因此该笔预支款与黑龙江水道委员会的技术性活动并无关系。

　　5. 1927 年 3 月，黑龙江水道委员会的年度财务报表照例呈报给道尹（兼黑龙江水道委员会委员长）。同时，瑷珲关在致海关总税务司署第 313 号呈中附上了该报表的抄件。除了该年度财务报表外，当时还有一份哈尔滨关预支款项报表，仅供海关总税务司署参阅，其中便包括贾登先生巡查黑龙江的旅费（哈尔滨关于该预支款报表中将该笔款项记入黑龙江航路标志账户项下）。道尹收到该报表的译本后，得知哈尔滨关将 8907.39 海关两的未结账款记入黑龙江航路标志账户，遂于 1927 年 5 月 7 日向本署致函（兹附道尹信函抄件），表示已将此事呈报吉林省政府，并指出所有关于航路标志的支出都应该在第一时间得到省政府的批准。

6. 本署于 1927 年 5 月 9 日就该笔预支款之情况向道尹致函（兹附该信函抄件）。本署于回函中说明，若道尹认为该笔款项在未获其批准的情况下便已记入黑龙江航路标志账户，则实属误解，因为哈尔滨关将该笔款项记入黑龙江航路标志账户之举实际上仅为账面交易，而且只有当黑龙江水道委员会有足够的支付能力时，才有可能对该笔预支款予以结付。同时，本署请道尹将此回复信函作为补充材料，一并呈送至省政府。

7. 道尹遂将本署信函呈送至省政府，并于 1927 年 6 月 7 日回函传达省长之回复（兹附省长回函抄件），大意为：贾登先生前往大黑河的目的乃是为了调查建立港务课一事的可行性，因此其旅费不应该由黑龙江航路标志资金偿付，而是应该由相关的派遣司支付。

8. 在收到回复后，本署拜访了道尹，指出省长如此理解，确有误解之处：当时大黑河建立港务课仍属悬而未决之事（参阅海关总税务司署致江海关第 10766/73071 号令），并非贾登先生前往黑龙江巡查之主要目的。该笔预支款所涉支出包括：自拉哈苏苏至漠河廷河段的勘测费用，摩托艇的费用（为勘测工事而从哈尔滨关带来的摩托艇），贾登先生的薪俸及其他相关费用。由此看来，该笔款项确与航路标志事宜相关。

9. 道尹认为，哈尔滨关预支贾登先生巡查黑龙江之旅费时，黑龙江水道委员会尚未成立，此事是哈尔滨关税务司与黑龙江省政府之间的事情，又或者说是黑龙江省政府与海关总税务司署（通过税务处）之间的事情。道尹坦言，因有关此事的记录十分模糊，所以他也无法给出明确的见解，但是他仍愿意促成此事。在后续的会面中，道尹表示他已无法与省政府重新讨论这一问题，但如果本署仍欲致函省政府，他也乐于代呈。此次，道尹考虑亲自前往齐齐哈尔，本署相信道尹会向相关部门说明此事。

10. 然而道尹前往齐齐哈尔一事却因故延迟。1927 年 10 月 25 日，本署再次致函道尹（兹附该信函抄件，包括在道尹建议下的修正版），重申了本署在与道尹初次会面时所持的观点以及后来陆续向道尹提出的种种意见。1928 年 1 月 20 日，本署收到道尹的回函（兹附道尹信函抄件），从信函中可知，在大黑河建立港务课一事再次被视为该笔预支款支出的主要原因，而贾登先生巡查航路标志一事却被忽略。道尹还表示，鉴于江捐税收除须用于当前必要事宜以外，还须偿还自松花江航路标志资金所借贷款，因此该笔预支款的相关事宜均须呈报税务处，并由税务处来负责预支款偿还事宜。

11. 尽管贾登先生逝世之时，本署已于哈尔滨关任职，且更于之后接管了瑷珲关，但是本署对于贾登先生生前所处理的工作却已经印象模糊。从预支款报表（兹附该预支款报表）来看，贾登先生共在黑龙江上巡查了两次，第一次是于 1918 年由哈尔滨关出发，乘坐"黑龙"号摩托艇至漠河廷；第二次是于 1919 年由哈尔滨关出发，乘坐轮船至大黑河。贾登先生第二次巡查时有妻子随行，抵达大黑河之后，便停留于此。

12. 黑龙江省政府似乎早于 1918 年就已提出巡查黑龙江之事，当时要求哈尔滨关税务司予以协助，巡查黑龙江上已安设之航路标志，其目的是为在黑龙江上开展中国航运工作做准备。1918 年 3 月 12 日哈尔滨关致海关总税务司署第 1706 号呈，报告了哈尔滨关税务司柯必达（Grevedon）先生对此事的态度，并附上了柯必达先生与海关监督之间往来信件的抄件。1918 年 7 月 30 日海关总税务司署致哈尔滨关第 1879/70042 号令指示："黑龙江督军要求 7 月自松花江至漠河廷的巡查事宜由海关负责，以便海关可以详细了解并记录俄国政府所建航路标志的具体情况。"此令文还说明，已选定贾登先生负责该巡查事宜，而支付给他的预支款，将以税收账户中的资金来偿还（参阅海关总税务司署致哈尔滨关第 1879/70042 号令第 4 章）。海关总税务司署致哈尔滨关第 2111/74778 号令告知哈尔滨关中俄当局签订临时协议一事的协商进程。根据该协议，中国轮船在黑龙江上的航行范围将与俄罗斯轮船在松花江上的航行范围相一致。兹附税务处与海关总税务司署就 1919 年 8 月 29 日呈文中的黑龙江问题互通信函之英文摘要（该呈抄件最近才由哈尔滨关税务司发送至本署）。

13. 回顾哈尔滨关税务司柯必达先生与满士斐（Mansfield）先生之间的往来机要信件，可知满士斐先生在出任哈尔滨关代理税务司期间，对于贾登先生在黑龙江上的巡查活动并无太多关注，所以关于贾登先生 1918 年的巡查活动没有任何记载。满士斐先生在 1919 年 5 月 27 日致哈尔滨关的机要文件中，第一次间接提到了贾登先生在黑龙江上的巡查活动，据满士斐先生说，贾登先生于 5 月 20 日到达大黑河，且巡查期间一直与满士斐先生住在一起，并在满士斐先生的引导下拜访了道尹，只是道尹却并未与之进行正式的沟通。道尹当时似乎忙于委任理船厅作为航路标志的监事员。贾登先生向道尹说明已呈交了巡查报告，另外交通部要求贾登先生在离开上海之前再提交一份报告的抄件。道尹似乎认为贾登先生有可能再次被委任去协助处理黑龙江航路标志事宜，那么既然贾登先生在此，无疑就给许多亟待解决的问题提供了一个得以解决的好机会，比如港口限制问题以及中国管辖权的范围等。

14. 柯必达先生收到满士斐先生的机要信件之后，似乎已于私下向海关总税务司致函

（兹附信函抄件）。海关总税务司的电令批复抄件已随哈尔滨关1919年6月9日机要文件发送至瑷珲关。该机要文件内容为：海关总税务司署6月7日电令抄件（回复哈尔滨关6月3日信函）：请贾登先生尽一切可能就港口管控事宜与满士斐先生及道尹进行磋商。同时请贾登先生根据通商口岸之惯例，对大黑河港口界限的设定以及《理船章程》的制定提出与当地情况相宜之建议。注：须待中国政府与俄国当局解决相关问题之后，方有处理航路标志问题之可能。

15. 据满士斐先生1919年6月5日致哈尔滨关的机要文件陈述："贾登（H.G.Garden）先生之任命：道尹的翻译员一直在大黑河，其告知本人道尹已收悉交通部关于贾登先生任命一事的电报。税务处称已有于瑷珲关建立港务课之提议，且已将此事呈报至海关总税务司署征求意见。兹认为任命贾登先生的指令不日将至。"然而，关于贾登先生被任命的具体职位还不清楚，因此尚无法确定其职位是否与航路标志事宜或者港口事务有关。

16. 据满士斐先生1919年7月17日致哈尔滨关的机要文件陈述："港务与航务：贾登（H.G.Garden）先生已收到道尹秘书沈先生的来信，并将此信函抄件及附件呈送至哈尔滨关。由该信函可知，俄国公使已命郝沃斯（Howarth）将军与戊通航业公司一起开始调查航路标志的有关情况。昨日道尹来函，告知即将就港务等事宜前来拜访；为节省时间，本人与贾登先生主动去拜访了道尹。道尹出示了来自外交部的令文，该令文的内容与沈先生信函所附交通部电报之内容不太一致。由外交部致道尹的令文中可知，在驻符拉迪沃斯托克公使林先生的促使下，外交部建议中国当局与俄方政府（本署推测为高尔察克政府）共同起草有关黑龙江航道中国航运事宜的临时章程。鉴于哈尔滨关税务司与黑河道尹对中国在黑龙江上的航运问题十分熟悉，故二人已接受委派参与到有关临时章程的协商之中。外交部还表示，已要求税务处向哈尔滨关下达相关指令。故本人猜测，海关总税务司署不日将下达包含该指令的令文。外交部所提及之黑龙江上的中国航运相关事宜与航路标志问题相关，但与大黑河《理船章程》（此乃中国政府全权负责之事）却并无干系，即便有，亦非直接干系。"

海关总税务司署致哈尔滨关第2089/74295号令（此令抄件已于瑷珲关存档）批准支出大黑河港口测量工事所需费用，测量工作交由贾登先生负责。然而因贾登先生身患重病，大黑河港口测量工作未能如期开展。

17. 综上所述，或可推断出：贾登先生于1918年前往黑龙江巡查之目的完全是为了勘测黑龙江航道上当时已安设的航路标志之状况。然而贾登先生1919年再次巡查之由则令人十分困惑，而且因其突然不幸离世，第二次巡查所做之事亦仅限于起草《理船章程》

以及提供相关建议而已。据海关总税务司与税务处之间有关黑龙江问题的往来信件摘要可知,道尹于 1919 年 4 月 22 日致税务处第 82 号文中表示:"虽然海关总税务司目前尚未发现于瑷珲关(大黑河)设立理船厅一职对解决大黑河港务问题带来任何的帮助,但考虑到若瑷珲关有技术人员可供咨询,亦会有所助益,因此仍愿派遣贾登先生前往瑷珲关停留数月。"据道尹于 1919 年 6 月 5 日致税务处第 884 号文和于 1919 年 6 月 14 日致税务处第 134 号文的摘要显示,当时贾登先生之精力皆集中于筹建港务课一事上而非航路标志相关问题之上。

18. 在与道尹通信后,本署又收到了海关总税务司署致哈尔滨关第 3938/115668 号令的抄件。该令文指示哈尔滨关将江海关账户中预支给贾登先生的未结款账 1024.43 海关两(该笔预支款为贾登先生巡查黑龙江航路标志之准备和计划工作的相关费用)记入瑷珲关黑龙江江捐账户。兹认为应将此事汇报道尹,本署将待海关总税务司署下达进一步指示之后再行动。

您忠诚的仆人

铎博赉(R. M. Talbot)

瑷珲关署理税务司

瑷珲关致海关总税务司署第 359 号呈附表 6

黑龙江巡查账户

（根据海关总税务司署致哈尔滨关第 1861/69669 号令、第 1879/70042 号令、第 1493/60873 号令，以及致江海关的第 73071 号令）

（1919 年 4 月 22 日至 1919 年 5 月 9 日）

日期	支付对象	明细	卢布	海关两
1918 年 7 月 31 日	贾登（H.G.Garden）巡江工司	1918 年 7 月薪俸	5840.00	
1918 年 7 月 31 日	贾登巡江工司	调口津贴	1062.50	
1918 年 8 月 5 日	贾登巡江工司	黑龙江巡查预支款	10000.00	
1918 年 8 月 16 日	标准石油公司	汽艇所需煤油	13457.01	
1918 年 9 月 7 日	标准石油公司	"黑龙"号摩托艇所需煤油	30839.68	
1918 年 10 月 19 日	秋林公司	巡查活动所需商品	5734.90	
1918 年 10 月 19 日	贾登巡江工司	巡查活动所需杂物	1130.25	
1918 年 10 月 19 日	贾登巡江工司	晾衣麻绳	30.90	
1918 年 10 月 19 日	贾登巡江工司	差旅费	8010.55	
1918 年 10 月 19 日	贾登巡江工司	预支款退款	*−10000.00	
1918 年 10 月 19 日	贾登巡江工司	空锡罐售卖收益	*−3557.00	

续表

日期	支付对象	明细	卢布	海关两
1918 年 10 月 28 日	贾登巡江工司	1918 年 10 月薪俸	5884.00	
1918 年 10 月 28 日	贾登巡江工司	至上海的运费津贴	460.80	
1918 年 10 月 28 日	贾登巡江工司	旅店费用	556.00	
1918 年 10 月 28 日	铁路卧车	贾登先生至上海的旅费	490.35	
1918 年 11 月 18 日	纯医员	医疗护理	28.39	
1918 年 12 月 4 日	江海关工程局	两套方形绘图笔	79.31	
1919 年 5 月 12 日	贾登先生	调口津贴	3250.00	
1919 年 5 月 31 日	贾登先生	1919 年 5 月薪俸 400 海关两	16041.60	
1919 年 6 月 28 日	贾登先生	1919 年 6 月薪俸 400 海关两	15818.80	
1919 年 7 月 30 日	贾登先生	1919 年 7 月薪俸 400 海关两	21789.84	
1919 年 8 月 30 日	贾登先生	1919 年 8 月薪俸	26513.20	
1919 年 8 月 19 日	中国邮局	测量仪器运输费	279.95	
1919 年 7 月 15 日	贾登先生	报销旅费	1885.00	
1919 年 9 月 29 日	贾登先生	1919 年 9 月 部分薪俸	15328.40	
1919 年 9 月 29 日	贾登先生	丧葬费	57482.40	

续表

日期	支付对象	明细	卢布	海关两
1919年 9月30日	贾登夫人	旅费 （大黑河至哈尔滨）	651.00	
1919年 9月30日	贾登夫人	房租津贴	9180.00	
1919年 9月30日	铁路卧车	贾登夫人至上海的旅费	3104.30	
1919年 11月12日	戴纳格（J.Steinscher）	贾登先生行李货车运费	30.00	
1919年 11月15日	账户A	测量仪器货车运费	14.36	
1919年 12月2日	中国电报管理局	9月至11月电报费	129.60	
1919年 12月24日	中国电报管理局	电报费	3161.00	
		总计	258264.09	
		扣除预支款退款*	-13557.00	
		预支款总额（卢布）	244707.09	
		@机动汇率=		8102.07
1918年 8月30日	贾登巡江工司	1918年8月薪俸 445.60海关两		400.00
1918年 9月30日	贾登巡江工司	1918年9月薪俸 445.60上海两		400.00
1920年 12月17日	铎博赉（R. M. Talbot） 帮办	测量仪器检修费		5.32
		预支款总额（海关两）		8907.39

*1921年6月12日总预支款244707.09卢布已按机动汇率折合成海关两。

该抄件内容真实有效，特此证明

录事：屠守鑫四等帮办后班

注：该附录标题中的日期乃由哈尔滨关所提供。

9. 为自 1929 年春天起增加江捐税率及黑龙江省政府指令事

RIVER DUES TARIFF: increase of, from the opening of
navigation, 1929, reporting; instructions of Provincial
Authorities in re, transmitting.

432.

I. G.   Aigun   4th   July,   1929.

Sir,

       I have the honour to append copies of
two letters received from the Mayor (formerly
Taoyin), as President of the Chinese Aids
Commission, dated the 20th May and 25th June, 1929.
The first letter is to the effect that, owing
to heavy expenditure Amur Aids funds have not
been sufficient and that, to increase the income
of the Commission, and to bring the Amur - Ussuri
River Dues Tariff more into line with that
applying to the Sungari, dues on timber and
firewood should be increased. The second letter
informed this office that the increases, as drawn
up, had been approved by the Heilungchiang
Authorities.

       The increases authorised by the Mayor, as
compared with the dues levied last year, were as
follows:

	1928	1929
Planks, sup.sq.ft..1" and in proportion,	$0.00035	$0.0005
Round Beams, cubic feet,	0.0035	0.006
Firewood, up to ¾ arshine long, per sajen,	0.15	0.20
" " 1 " " " "	0.20	0.30

These rates were put into effect on the opening

of

THE INSPECTOR GENERAL OF CUSTOMS,
     SHANGHAI.

Appendix No.1.

Appendix No.2.

of navigation this spring after the receipt of your telegram of the 5th May instructing me to follow the precedents of 1925 and 1927, when the River Dues Tariff was increased on the instructions of the Heilungchiang Authorities.

In accordance with the instructions of I.G. telegram of 3rd June, 1927, I have written the Mayor requesting that he report the increase in the River Dues Tariff to the Kuan-wu Shu; a copy of this letter is appended.

I have the honour to be,

Sir,

Your obedient Servant,

Acting Commissioner.

Appendix No.3.

Appendix.

呈海关总税务司署 <u>432</u> 号文   瑷珲关 1929 年 7 月 4 日

尊敬的海关总税务司（上海）：

兹附 1929 年 5 月 20 日及 6 月 25 日两封黑河市政筹备处处长（前道尹）兼黑龙江水道委员会委员长发来的信件副本（附录 1）。第一封信大意是鉴于开支高昂，黑龙江航路标志资金已不足，以及要增加黑龙江水道委员会收益，还要调整黑龙江 - 乌苏里江江捐税率，使其与松花江一致，认为应该增加木桦与柴火税。第二封信告知瑷珲关，黑龙江省政府已批准按拟议协议增加税收（附录 2）。

与去年征税相比，黑河市政筹备处处长授权的增税如下：

	1928 年	1929 年
厚木板，按比例最大 1 平方英尺	0.00035 银圆	0.0005 银圆
圆横梁，立方英尺	0.0035 银圆	0.006 银圆
木桦，每俄丈最多 3/4 俄尺长	0.15 银圆	0.20 银圆
木桦，每俄丈最多 1 俄尺长	0.20 银圆	0.30 银圆

已经收到海关总税务司署 5 月 5 日的电报，指示瑷珲关遵照 1925 及 1927 年惯例，按黑龙江省政府指示增加江捐税率，今年春天开航便施行了新税率。

本署已致信黑河市政筹备处处长，请其向关务署报告江捐税率增加事宜；随呈附上该信函副本（附录 3）。

您忠诚的仆人

铎博赉（R. M. Talbot）

瑷珲关署理税务司

录事：黎彭寿 四等一级帮办

10. 为黑河市政筹备处处长要求每月扣除 10% 海关征税佣金后向其移交江捐税款事

Copy for Aigun Commissioner.

JUL 22 1930

M E M O R A N D U M.

Custom House,	To
H A R B I N, 11th July 1930.	The Chief Secretary,
	S H A N G H A I.

Harbin Commissioner's Comments on Aigun despatch
No. 492/I.G. dated the 14th June, 1930 and
docketed:

AIDS TO NAVIGATION: request of Provisional Mayor
conveyed through Superintendent that River Dues
be collected at increased rate/to signing of
annual local International Agreement and also
that River Dues less Customs 1/10th Cost of
Collection be handed over to him monthly,
reporting. First request acceded to under
certain conditions. Approval solicited.
Dissertation on advisibility of acceding to
2nd request and on effect of so doing both on
repayment of Sungari Aids loans to Amur Aids
and on position of Technical Adviser. Instructions
requested.

TECHNICAL ADVISER TO AMUR AIDS: question of
renewal of I.G. agreement with on 16th September
1930 on revised terms much effected by proposed
handing over of River Dues funds. Instructions
requested.

$ 25,000 - out of the $ 40,000 authorised by
I.G. - have already been advanced by the Sungari
Aids to the Amur Aids. After Mr. Fletcher's
very lucid expose of the situation of the Amur
Aids, it is very much hoped that the Sungari
Aids will not be called upon for a further

advance

advance. As the Sungari Aids may pass into the hands of the Conservancy Bureau at any moment, it becomes necessary to hold on to its reserve funds for the eventual superannuation of the Aids Staff. The indebtedness of the Amur Aids should not be lost sight of and the President of the Amur Aids Commission should have his memory refreshed from time to time. It is not out of place to remark here that the advances from Sungari to Amur Aids have been made solely on the authority of the I.G. and that the authority of the latter for such advances may be questioned sooner or later by the Provincial Authorities. In the matter of repayment it should be remembered that a sub-port of Harbin, Lahasusu, collects Amur and Ussuri river dues on behalf of the Amur Aids and that the suggestion made by my predecessor that we might obtain a lien on this collection is well worth consideration.

(Rene d'Anjou)
Commissioner.

Copy of these Comments is being sent to the Aigun Commissioner.

492

I.G.

A I G U N   14th June 1930.   492/I.G.

Rep. C.Y.

Sir,

1.   With reference to your despatch No.524/127,220 of 3rd April 1930 :

> Authorising me to start collecting River Dues at the existing rate, or at an increased rate if so desired by the Provincial Authorities, before the Annual International Agreement is signed, but instructing me to request the Superintendent to report the matter to the Kwan-wu Shu for approval or record :

Append A.

I have the honour to append copy of a letter from the Superintendent dated 3rd June 1930 in which he requests me to collect River Dues at the increased rate of 5% _ad valorem_ on direct imports from, and exports to, Russia, the Dues on other classes of goods remaining unchanged. He states that he is requesting the Provincial Authorities to report this increase to the Kwan-wu Shu. He also requests me at the end of each month to transfer to the Mayor the River Dues collection, after deducting the Customs one-tenth as Cost of Collection, stating that he will attend to all expenditure, including the salary of the Technical Adviser.

                                                Immediately

The Inspector General of Customs,

     S H A N G H A I.

C.Y.

Immediately after my arrival here on 30th May
I had called on the Superintendent -- who is also
Provisional Mayor (ex-Taoyin) and President of the
Chinese side of the Amur Aids Commission -- and conferred
with him whether I was to collect River Dues on the
following day.   He feigned surprise that there should
be any question about it.   I therefore pointed out
the Customs position, i.e., that we normally collect
River Dues on behalf of the Provincial Authorities
under the authority of the Kwan-wu Shu conveyed after
the signing of the Annual International Agreement.
But I added that, though no International Agreement
had yet been negotiated this year, I would continue
to collect if he, as Superintendent, shouldered the
responsibility for the collection and undertook to
report the matter to the Kwan-wu Shu.   He was at
first inclined to argue the question whether the
Provincial Authorities had the right to collect these
Dues but I refused to be drawn into this snare,
saying that the Customs had nothing to do with that
abstract question and only became concerned when they
were requested to collect the Dues.   He then agreed
to accept responsibility and to report to the Kwan-wu.
Shu.   The present letter is the outcome.   It will
be noted that in spite of my insistence on the
paramount importance of his office of Superintendent as
far as we are concerned, the whole tone of his letter
is couched in the language of the Mayor -- it is true
that he uses both offices in the heading but he refers
to this office as 貴關 (kuei Kuan) instead of 本關 (pen
kuan), to me as 愛琿關稅務司 (Aigun Commissioner)
instead of 本關稅務司 (pen kuan shui wu ssu), and

to

to the Mayor as 本處 (pen ch'u) instead of 黑河市政善備處
(Heiho Mayor).   He also uses the Mayor's seal.   He
does not promise to report to the Kwan-wu Shu but
only to suggest such a course to the Manchurian
Authorities, the same procedure that he adopted in 1927,
<u>vide</u> Aigun despatch No.325, though a more satisfactory
one than his ignoring of a similar request in 1929,
<u>vide</u> Aigun despatch No.478, bottom of page 7.   In
addition, he introduces the question of handing over
the funds monthly.

Append B.

On the 7th June I replied, copy appended,
that I would draft a joint notification to be issued
by him, as Superintendent, and myself stating that
River Dues would be collected at an increased rate at
the request of the Mayor.   As regards the proposed
change of procedure in so far as the custody of the
funds is concerned, I requested him to wait while I
referred the matter to you.

Append C.

On the 12th June the Mayor, i.e., the
Superintendent using the language and phraseology of
the Mayor, replied that he was quite willing to issue
a Joint Notification.   Nevertheless, I had the Joint
Notification made out in the name of the Superintendent
and sent it to his office by the hand of the Writer
who was requested to point out that it was the
Superintendent's seal that I required, not the Mayor's.
There was no difficulty: the Superintendent's seal was
affixed.

2.   I therefore have the honour to suggest that
everything possible has been done as regards Customs
collection at an increased rate prior to the signing
of the Annual International Agreement and prior to

receipt

receipt of Kwan-wu Shu authority. I presume that the Superintendent finds himself unable to address the Kwan-wu Shu direct, though I cannot but admit that this causes me some little surprise since, as far as I know, Manchuria does not now profess to occupy the same independent position that it did in 1927 and 1929.

3.　　　　As regards the handing over of the collection, it becomes necessary for me to quote some of the references to which I drew your attention in my semi-official letter No.125 of 11th February 1930.

The Joint Amur Aids Commission consists, as you are aware, of four representatives from the Chinese side and four from the Russian side. The Mayor (ex-Taoyin) is President of the Chinese side and the Customs Commissioner is Vice-President. The Technical Adviser is one of the other two members, and the Mayor's Secretary is the fourth. The Russian side also has its President and Vice-President.

The original Provisional Agreement of 1922, Art. 7, and also the Additional Regulations of 1922, Art. 1, laid down that the total of the River Dues collection was to be used for Joint Aids (vide Aigun despatch No. 67, Appends 1 and 4, respectively). This was modified by the Provisional Agreement of 1923/4, Annex 2, §§ 13, 14 and 15, to read "Collection less one-tenth cost of collection less expenses of Technical Adviser's Office (estimated at $8,000 p.a.) less expenses of Chinese President's Office (estimated at $2,000 p.a.)", vide Aigun despatch No.144, Enclosure 1. But subsequent Agreements call upon the Chinese Commission to furnish fixed annual sums, so that nowadays the Chinese Commission is, I understand, associated with the Russian

Commission

Commission only so far as expenditure on Joint Aids is concerned.   It follows, then, that the balance of the River Dues, which are the source from which the annual fixed sum is obtained, do not belong in any way to the Joint Commission, but to the Chinese Commission.

I. G. despatch No.59/90,055 of 28th June 1922 issues directions for the accounts treatment of the River Dues Collection which is to form a Local Moneys Account in A/c. D.   That, I take it, constitutes the Commissioner Treasurer of the Aids funds but does not definitely assign him a preponderating voice in the disposal of the collection which, at that time, was, as I have shown, all accounted for under Joint Aids. It was not till later that the institution of fixed sums for Joint Aids left the River Dues Account with a credit or debit (!) balance annually.   In practice the Mayor "controls" the funds, for he is President, has the fourth member (his Secretary) in his pocket, and can make himself exceedingly unpleasant in his rôle of Superintendent if the Commissioner, in his capacity as Treasurer of Aids funds, rouses his antagonism.   He even, I am credibly informed from several sources, is offended at the Commissioner referring any special item of expenditure to yourself, considering that his desires should be met unchallenged.   And I am not even quite sure whether you wish to have any proposed expenditures or refunds of expenditure referred to you.   Certain it is, in my humble opinion, that no practical control at all can be exercised at this end unless such references are insisted upon by you.   I therefore said in my semi-official letter No.126, pages 8 and 9, that I considered that the best course would be for the

Commissioner

Commissioner to have nothing to do with the expenditure of the balance. He should collect, of course, and then hand over the Collection, less one-tenth for Cost of Collection, to the Chinese Authorities, e.g., the Mayor, for them to deal with. Now, without any prompting on my part, the Mayor takes the same view, and, were it not for two points, I would be whole-heartedly in favour of Customs concurrence. These two points are : (1) your loans from Sungari Aids Account to Amur Aids Account and (2) the status of the Technical Adviser. A discussion thereon follows.

4.   I. G. despatch No.253/104,793 of 21st September 1925 authorised an advance to Amur Aids Account from Sungari Aids Account of $20,000 and I. G. despatch No. 300/108,242 of 29th June 1926 authorised a further advance of $20,000. $25,000 of these $40,000 have been drawn ($10,000 on 1/4/26, $10,000 on 18/8/26, and $5,000 on 5/3/27), leaving $15,000 still available. No repayment has ever been effected, budgeted for, or, as far as I can see, seriously contemplated.

I. G. despatch No.350/112,642 of 18th May 1927 says that Harbour improvement works should only have been proceeded with after the Taoyin had actually provided the necessary funds from local sources, seeing that the funds remaining in Aids Account were specially advanced from Sungari Aids Account to meet a clearly defined programme of Aids work on the Amur and if these funds are not required for the purpose for which they were allocated they should properly be returned to the Sungari Aids Account.

Aigun despatch No.359 of 23rd February 1928 reports the reluctance of the Provincial Authorities to acknowledge

acknowledge the indebtedness of the Amur Aids Commission for the expenditure of Hk.Tls.8,907.39 incurred over the late River Inspector Garden's inspection trips on the Amur in 1918/19 and, consequently, of a further sum of Hk.Tls.1,024.43 expended in the same connection, though they acknowledge, $10, the Commission's indebtedness for loans from the Sungari Aids funds, to be repaid from Amur River Dues Collection. I. G. despatch No.393/116202 of 8th March 1928 instructs the Commissioner to inform the Taoyin that for purposes of accountancy a further sum of Hk.Tls.1,024.43 has been added to the advances (Hk.Tls.8,907.39) appearing in the Harbin books to the debit of the Amur Aids but that at this juncture there is no question of pressing for repayment. It also states that it should be made clear to the Taoyin that the recording of these advances is for the time being in the nature of a book transaction and that when the time comes for a definite settlement no doubt a basis of agreement will be arrived at satisfactory to all parties concerned.

I. G. despatch No.416/117,614 of 4th July 1928, commenting on the Budget for 1928 of the Amur and Ussuri Aids to Navigation, says that it is not reassuring to know that so far no repayment of any kind has been made to the Sungari Aids Commission for sums advanced; that this indebtedness must not be lost sight of, the fact that no provision has been made towards its liquidation in the Commission's budget for 1928 not auguring well; and that the evident tendency of the Commission to launch into expenditure far beyond its income should be kept firmly in check.

Aigun despatch No.439 of 5th August 1929

records

records your telegram of 4th May 1929 stating that
you had no objection to the proposed Taheiho bunding
scheme (to be paid from Amur Aids funds) provided that
the Amur did not suffer thereby and that the Sungari
Aids did not demand immediate refund of the advances
made. (This telegram of yours was sent in answer to
Aigun S/O letter No.106 of 20th April 1929 on which
the Harbin Commissioner had "commented" that "the
Sungari Aids funds are in such condition that the
repayment of the $15,000 -- really $10,000 plus $15,000 =
$25,000 -- owed by the Amur Commission is by no means
pressing", Harbin S/O 759 to I.G.). This same
despatch points out that the Taoyin had been notified
that the Sungari Aids had a prior claim on all
surplus for the repayment of the $15,000 ($25,000 !)
advanced to the Amur Aids but that whilst acknowledging
this he held that the urgency of the work required
justified a further postponement of the repayment of
this loan. Your reply No.485/123,791 of 19th September
1929 remarks that it should not be overlooked that the
carrying out of this public utility, which benefits
Aigun only, has in reality been done at the expense
of the Sungari Aids Commission to whom the Amur Aids
Commission is in debt; that as the Chairman of the
latter Commission is also the Mayor (formerly Taoyin),
and the leading local authority, and as he understands
the situation and accepts full responsibility for this
use of Amur Aids money, the matter need not be
pressed in such a way as to cause friction and
unpleasantness; but that the debt should not be lost
sight of.

Aigun despatch No.440 of 7th August 1929 shows
an

an estimated surplus of $18,200 in the 1929 Amur Aids Budget and states that this may well be employed on very necessary work to be determined on later, including further bunding in Taheiho, though it is true that this is somewhat belatedly followed by the remark that though it would appear that the repayment of the $15,000 ($25,000 !) borrowed from the Sungari Aids Account is not pressing, yet recommendation will be made to the Taoyin when a copy of the budget is sent to him that part, at least, of the advance be refunded.

Aigun despatch No.451 of 29th November 1929 reports that the Mayor had, at the time of evacuation by the Customs, insisted on the Commissioner handing over to him $4,500 of the Amur Aids balance, saying in his letter of 9th November that as the future was uncertain he required this money for safeguarding (保管, pao kuan). At a previous interview the Mayor had stated that if the Amur Aids could not repay the $15,000 ($25,000 !) loan made by the Sungari Aids, the Heilungchiang Government would do so.

In Aigun despatch No.451 (Harbin No.3922) the Harbin Commissioner suggested that further advances should not be made by the Sungari Aids to the Amur Aids without some greater security than the personal opinion of the President of the Amur Aids that the Heilungchiang Government will effect repayment. He further suggested that the Sungari Aids be given a lien on the Amur and Ussuri River Dues collected on behalf of the Amur Commission by Harbin's Sub-port of Lahasusu. He also pointed out that the cash balance to the credit of the Amur Aids Commission was hardly sufficient to pay off the Technical Adviser.

From

From the foregoing it is sufficiently evident that, even with the Commissioner as Treasurer, no effort at repayment of Sungari Aids advances will ever be seriously considered or allowed by the Mayor so long as a measure of supported pressure is not brought to bear by the Commissioner. With the funds in the hands of the Mayor, it may be said that the last vestige of hope of recovery disappears. He will, of course, readily promise to refund out of any surplus available, but will at the same time arrange that there is never such an available surplus. So sure were my Chinese Staff of this denouement that I did not raise the point of refund in my reply letter, judging it preferable to take your views on the subject rather than extract a promise from him in the first instance and then, maybe, find myself in the difficult position of being obliged to question its efficacy, the logical inference from any possible insistence on further safeguards.

5.　　　　As regards the Technical Adviser, I should be greatly surprised were the Mayor's proposed control of expenditure not to result, sooner rather than later, in his discharge of Mr. Ignatieff. This, then, raises the question of the Technical Adviser's status and the attitude that you will adopt when the time comes for the renewal of his agreement on terms which your despatch No.530/127,497 (Pensions No.4094) states should be reconsidered.

　　　　Mr. P. I. Ignatieff was appointed Technical Adviser on Amur Aids to Navigation by Inspectorate despatch No.75/90,949 of 2nd September 1922 on a three years' contract.

Since

Since then that contract has been renewed annually as from 16th September, the last renewal from 16th September 1929 being notified in your despatch No.482/123,634.

There is nothing very definite on record to prove whether or not the Inspector General made this appointment at the request of the Chinese Authorities: though Clause 3 of the Technical Adviser's Agreement with you (Append to your despatch No.2928/90,948 to Harbin) states that the Harbin Commissioner of Customs is acting on behalf of the Inspector General as Agent for the Chinese Government. It appears, moreover, that the first reference to the source of his payment was the Audit Secretary's semi-official letter of 6th October 1922 directing that his pay be issued from the River Dues Account. Aigun despatch No.77, $6, of 1st November 1922, alluding to the above semi-official letter, states that the Joint Aids Commission had, subject to the Inspector General's final approval, verbally agreed in principle to the payment of his salary by River Dues Account. Your reply No.93/92,051 of 21st November 1922 ruled that since Mr. Ignatieff had been appointed Technical Adviser to the local Administration of the Amur Aids to Navigation, his salary, house-rent, etc., etc., are therefore to be charged to the River Dues Collection so long as he functions as such, i.e., so long as the Provisional Local Agreement is operative.

On 9th November 1929 the Chinese President of the Amur Aids Commission discharged the Technical Adviser with three months' pay in lieu of notice

(vide

(vide Aigun despatch No.451), your despatch No.504/ 125,340 acquiescing in this discharge. Your semi- official letter of 16th December 1929, however, required the question to be reconsidered; my semi-official letter No.123 presented you with the facts together with my conclusions deduced therefrom; and your despatch No.530/ 127,497 of 15th April 1930 recorded your telegram of 11th February 1930 temporarily appointing Mr. Ignatieff to Sungari Aids, laid down your treatment of the case, and stated that when the time comes for renewing Mr. Ignatieff's agreement the terms on which he is at present engaged should be reconsidered. .

        Now we have the Mayor's letter proposing himself as the Treasurer of the River Dues funds and it naturally becomes more than ever necessary for you to safeguard yourself against again having the Technical Adviser thrown on your hands.   At the same time I would do what I can for him, since all previous reports on, and references to, him are united in eulogising in high terms the services which he has rendered to the Amur Aids Commission.

        At the request of Mr. Ignatieff, who of course realises the uncertainty of his position and wishes to know as soon as possible how he stands in order that he may if necessary make other arrangements, I verbally asked the Mayor for an expression of his opinion about Mr. Ignatieff's future prospects.   For it is assumed both by Mr. Ignatieff and by myself that you will be unwilling to renew his Agreement if the control of River Dues funds passes out of my hands.   I therefore asked the Mayor whether, granting a satisfactory arrangement for the transfer of such

control/

control, Mr. Ignatieff's Agreement should in his
opinion be renewed with him or with you. He,
naturally enough, found it difficult to give an answer
before, as he said, he had negotiated the Annual local
Agreement with Russia and knew where he stood as
regards funds. He appeared, however, to be in favour
of the continuation of the present arrangement, i.e.,
an agreement between the Technical Adviser and yourself.
I pointed out that in that case I should have to
ask him to allow me to deduct the Technical Adviser's
salary as well as the Customs one-tenth Cost of
Collection before handing over the monthly Collection of
Dues. He agreed, in principle, willingly; but again
said that he could not give any definite reply at
present for the reason already given. He assumes, as
does everyone else, that the River Dues will this year
be insufficient for the Customs one-tenth and the
Technical Adviser's salary, let alone any payments to
Russia, so he does not wish to compromise himself in
any way.

As matters stand at present, it is exceedingly
difficult to offer any suggestions as to the tenour of
the altered terms to which you allude. If the
discharge of Mr. Ignatieff by the Mayor in November
1929 establishes a precedent, it would seem that
security of tenure of office is not affected, whether
the Technical Adviser's agreement be concluded with you
or with the Aids Commission. Further, not only does
it appear strange that an Agreement with you should
bind some other institution, the Amur Aids Commission,
to wit, to pay salary at a certain rate (a point not
lost sight of by the Mayor) but the very fact of
your

your fixing it at a rate that may possibly be higher
than that agreeable to the Commission (i.e., the Mayor)
must inevitably tend to precipitate a repetition of the
discharge incident. If, moreover, the control of the
funds passes out of my hands, it would appear more
than ever evident that renewal by you of the Agreement
is neither necessary nor desirable. But if you act
on these lines, I would certainly request your
consideration of the fact that Mr. Ignatieff has been
a contributor to the Pension Fund for eight years
and would venture to suggest that, besides refund of
Contributions, you treat him as liberally as possible
under the terms of Circular No.3006, §3, "Discharge".

6.　　　　Finally, I have the honour to request:

1) your approval of Customs collection of increased
River Dues under the circumstances reported;

2) your instructions re the Provisional Mayor's
request that the River Dues Collection, less Customs
one-tenth for Cost of Collection, be handed over to
him monthly; and

3) your instructions re the renewal of your
Agreement with the Technical Adviser on Amur Aids to
Navigation.

　　　　　　　I have the honour to be,

　　　　　　　　　Sir,

　　　　　　　Your obedient Servant,

　　　　　　　(H. G. Fletcher)
　　　　　　　Acting Commissioner.

　　　　　　　Append A.

通函

由：	致：
滨江关	总务科税务司（上海）
1930 年 7 月 11 日	

根据 1929 年 6 月 14 日瑷珲关致海关总税务司署第 492 号呈：

"航务：汇报海关监督兼暂代黑河市政筹备处处长之要求，在签订地方年度国际协议之前，提高征收江捐税率，江捐税收扣除 10% 海关征税佣金后，按月上交至暂代黑河市市政筹备处处长。兹请示可否同意于签订地方年度国际协议之前，提高江捐税率。汇报按月向暂代黑河市市政筹备处处长上交江捐税收（扣除 10% 海关征税佣金）一事的可行性，以及该事对黑龙江水道委员会向松花江水道委员会还款一事以及航务专门顾问一职的影响，请求指示。

黑龙江航务专门顾问：海关总税务司署与航务专门顾问于 1930 年 9 月 16 日的续约问题，合同条款的修订大多涉及江捐资金移交事宜，请求指示。"

海关总税务司署批准的 40000 银圆拨款中已有 25000 银圆从松花江航路标志账户预支给黑龙江航路标志账户。富乐嘉（Fletcher）先生明确分析黑龙江航路标志账户的情况之后，希望不要再从松花江航路标志账户预支款项了。而且松花江航路标志账户随时可能移交给东北水利局，因此必须持有储备金，以便最终支付航路标志职员的养老金。此外，松花江航路标志账户向黑龙江航路标志账户预支款项一事，只有海关总税务司署的单独授权，该授权恐怕迟早会遭到省政府的质疑。关于还款事宜，有两点需要考虑，首先，滨江关的拉哈苏苏分关是代表黑龙江水道委员会征收黑龙江及乌苏里江江捐的；其次，上一任税务司曾建议瑷珲关留置这一税收款项。

签字：覃书（R. C. L. d'Anjou）

滨江关税务司

此抄件发送至瑷珲关税务司

呈海关总税务司署 <u>492</u> 号文 　　　　　　　　瑷珲关（哈尔滨）1930 年 6 月 14 日

尊敬的海关总税务司（上海）：

1. 根据 1930 年 4 月 3 日海关总税务司署致瑷珲关第 524/127220 号令：

"批准瑷珲关以现行税率征收江捐，若省政府有要求，可于年度国际协议签署前，按提高的税率征收江捐，但请海关监督向关务署请示批准，或将此记录在案。"

兹附 1930 年 6 月 3 日海关监督来函副本，函中要求本署按提高的税率（值百抽五）向直接进出口俄国的货物征收江捐，其他江捐税率不变。海关监督说明已要求省政府向关务署汇报增税事宜，同时要求本署于每月月末扣除 10% 海关征税佣金后向黑河市政筹备处处长移交江捐税款，并称其会承担所有支出，包括航务专门顾问的薪俸。

本署于 5 月 30 日抵达后即刻拜访海关监督兼暂代黑河市政筹备处处长（前道尹）兼黑龙江水道委员会中方委员长，与之商议本署是否应于次日征收江捐。海关监督认为此事不应有任何疑问。本署说明按照常规，海关应于年度国际协议签署后，经关务署授权，代表省政府征收江捐，然而，虽然今年还未签订国际协议，但倘若海关监督承担起征税的责任，向关务署汇报此事，本署会继续征税。海关监督起初有意于讨论省政府是否有权征收江捐，但本署表示海关只关心征税问题。海关监督遂同意承担责任，表示会向关务署汇报此事并向本署致函（即为 1930 年 6 月 3 日海关监督信函）说明征税事宜。然而，尽管本署一再说明因此事涉及海关，其海关监督的身份至关重要，但其仍以黑河市政筹备处处长的口吻书写信函——函中称呼瑷珲关为"贵关"而非"本关"，称呼本署为"瑷珲关税务司"而非"本关税务司"，此外，还将"黑河市政筹备处"写成"本处"，最后亦加盖黑河市政筹备处处长之印章。但最终海关监督并未应允向关务署汇报，只是向满洲政府提出此建议，与其 1927 年所走程序相同（参阅瑷珲关第 325 号呈）。1929 年本署亦请海关监督向关务署汇报征税事宜，但其并未理会（参阅瑷珲关第 478 号呈，第 7 页底端），相比之下，海关监督今年之做法已相对较好。此外，海关监督还提出每月移交江捐资金之事。

兹附本署 6 月 7 日回函副本，本署回复将草拟一份联合声明"按照黑河市政筹备处处长要求，提高税率征收江捐"，由海关监督及本署发布。关于所提议的江捐资金管理权变更一事，本署请求其等待本署向海关总税务司署提交后再议。

6 月 12 日黑河市政筹备处处长兼海关监督，使用处长的口吻及措辞回复愿意发布联合声明。尽管如此，本署仍以海关监督的名义起草联合声明，由文案送至其办公室并向海关监督说明需使用海关监督印章而非黑河市政筹备处处长印章。

2.特此汇报,已完成在签署年度国际协议及收到关务署批准之前,提高税率征收税捐相关事宜。本署推测海关监督无法与关务署直接对话,这让人颇感意外,毕竟据本署所知,满洲现在并未像 1927 年及 1929 年那样宣布独立。

3.关于移交税款一事,需要引述 1930 年 2 月 11 日瑷珲关第 125 号机要信函之内容。

黑龙江水道委员会有 4 位中方委员及 4 位俄方委员。黑河市政筹备处处长(前道尹)任华方委员长,海关税务司任中方副委员长。另外两位成员分别是航务专门顾问和黑河市政筹备处处长的文案。俄方亦设有委员长及副委员长。

1922 年《临时地方工程协议》第 7 条以及 1922 年《附加章程》的第 1 条规定"江捐税收应全部用于联合维护航路标志工作"(参阅瑷珲关第 67 号呈,附录 1 及附录 4)。1923-1924 年《临时地方工程协议》附录 2(第 13、14、15 章)将此修改为"江捐税收扣除 10% 海关征税佣金,扣除航务专门顾问办事处办公经费(预计每年 8000 银圆),扣除中方委员长办公经费(预计每年 2000 银圆)"(参阅瑷珲关第 144 号呈的附件 1)。但随后签订的协议中要求中方委员会每年提供固定金额,如此一来,中俄委员会如今便只是在联合维护航路标志相关事宜上有所关联了。年度固定金额源自江捐税收,因此江捐税收余额无论如何都不属于联合委员会,而只属于中方委员会。

1922 年 6 月 28 日海关总税务司署第 59/90055 号令发布江捐税收入账办法指令,即在账户 D 设立地方公款清账一项。兹认为,如此一来,税务司便成为航路标志资金的司库,但却并未被明确赋予优先处置江捐税收的权力,且江捐税收当时全部归于联合航路标志项下,待中方按固定金额承担联合航路标志的维护费用之后,江捐账户每年方有可支配余额。黑河市政筹备处处长既是联合委员会的中方委员长,又可差遣委员会第四位委员(其文案),因此实际上"管控着"资金;但税务司以航路标志资金的司库身分行事时,又难免与其海关监督的身分发生冲突,使其不悦。据可靠消息称,海关监督认为自己的判断毋庸置疑,无论税务司向海关总税务司署请示任何特殊开支项目均会使其不满。此外,本署亦不确定贵署是否希望收到拟议支出或支出报销的相关报告。本署愚见,若不坚持让海关提交支出报告,最终将毫无实权。本署于瑷珲关第 126 号机要信函(第 8 页和第 9 页)中表示税务司最好不参与余额支出一事。当然,税务司应征收江捐,扣除 10% 海关征税佣金后将税款交于政府处置(如交于黑河市政筹备处处长)。目前本署虽未透露任何信息,但黑河市政筹备处处长已有同样的观点。海关总税务司署从松花江航路标志账户借款给黑龙江航路标志账户一事,以及航务专门顾问的职务问题,仍需解决。

4.1925 年 9 月 21 日海关总税务司署第 253/104793 号令批准从松花江航路标志

账户预支给黑龙江航路标志账户 20000 银圆；1926 年 6 月 29 日海关总税务司署第 300/108242 号令再次批准预支 20000 银圆。该 40000 银圆预支款中已支出 25000 银圆（1929 年 4 月 1 日支出 10000 银圆；1926 年 8 月 18 日支出 10000 银圆；1927 年 3 月 5 日支出 5000 银圆），可用余额 15000 银圆。黑龙江航路标志账户迄今仍未还款，亦未有还款预算，据本署所知，甚至未曾认真考虑还款一事。

1927 年 5 月 18 日海关总税务司署第 350/112642 号令说明，鉴于黑龙江航路标志账户的余额是松花江航路标志账户的预支款项，专门用以支付明确规定的黑龙江航路标志工作项目；若非如此，则应将余额返还松花江航路标志账户，故应在收到道尹的地方经费之后，再开展港口改建工作。1928 年 2 月 3 日瑷珲关第 359 号呈汇报省政府不愿承认黑龙江水道委员会的债务，包括已故的巡江工司贾登（Garden）先生于 1918-1919 年巡查黑龙江时的费用（8907.39 海关两）以及另一笔同类支出（1024.43 海关两），但承认（第 10 章）从松花江航路标志账户所借债款，并计划用黑龙江江捐税收支付。1928 年 3 月 8 日海关总税务司署第 393/116202 号令命税务司告知道尹，黑龙江航路标志偿还给滨江关的款项（8907.39 海关两）中额外增加了 1024.43 海关两，但并无催款之意，同时向道尹说明，这些款项是按当前账户交易性质记录，最终账款清算时，以协商一致为原则，达到相关各方均满意之结果。

1928 年 7 月 4 日海关总税务司署第 416/117614 号令对 1928 年黑龙江及乌苏里江航务预算给出意见，表示不确定黑龙江水道委员会从松花江水道委员会预支的款项是否仍未偿还；不可忽视此项债务，且黑龙江水道委员会在 1928 年预算中并未涉及清算问题，此非吉兆；对黑龙江水道委员会入不敷出的趋势，须严格控制。

1929 年 8 月 5 日瑷珲关第 439 号呈记载 1929 年 5 月 4 日海关总税务司署电令（回复 1929 年 4 月 20 日瑷珲关第 106 号机要信函。滨江关税务司于滨江关至海关总税务司署第 759 号机要文件中给出对瑷珲关第 106 号机要信函的意见，即"黑龙江水道委员会应向松花江航路标志资金账户还款 15000 银圆——实际为 10000 银圆加 15000 银圆 =25000 银圆，并无催款之意"）。该电令声明海关总税务司署对筑堤方案（由黑龙江航路标志资金支付）的提议无反对意见，前提是松花江水道委员会不要求即刻还款，且黑龙江航路标志的维护工作不会受到影响。瑷珲关第 439 号呈中说明已告知道尹，黑龙江航路标志账户的余额应优先偿还松花江航路标志的预支款 15000 银圆（25000 银圆！）。道尹表示认同，但坚持认为筑堤工程为当务之急，不得不推迟还款。1929 年 9 月 19 日海关总税务司署第 485/123791 号令中回复，不容忽视的是，开展此项公共事业，仅有利于瑷珲关发展，这实际上是以牺牲向黑龙江水道委员会出借款项的松花江水道委员会为代价的；鉴于黑龙江水道委员会委员长亦为黑河市政筹备处处长（前道尹）兼任地方长官，对目前状况表示理解，并对使用黑龙江航路标志账款承担全部责任，因此无需催促，以免造成摩擦与不愉快；但不应忽视此项债务。

1929 年 8 月 7 日瑷珲关第 440 号呈中指出 1929 年黑龙江航路标志预算预计结余 18200 银圆，并说明此项结余大可用于日后必要工作，包括大黑河下一步筑堤工程；虽然从松花江航路标志账户所借 15000 银圆（25000 银圆！）并未催还，但本署会在向道尹将发送该预算副本时提议至少偿还部分借款。

1929 年 11 月 29 日瑷珲关第 451 号呈汇报海关撤离大黑河时，黑河市政筹备处处长执意让税务司移交黑龙江航路标志账户余额 4500 银圆，并在其 11 月 9 日信函中表示因将来难测，欲保管余额。黑河市政筹备处处长早在之前的一次会谈中就声明若黑龙江航路标志账户无法偿还松花江航路标志账户的 15000 银圆（25000 银圆！）债款，那么黑龙江政府将会代之还款。

在瑷珲关第 453 号呈（滨江关第 3922 号呈）中，滨江关税务司建议若松花江航路标志需要再次预支给黑龙江航路标志款项，则应有更大的保证，而非只是黑龙江水道委员会委员长个人认为黑龙江政府将会还款。另建议松花江航路标志机构应有权留置由滨江关的拉哈苏苏分关代表黑龙江水道委员会所征收的黑龙江及乌苏里江江捐税款。滨江关税务司还指出黑龙江水道委员会账户现金余额不足以付清航务专门顾问的薪俸。

如上所述，显然即使税务司任司库，若得不到一定的支持，黑河市政筹备处处长对偿还松花江航路标志借款一事仍不会认真考虑，亦不会允许还款。现黑河市政筹备处处长手握资金，可以说收回债款的最后一丝希望也破灭了。当然其会欣然答应若有可用余额必会还款，但同时亦会安排永无可用余额。如此一来，瑷珲关华籍职员便确信本署认为与其先得到黑河市政筹备处处长的承诺，不如先征求贵署之意见更为妥当，遂未于回函中提及还款一事。但本署也因此陷入窘境，不免要质疑此法是否有效，将来又应如何保障还款事宜。

5. 关于航务专门顾问，本署相信黑河市政筹备处处长提出管理支出后，迟早会解雇易保罗（Ignatieff）先生。如此则需考虑航务专门顾问的职务问题，海关总税务司署第 530/127497 号令（养老储金编号 4094）声明会重新考虑航务专门顾问续约事宜，贵署届时会如何应对此事。

根据 1922 年 9 月 2 日海关总税务司署第 75/90949 号令，易保罗先生担任黑龙江航务专门顾问一职，任期三年。此后，合同于每年9月16日续约，1929年9月16日为最后一次续约，由海关总税务司署第482/123634号令通知。

无明确记录证明总税务司是否是按照中国政府要求才有此协定：海关总税务司署致滨江关第2928/90948号令之附录，即航务专门顾问与海关总税务司署之间的合同，说明滨江关税务司谨代表中国政府之代理——总税务司。1922年10月6日会计科税务司的机要信函中指示从江捐账户支付航务专门顾问薪俸，该处似乎是首次提及其薪俸来源。1922年11月1日瑷珲关第77号呈（第6章）提及上述机要信函，说明联合水道委员会已经口头表示，原则上同意从江捐账户中支付其薪俸，但需经总税务司最终批准。1922年11月21日海关总税务司署第93/92051号令回复，因易保罗先生担任黑龙江航务专门顾问一职，故只要其从事本职工作（即只要《临时地方工程协议》仍在生效中），其薪资、房屋租赁费等应由江捐征收项下支出。

1929年11月9日，黑龙江水道委员会委员长解雇航务专门顾问，直接发放其3个月的薪俸（参阅瑷珲关第451号呈），海关总税务司署第504/125340号令予以批准。1929年12月16日海关总税务司署机要信函提出重新考虑此问题；本署于瑷珲关第123号机要信函中向海关总税务司署说明实际情况及结论；1930年4月15日海关总税务司署第530/127479号令记录1930年2月11日海关总税务司署电报，即易保罗先生暂时任职于松花江水道委员会，待续约时，再重新考虑当前合同所定条款。

黑河市政筹备处处长来函提议自己担任江捐资金司库，因此，贵署务必保己周全，以免再次负责航务专门顾问一事。同时本署亦会尽量帮助航务专门顾问，而且相关报告及资料一致高度赞扬了航务专门顾问在黑龙江水道委员会的工作表现。

易保罗先生当然意识到自己职务的不确定性，希望尽快明晰，也好另作安排。本署按照其请求，向黑河市政筹备处处长口头询问易保罗先生日后的工作应如何安排。易保罗先生及本署均认为若瑷珲关不再管理江捐资金，海关总税务司署则不会再愿意续约。本署遂向黑河市政筹备处处长询问，若能称心安排管理权移交事宜，易保罗先生是否应与其续约，还是应与海关总税务司署续约。黑河市政筹备处处长表示，在未与俄方协定年度地方协议，且不知在资金问题上自己所处位置的前提下，难以答复。但其似乎倾向于目前的安排，即航务专门顾问与海关总税务司署续约，本署遂指出，若如此安排，则应允准每月移交江捐资金之前扣除航务专门顾问薪俸及10%的海关征税佣金。黑河市政筹备处处长表示原则上愿意同意，但再次说明基于上述原因，目前无法给出确切答复，但也认为今年的江捐税款不足以支付10%的海关征税佣金以及航务专门顾问的薪俸，更不用提向俄方付款一事，因此不希望做出任何让步。

就目前形势而言，关于贵署所提变更合同条款事宜，实难给出建议。若 1929 年 11 月黑河市政筹备处处长首开先例，解雇易保罗先生，那么航务专门顾问的合同无论是与海关总税务司署签订还是与黑龙江水道委员会签订，似乎都不会影响其任职保障。若航务专门顾问与海关总税务司署签订合同，必会约束某些机构，即黑龙江水道委员会，按照特定税率支付薪俸（黑河市政筹备处处长不会忽视此处），贵署按税率所定薪俸很有可能高于委员会（即黑河市政筹备处处长）同意的金额，由此必致解雇事件重演。此外，若本署不再管理江捐资金，贵署则更不必亦不宜参与续约一事。若贵署仍欲为之，还望考虑易保罗先生已缴 8 年养老储金，届时除退还养老储金之外，还需根据第 3006 号通令（第三章）"解雇"所定条款安置易保罗先生。

6. 最后，兹请求：

（1）按照报告情况，批准海关提高税率征收江捐；

（2）请指示如何回复暂代黑河市政筹备处处长关于每月扣除 10% 海关征税佣金后向其移交江捐税款之要求；

（3）请指示航务专门顾问续约事宜。

您忠诚的仆人

富乐嘉（H. G. Fletcher）

瑷珲关署理税务司

录事：陈培因 三等二级税务员

11. 为批准提高江捐及黑龙江政府提议松花江水道委员会
免除黑龙江航路标志委员债务事

COMMRS. No. 132,077

Aigun No. 569

No.

SHANGHAI OFFICE OF THE

INSPECTORATE GENERAL OF CUSTOMS. 19th December, 1930.

SIR,

 With reference to your despatch No. 492:

  reporting the proposals of the Provisional
  Mayor, - who acts also as Superintendent, -
  that River Dues be collected at increased rate
  prior to signing of annual agreement by the
  local Chinese and Russian authorities, and that
  the River Dues collection, less 1/10th for
  Customs cost of collection, be turned over to
  him monthly; and pointing out probable effects
  if the latter proposal be accepted, especially
  as regards the continued employment of Mr.
  Ignatieff, the Technical Adviser;

and to your despatch No. 504:

  reporting the renewal of the annual Sino-Soviet
  agreement for the joint upkeep of the Amur
  Aids; and forwarding copies of this document;

I have now to inform you that on receipt of your
former despatch, I at once laid before the Kuan-wu Shu
a statement of the case, and while requesting their
decision on the Mayor's proposal pointed out at the
same time the extent of the indebtedness of the Amur
Aids Commission to the Sungari Aids Commission, and
suggested that the Aigun Commissioner should be

            authorised

...missioner of Customs,

  A I G U N.

authorised to deduct from each month's River Dues collection one-tenth, - in addition to the one-tenth cost of collection, - in order to repay the outstanding debt to the Sungari Aids Commission.

Correspondence then ensued between the Kuan-wu Shu and myself on the subject of the Amur Aids generally and between the Kuan-wu Shu and the North Eastern Executive Council, which as will be seen from the appended copy of Kuan-wu Shu despatch No. 3,926, supports the view taken by the Heilungchiang Government (1) that on account of the insufficiency of River Dues revenue, the proposal to deduct one-tenth from that annual revenue to repay the debt to the Sungari Aids Commission is not acceptable; and (2) that as navigation on the Amur and the Sungari is in both cases a concern of the Government, and as the Aids Commissions for both these rivers have kindred aims in view, the Sungari Commission should not only cancel the outstanding indebtedness of the Amur Commission, but also, as the Amur Aids funds are so low, should make a further appropriation from its funds of $ 30,000 for the benefit of the Amur Aids.

I have accordingly to request you to note:

 (1) that the proposed increase in the River Dues rates is approved by the Government;

 (2) that there is no objection to handing over to the Mayor at the close of each month the Dues collected, minus one-tenth for Customs cost of collection;

 (3) that Mr. Ignatieff is to continue to be employed and that his salary and allowances are

are to be paid from the net collection of the River Dues, that is from the sums turned over monthly to the Mayor;

(4) that you are to approach the Sungari Aids Commission, through the Harbin Commissioner, to see whether arrangements can be made in regard to the proposal of the Heilungchiang Government that the outstanding indebtedness of the Amur Commission to the Sungari Commission should be cancelled and whether the latter Commission should extend further financial help to the extent of $ 30,000 to the Amur Commission; and

(5) that on reaching an understanding with the Sungari Aids Commission, you are to report the result to me by despatch, with Chinese version in duplicate.

It is quite possible that as a result of these developments, the Mayor may on the grounds of economy decide to dispense with the services of Mr. Ignatieff, the Technical Adviser. Should there be any sign of this eventuating, you are to report the matter at once to me by despatch.

I am,

Sir,

Your obedient Servant,

Inspector General.

Appendix.

致瑷珲关第 <u>569/132077</u> 号令　　　　海关总税务司署（上海）1930 年 12 月 19 日

尊敬的瑷珲关税务司：

根据第 492 号呈：

"黑河市政筹备处处长，兼任海关监督提议，在当地中国政府与俄罗斯政府签订年度协议之前，先提高江捐税率并完成征收；所收江捐在扣除 10% 佣金后，按月转交给黑河市政筹备处处长；并指出，若第二个提议被采纳，可能产生的影响有哪些，以及是否继续聘用航务专门顾问易保罗（P. I. Ignatieff）先生的问题。"

以及贵署第 504 号呈：

"中苏联合维护黑龙江航路标志年度协议续签；并呈送此协议副本。"

谨通知，收悉贵署上一呈后，本署立即针对此事向关务署致函，请求对方决策是否批准黑河市政筹备处的提议，同时指明黑龙江水道委员会欠松花江水道委员会的债务总量，提议授权瑷珲关税务司从江捐征收中扣除十分之一佣金外再按月扣留十分之一，以偿还黑龙江水道委员会欠松花江水道委员会的巨额债务。

而后，关务署与本署，关务署与东北政务委员会大致就黑龙江航路标志问题往来多封信函，信函见关务署第 3926 号令副本的附件，此令支持黑龙江政府所提观点。（1）由于江捐税款紧缺，无法接受扣除十分之一江捐税款以偿还债务的提议；（2）因政府对黑龙江航运与松花江水道委员会二者都很关注，而两条江上的水道委员会的期望目标类似，故松花江水道委员会不仅应该免除黑龙江水道委员会的巨额债务，并且因黑龙江航路标志的资金紧缺，松花江水道委员会应考虑黑龙江航路标志的利益，进一步从自己账户拨款 30000 银圆供黑龙江航路标志使用。

据此，请贵署注意：

（1）政府已批准提高江捐税率的提议；

（2）同意每月月末扣除 10% 海关佣金后向黑河市政筹备处移交所收税款；

（3）易保罗先生应继续聘用，他的员工薪资与技术顾问津贴由按月移交给黑河市政筹备处的江捐征收净值中支出；

（4）贵署应通过滨江关税务司联系松花江水道委员会，看是否能就黑龙江政府提议免除黑龙江水道委员会欠松花江水道委员会的巨额债务问题达成协议，以及松花江委员会是否应继续对黑龙江委员会进行金额为 30000 银圆的资金援助；并且

（5）若与松花江水道委员会达成协议，贵署应向我署呈送报告，附中文版本，一式两份。

因事情有新进展,黑河市政筹备处很可能因资金不足免除易保罗先生航务专门顾问的职务,贵署应立即向我署呈报告。

您忠诚的仆人

华善(P. R. Walsham)

总务科税务司

12. 为汇报自 1931 年 6 月 10 日起以新税率征收江捐事

AMUR AIDS TO NAVIGATION:River Dues(now called Navigation
Fees) to be collected at increased rates from 10th June
1931, reporting; correspondence from Mayor in re, together with translation of new tariff, forwarding.

567
                                                              567
                                                              I.G.
I.G.   A I G U N   12th June 1931.

     Sir,

     1.   With reference to previous correspondence on
          the subject of increases in the rates of the River
          Dues Tariff, and with special reference to Aigun
          despatch No. 492 :

                    reporting, inter alia, that the Provisional
               Mayor had requested the collection of River
               Dues at the increased rate of 5% ad valorem
               on direct imports from, and exports to,
               Russia :

          and to your despatch No. 569/132,077 :

                    replying that the proposed increase in the
               River Dues rates was approved by the
               Government :

          I have the honour to forward, appended hereto, copy
          of a letter of the 4th June 1931, from the Provisional
          Mayor :

                    informing me that, owing to the insufficiency
               of the River Dues collection in the past,
               the North-Eastern Political Council has now,
               in response to his request, authorised the
               collection of Navigation Fees (航务费),
               vice River Dues, at increased rates;
               forwarding particulars of the new rates; and
               requesting that they be enforced from the
               10th June 1931 :

          and to report that a Joint Notification, stating that
                                                              in

The Inspector General of Customs,

     S H A N G H A I.

in compliance with the above request, Navigation Fees
at the new rates would be collected from the 10th
instant, was issued with the Superintendent.   I have
also requested the Harbin Commissioner to instruct the
Lahasusu Sub-port to introduce the new tariff from
the same date and to note that the collection will
in future be known as "Navigation Fees" instead of
"River Dues".   For accounts purposes, the new name
will be used here from the beginning of the next
September Quarter.

2.   It will be seen from the new tariff, an
English translation of which is also appended hereto,
that the North-Eastern Political Council has now
authorised the levy of Navigation Fees on trans-frontier
cart-borne traffic during the winter.   This innovation
was formerly proposed by the Provisional Mayor in
November 1930, as reported in my telegram of the 28th
November 1930, but it was disallowed by the Heilung-
kiang Provincial Authorities.

3.   In accordance with the instructions of your
despatch No. 524/127,220, the Superintendent has been
requested to report the matter to the Kuan-wu Shu.

                                I have the honour to be,

                                        Sir,

                                Your obedient Servant,

                        (Signed) C. B. Joly

                                (C. H. B. Joly)

                                Acting Commissioner.

                                                    Appendix No. 1

APPENDIX No.1.

AMUR AND USSURI RIVERS NAVIGATION FEES TARIFF:

(Rates for one section for steamers & barges)

Name	Classifier	Former rate $	New rate Foreign $	New rate Chinese $
Category I: Building materials, Iron, Cast iron, Steel- & Lead-ware, Salt, Flour, Cereals, Hay & Fodder, Vegetables, Charcoal, Agricultural Machines other than wooden, Coal:	Pood	0.015	0.05	0.25
Category II: other goods	"	0.05	0.10	0.05
Timber: 1" thick or under	Sup.Sq.Ft.	0.0005	0.001	0.0005
Over 1" thick, not exceeding 2"	"	0.001	0.002	0.001
" 2" " " " 3"	"	0.0015	0.003	0.0015
" 3" " " " 4"	"	0.002	0.004	0.002
" 4" " " " 5"	"	0.0025	0.005	0.0025
" 5" " " " 6"	"	0.003	0.006	0.003
Beams:	Cubic Ft.	0.006	0.012	0.006
Poles:	Piece	...	0.03	0.015
Gold:	Catty	2.00	4.00	4.00
Ginseng:	Duty	10%	10%	10%
Deer Horns & Musk:	"	20%	20%	20%
Benzine & Kerosene:	Pood	0.03	0.15	0.15
Fungus:	"	0.03	0.25	0.25
Lath:	"	0.015	0.02	0.01
Firewood: ½ arsine long	Sq.sajen	0.20	0.80	0.40
Up to one " "	"	0.30	1.20	0.60
Live stock: Large (horse & cattle)	Head	0.30	0.30	0.30
Small (pigs, sheep & goats)	"	0.15	0.15	0.15
Fowls:	Piece	0.01	0.01	0.01
Passenger Tickets:	Ad.val.	7½%	7½%	7½%

1st Section: Pokrovka to Taheiho
2nd Section: Taheiho to Kasakevich Waterway
3rd Section: Lahasusu to Hulin

Note: Goods moved between Chinese side and Soviet side, either carried by Steamer/Barges or Junks/Rafts, or by cart during winter, pay full Navigation Fee (same rate as carried by Steamer/Barges imported from, or exported to, Amur and Ussuri ports).
Goods carried by Junks/Rafts exported to, or imported from, the places on the Chinese side of the Amur and Ussuri pay Navigation Fee at half Steamer/Barge rate.

Appendix No.2

呈海关总税务司署 <u>567</u> 号文   瑷珲关 1931 年 6 月 12 日

尊敬的海关总税务司（上海）：

1. 根据先前有关提高江捐税率的函文及瑷珲关第 492 号呈：

"特汇报暂代黑河市政筹备处处长要求对直接往来俄国的商品按值百抽五征收江捐。"

及海关总税务司署第 569/132077 号令：

"政府已批准提高江捐税率之提议。"

兹附 1931 年 6 月 4 日暂代黑河市政筹备处处长公函抄件：

"因过去江捐税收不足，入不敷出，东北政务委员会现已批准增加航务费（即江捐）税率；随附新税率表；自 1931 年 6 月 10 日起以新税率征收航务费（即江捐）。"

兹汇报，本署已与海关监督发布联合声明，说明按照黑河市政筹备处处长指示，自 6 月 10 日起以新税率征收航务费，另已请滨江关税务司将该指示传达给拉哈苏苏分关，并说明日后"江捐"将更名为"航务费"（Navigation Fees）。然为便于记账，瑷珲关将于第三季度初开始使用该新名称。

2. 根据新税率表可知，东北政务委员会已批准冬季向跨境运输货车征收航务费，随附新税率表的英文译本。关于该项征税，暂代黑河市政筹备处处长早于 1930 年 11 月便提议过（参阅瑷珲关 1930 年 11 月 28 日电报），但当时被黑龙江省政府驳回。

3. 本署已照海关总税务司署第 524/127220 号令指示，请海关监督将此事汇报给关务署。

您忠诚的仆人

周骊（C. H. B. Joly）

瑷珲关署理税务司

附录1

黑龙江及乌苏里江航务费税率表

（轮船及驳船一段路程的税率）

名称	单位	旧税率	新税率	
			洋货	土货
		银圆	银圆	银圆
类别一： 建筑材料,铁,铸铁,钢及铅制品,盐,面粉,谷物,干草饲料,蔬菜,木炭,非木质农机,煤	普特	0.015	0.05	0.025
类别二： 其他货物	普特	0.03	0.10	0.05
木料： 厚度不超过1英寸	1平方英尺	0.0005	0.001	0.0005
厚度为1-2英寸	1平方英尺	0.001	0.002	0.001
厚度为2-3英寸	1平方英尺	0.0015	0.003	0.0015
厚度为3-4英寸	1平方英尺	0.002	0.004	0.002
厚度为4-5英寸	1平方英尺	0.0025	0.005	0.0025
厚度为5-6英寸	1平方英尺	0.003	0.006	0.003
大木梁：	1立方英尺	0.006	0.012	0.006
木杆：	每支	…	0.03	0.015
黄金：	每斤	2.00	4.00	4.00
人参：	按税	10%	10%	10%
鹿角及麝香：	按税	20%	20%	20%
石油醚及煤油：	普特	0.03	0.15	0.15
菌类：	普特	0.03	0.25	0.25
板条：	普特	0.015	0.02	0.01
薪柴： 3/4胛长	1平方俄丈	0.20	0.80	0.40
1胛长	1平方俄丈	0.30	1.20	0.60

续表

名称	单位	旧税率	新税率	
			洋货	土货
		银圆	银圆	银圆
家畜： 大型（牛、马）	每头	0.30	0.30	0.30
小型（猪、绵羊及山羊）	每头	0.15	0.15	0.15
家禽：	每只	0.01	0.01	0.01
客票：	从价	7.5%	7.5%	7.5%

黑龙江和乌苏里江将分为三段路程征税：

第一段：自波克罗夫卡至大黑河；

第二段：自大黑河至嘎杂克维池水道；

第三段：自拉哈苏苏至虎林。

注：

凡中俄两岸往来货物（无论使用轮船／驳船，民船／木筏或冬季时使用二轮手推车运输），皆需支付全额航务费（其税率与使用轮船／驳船运输货物往来黑龙江及乌苏里江之税率相同）。

凡使用民船／木筏运输货物往来华岸黑龙江及乌苏里江者，皆需按轮船／驳船税率之半数缴纳航务费。